JOURNAL

OF
SOVIET AND POST-SOVIET
POLITICS AND SOCIETY

Vol. 8, No. 1 (2022)

Special Sections

Russia's Annexation of Crimea III

A Debate on Prospect Theory and Explaining Russia's Annexation of Crimea

GENERAL EDITOR AND ISSUE EDITOR-IN-CHIEF:
Julie Fedor, University of Melbourne

GUEST EDITORS:
Andreas Umland, National University of Kyiv-Mohyla Academy
Gergana Dimova, Florida State University (London Program)

JSPPS Editorial Team

Julie Fedor, *University of Melbourne* (General Editor)
Andriy Portnov, *European University Viadrina* (Russian Language Editor)
Andreas Umland, *National University of Kyiv-Mohyla Academy* (Consulting Editor)

JSPPS Advisory Board

Timofey Agarin, Queen's University, Belfast
Mikhail Alexseev, San Diego State University, CA
Catherine Andreyev, University of Oxford
Anne Applebaum, The Legatum Institute, London
Anders Åslund, Peterson Inst. for International Economics
Margarita Balmaceda, Seton Hall University, NJ
Harley Balzer, Georgetown University, DC
Timm Beichelt, European University Viadrina, Frankfurt (Oder)
Mark R. Beissinger, Princeton University, NJ
Thomas Bohn, Justus Liebig University, Giessen
Giovanna Brogi, University of Milan
Paul Chaisty, University of Oxford
Vitaly Chernetsky, University of Kansas, Lawrence
Ariel Cohen, Institute for the Analysis of Global Security, MD
Timothy J. Colton, Harvard University, MA
Peter J.S. Duncan, University College London
John B. Dunlop, Stanford University, CA
Gerald M. Easter, Boston College, MA
Alexander Etkind, European University Institute, Florence
M. Steven Fish, University of California at Berkeley
Gasan Gusejnov, Higher School of Economics, Moscow
Nikolas K. Gvosdev, U.S. Naval War College, RI
Michael Hagemeister, Ruhr University, Bochum
Stephen E. Hanson, College of William & Mary, VA
Olexiy Haran, Kyiv-Mohyla Academy
Nicolas Hayoz, University of Fribourg
Andreas Heinemann-Grüder, University of Bonn
Stephen Hutchings, University of Manchester, UK
Stefani Hoffman, The Hebrew University of Jerusalem
Mikhail Ilyin, Higher School of Economics, Moscow
Wilfried Jilge, University of Basel
Markku Kangaspuro, University of Helsinki
Adrian Karatnycky, Atlantic Council, New York
Andrei Kazantsev, MGIMO, Moscow
Jeffrey Kopstein, University of Toronto

Hrant Kostanyan, Centre for European Policy Studies
Paul Kubicek, Oakland University, MI
Walter Laqueur, Georgetown University, DC
Marlene Laruelle, George Washington University, DC
Carol Leonard, Higher School of Economics, Moscow
Leonid Luks, The Catholic University of Eichstaett-Ingolstadt
Luke March, University of Edinburgh
Mykhailo Minakov, Kyiv-Mohyla Academy
Olga Onuch, University of Manchester
Mitchell Orenstein, Northeastern University, MA
Nikolay Petrov, Higher School of Economics, Moscow
Andriy Portnov, Humboldt University, Berlin
Serhii Plokhii, Harvard University, MA
Alina Polyakova, Atlantic Council, DC
Maria Popova, McGill University, Montreal
Alex Pravda, University of Oxford
Mykola Riabchuk, Ukrainian Academy of Sciences, Kyiv
Per Anders Rudling, Lund University
Ellen Rutten, University of Amsterdam
Jutta Scherrer, École des Hautes Études en Sciences Sociales
Dieter Segert, University of Vienna
Anton Shekhovtsov, The Legatum Institute, London
Oxana Shevel, Tufts University, MA
Stephen Shulman, Southern Illinois University, Carbondale
Valerie Sperling, Clark University, MA
Susan Stewart, SWP, Berlin
Lisa M. Sundstrom, University of British Columbia
Mark Tauger, West Virginia University, Morgantown
Vera Tolz-Zilitinkevic, University of Manchester
Amir Weiner, Stanford University
Sarah Whitmore, Oxford Brookes University, UK
Andrew Wilson, University College London
Christian Wipperfürth, DGAP, Berlin
Andreas Wittkowsky, ZIF, Berlin
Jan Zielonka, University of Oxford

Bibliographic information published by the Deutsche Nationalbibliothek
The Deutsche Nationalbibliothek lists this publication in the Deutsche Nationalbibliografie; detailed bibliographic data are available on the Internet at http://dnb.dnb.de.

Bibliografische Information der Deutschen Nationalbibliothek
Die Deutsche Nationalbibliothek verzeichnet diese Publikation in der Deutschen Nationalbibliografie; detaillierte bibliografische Daten sind im Internet über http://dnb.d-nb.de abrufbar.

Cover picture: © Dmitry Bogatyrev | Unsplash

Journal of Soviet and Post-Soviet Politics and Society
Vol. 8, No. 1 (2022)

Stuttgart: *ibidem*-Verlag / *ibidem* Press

Erscheinungsweise: halbjährlich / Frequency: biannual

ISSN 2364-5334

Ordering Information:
PRINT: Subscription (two copies per year): € 58.00 / year (+ S&H: € 6.00 / year within Germany, € 10.00 / year international). The subscription can be canceled at any time.
Single copy or back issue: € 34.00 / copy (+ S&H: € 3.00 within Germany, € 4.50 international).

E-BOOK: Individual copy or back issue: € 19.99 / copy. Available via amazon.com or google.books.
For further information please visit www.jspps.eu

© *ibidem*-Verlag / *ibidem* Press
Stuttgart, Germany 2022

Alle Rechte vorbehalten
Das Werk einschließlich aller seiner Teile ist urheberrechtlich geschützt. Jede Verwertung außerhalb der engen Grenzen des Urheberrechtsgesetzes ist ohne Zustimmung des Verlages unzulässig und strafbar. Dies gilt insbesondere für Vervielfältigungen, Übersetzungen, Mikroverfilmungen und elektronische Speicherformen sowie die Einspeicherung und Verarbeitung in elektronischen Systemen.

All rights reserved

No part of this publication may be reproduced, stored in or introduced into a retrieval system, or transmitted, in any form, or by any means (electronical, mechanical, photocopying, recording or otherwise) without the prior written permission of the publisher.
Any person who performs any unauthorized act in relation to this publication may be liable to criminal prosecution and civil claims for damages.

CONTENTS

SPECIAL SECTION: RUSSIA'S ANNEXATION OF CRIMEA III

Introduction. Perspectives on Russia's 2014 Annexation of Crimea: Empirical and Theoretical Explorations
GERGANA DIMOVA and ANDREAS UMLAND 1

The Personal Stakes of Political Crisis: The 2014 Attempted Annexation of Crimea
GRETA LYNN UEHLING 13

"Dark" and "Golden" Times: The Crimean Tatar Population under Tsarist and Soviet Rule (1783–1941)
KERSTIN S. JOBST 45

Agents of Separatism: Social Background to the Pro-Russian Movements in Crimea and the Moldovan Dniester Valley in Comparison (1989–95)
JAN ZOFKA 73

A Debate on Prospect Theory and Explaining Russia's Annexation of Crimea

Loss Aversion, Neo-Imperial Frames, and Territorial Expansion: Using Prospect Theory to Examine the Annexation of Crimea
ION MARANDICI 111

DISCUSSION

Competing Theoretical Frameworks for Clarifying Russia's Annexation of Crimea
PETER RUTLAND 151

On Reading Yanukovych and the Rhetoric of *Novorossiia* Right
TOR BUKKVOLL 156

How Rational was Putin's Strategy of Crimea Annexation? Prospect Theory and Security Dilemma Perspectives
MYKOLA KAPITONENKO 161

A Constructivist International Relations Contribution to Understanding the Annexation of Crimea
RUMENA FILIPOVA 172

On the Application of Prospect Theory to the Annexation of
Crimea: Possibilities for Optimization

MARTIN MALEK 177

Follow-up Observations on Prospect Theory, the Annexation
of Crimea, and the Second Invasion of Ukraine

ION MARANDICI 181

ARTICLES

Mikhail Putin (1894–1969) and Socialist Competition:
Exploring a Neglected Branch of the Putin Family Tree

CHRIS MONDAY 193

REVIEWS

Elizabeth Buchanan (Ed.), *Russian Energy Strategy in the Asia-Pacific: Implications for Australia*

INNA CHUVYCHKINA 257

Juliane Fürst, *Flowers through Concrete: Explorations in Soviet Hippieland*

BRENDAN M. MCELMEEL 260

Hubertus Jahn (ed.), *Identities and Representations in Georgia from the 19th Century to the Present*
OLGA KHABIBULINA 262

Natalia Knoblock (ed.), *Language of Conflict: Discourses of the Ukrainian Crisis*
ELISE WESTIN 265

Andrei Kozyrev, *The Firebird: The Elusive Fate of Russian Democracy*
MANNE WÄNGBORG 268

Anna Matveeva, *Through Times of Trouble: Conflict in Southeastern Ukraine Explained from Within*
GIULIA PRELZ OLTRAMONTI 272

David Rainbow, *Ideologies of Race: Imperial Russia and the Soviet Union in Global Context*
KIMBERLY ST. JULIAN-VARNON 275

Josephine von Zitzewitz, *The Culture of Samizdat: Literature and Underground Networks in the Late Soviet Union*
JOHN (IVAN) JAWORSKY 278

Jessica Zychowicz, *Superfluous Women: Art, Feminism, and Revolution in Twenty-First-Century Ukraine*
YANA OSTAPENKO 279

Vladislav M. Zubok, *Collapse: The Fall of the Soviet Union*
DIMA KORTUKOV 282

ABOUT THE GUEST EDITORS 285
ABOUT THE THE CONTRIBUTORS 286

RUSSIA'S ANNEXATION OF CRIMEA III

EDITED BY

GERGANA DIMOVA AND ANDREAS UMLAND

Introduction

Perspectives on Russia's 2014 Annexation of Crimea: Empirical and Theoretical Explorations*

Gergana Dimova and Andreas Umland

This is the third installment of a series of *JSPPS* special sections dedicated to various aspects of the pre-history, course, and aftermath of Russia's armed capture of Crimea, in February–March 2014. The first special section, published in 2019, focused on judicial issues including the sanctions imposed on the annexed peninsula.[1] The second special section, published in 2020, centered on the interpretation of select issues concerning Crimea's recent past, namely the status of the Crimean Tatars, the 1954 transfer of the Black Sea peninsula from the Russian to the Ukrainian Soviet republic, and Germany's reaction to Russia's 2014 attack on Ukraine.[2]

---

* We are grateful to *JSPPS* general editor Julie Fedor for her careful editorial work on this and the previous two special sections "Russia's Annexation of Crimea."
[1] Gergana Dimova, "Legal Loopholes and Judicial Debates: Essays on Russia's 2014 Annexation of Crimea and Its Consequences for International Law," Agata Kleczkowska, "The Obligation of Non-recognition: The Case of the Annexation of Crimea;" Dasha Dubinsky and Peter Rutland, "Russia's Legal Position on the Annexation of Crimea;" Maria Shagina, "Business as Usual: Sanctions Circumvention by Western Firms in Crimea," *Journal of Soviet and Post-Soviet Politics and Society* 5, no. 1 (2019): 1-120.
[2] Gergana Dimova and Andreas Umland, "Russia's 2014 Annexation of Crimea in Historical Context: Discourses and Controversies;" Natalya Belitser, "The Status of the Crimean Tatars in Ukrainian and International Law;" Alina Cherviatsova, "The 1954 Transfer of Crimea: Debunking the Myth of a 'Royal Gift' to Ukraine;" Maryna Rabinovych, "How the Federal Republic Reacted to Russia's Annexation of Crimea: Berlin's Diplomatic Response and German Media Representations in

The current third installment is different from the first two in view of its publication's political context as well as in terms of its substantive foci. This third special section on the Russian annexation of Crimea goes to print in the aftermath of Moscow's extension of its hybrid assault on Ukraine, underway since 2014, to an open and full-scale war of annihilation (German: *Vernichtungskrieg*). After 24 February 2022, the crucial role of the Russian state and army in the destruction of the Ukrainian state is no longer concealed by the Kremlin and its propaganda channels, as had been the case with Russia's annexation of Crimea and triggering of a pseudo-civil war in the Donbas in spring 2014. The enormous escalation of Moscow's eight-year attack on Ukraine in 2022 will presumably also have repercussions for future scholarly assessments of the recent history and annexation of Crimea.

Readers of the following texts should keep in mind that, except for the last contribution to this special section, these texts were written and submitted before 24 February 2022. They thus document the state of deliberation about Crimea's recent fate before, what has in Germany famously been called, the *Zeitenwende*—a change of times, or historical turning point.[3] Possibly, some, most, or even all of the below texts would have been written more or less differently after this fateful date. Only Ion Marandici's concluding essay responding to comments on his 2020 paper on the annexation of Crimea already incorporates reflections on the new situation after the start of Russia's massive offensive in early 2022.

2014–2020," *Journal of Soviet and Post-Soviet Politics and Society* 6, no. 2 (2020): 145-242.

[3] Paul Maurice, "Un 'changement d'époque'? Vers une réorientation de la politique étrangère allemande après l'invasion russe en Ukraine," *Briefings de l'IFRI*, 7 March 2022, www.ifri.org/fr/publications/briefings-de-lifri/un-changement-depoque-vers-une-reorientation-de-politique-etrangere; Mario Bisiada, "The Discursive Construction of a New Reality in Olaf Scholz's *Zeitenwende* Speech," *SciELO Preprints*, 25 March 2022, https://doi.org/10.1590/SciELOPreprints.3852; and Tobias Bunde, "Lessons (to be) learned? Germany's *Zeitenwende* and European security after the Russian invasion of Ukraine," *Contemporary Security Policy*, 26 June 2022, DOI: 10.1080/13523260.2022.2092820.

Greta Lynn Uehling's article "The Personal Stakes of Political Crisis: The 2014 Attempted Annexation of Crimea" complements earlier discussions, in this series of special sections, of various political, legal, and humanitarian repercussions of Russia's 2014 occupation of the Ukrainian peninsula in the Black Sea. Uehling examines scrupulously how the annexation affected inter-personal relationships of the peoples who are or were living on Crimea. Her paper is based on extensive Crimea-related interviews.

Uehling argues that the annexation sparked a reorganization of all three of the most basic types of personal relations—those between intimate partners, between children and parents, and between friends. In most of the cases studied by Uehling, the main result of the annexation's impact on family ties and friendships, was alienation between formerly close people. The severing of their bonds often happened in connection with or as a result of emigration from Crimea by a family member, life partner, or friend. Uehling provides many touching examples for these break-ups. One is that of a father who disowned and disinherited his son because he had not voted in the 16 March 2014 pseudo-referendum that provided the pretext for Russia's formal capture of the peninsula two days later.

One of Uehling's most intriguing findings is that, in 75% of her extensive interviews, the word "traitor" comes up. Uehling explains the dominance of the traitor denomination attributed to pro-Ukrainian Crimean citizens with reference to lingering after-effects of earlier traumatic periods in Crimea's recent history. Thus, there remains a lack of historical clarity, in the memory of many Crimeans, with regard to who was a perpetrator and who was a victim in two critical periods of Crimea's past—during the Crimean War in 1853–54 and the Nazi occupation of Crimea in 1941–44.

A continuing ambiguity in the remembrance of the latter case, for example, concerns 20,000 Crimean Tatars who are believed to have been recruited by the German occupiers as collaborators during World War II. In contrast, far less attention is given to another approximately 20,000 Crimean Tatars who became part of the Red Army and other Soviet armed forces. Selective and politicized historical memories such as these are often fed by Soviet and post-Soviet Russian propaganda.

Until today, conflicting historical narratives are affecting personal relationships through various psychological mechanisms. Uehling invokes Jacques Derrida's idea of "haunting" to show that remnants from the past "haunt" today's inter-personal ties. She refers to Alexander Etkind's concept of "warped mourning" to maintain that in formerly Soviet areas, the past remains uncannily present because of a, so far, incomplete processing of the past.

Kerstin Jobst's article "'Dark' and 'Golden' Times: Crimean Tatars under Tsarist and Soviet Rule (1783–1941)" examines Tatar life and St. Petersburg's/Moscow's policy on the Black Sea peninsula across the span of almost three centuries. Jobst demonstrates that the Tatars had varied experiences in Crimea under the tsarist regime from 1783 until the First World War, and under Soviet power, until Nazi Germany's invasion of the USSR in 1941. Her argument complements earlier assessments of the Crimean Tatars' colonial experience that focused heavily on their deportation, by the Stalinist regime, from the peninsula in May 1944, the harsh and often deadly conditions of their transport to and life in Central Asia, as well as their inability to return to Crimea for decades. Jobst suggests that, while Stalin's genocidal action and its aftermath constituted the greatest collective trauma for the Crimean Tatars, it is not the only reference point for a full understanding of their fate under Russian rule.

Unfolding a rich historical narrative, Jobst uncovers a number of important nuances. It starts with the first annexation of the peninsula to the Russian empire in 1783 and argues that it had differing consequences depending on which segment of the Crimean Tatar population one considers. The clergy seems to have been a partial winner as, for example, its property was exempt from state taxes. The Crimean Tatar secular elites were given *de jure* rights equal to those of the Russian elites. However, in practice, they could not fully benefit from these rights. Crimea's pre-1783 peasantry was one of the losers from the annexation as it was more and more replaced with immigrating Russian peasants.

The article shows that the early massive exodus of Tatars from Crimea during the tsarist period was due to economic reasons as well as to fear and distrust towards the Russians on the part of the titular population. It adds though an important element not aligning with these factors. Some Crimean Tatars willingly left for the Ottoman Empire for religious reasons and because they wanted to avoid mandatory military service in the tsarist army. St. Petersburg limited the Muslim population's autonomous political activity. Yet, the Crimean Tatars still possessed a modicum of independence. The Muslim Reform movement which the Tatars used to gain some self-government demonstrated that the times were neither entirely "golden" nor fully "dark."

The article juxtaposes the Tatar experience under tsarist and Soviet rule. It divides the latter period into two sub-periods: the "golden" times which lasted from about 1922 until 1928, followed by a dark period which ended in the notorious 1944 deportation. The author links the genesis of the "golden" phase to Stalin's initial nationalities policy coupling nationality with territory, and to the policy of indigenization, which sought to integrate non-Russian nationalities into Communist party and Soviet administrative structures. As a result of these policies, the Crimean Tatars played a greater role in public life than they had in tsarist times.

The subsequent turnaround in Moscow's nationalities policy and the beginning of massive purges resulted in the repression of 30,000 to 40,000 Crimean Tatars. Nevertheless, the article argues, the Russian–Crimean encounter was not only an encounter between an imperial power and a colonial object. As the Crimean Tatars had, at least during certain periods, a noteworthy degree of agency, a more nuanced approach to a comprehensive assessment of their fate under tsarist and Soviet rule is necessary.

Jan Zofka's article "Agents of Separatism: The Social Background to the Pro-Russian Movements in Crimea and the Moldovan Dniester Valley in Comparative Perspective (1989–95)" seeks to resolve the intriguing puzzle of diverging degrees of local support for separatism in two early post-Soviet secessionist regions. It compares two cases of pro-Russian separatism in the years after 1989. Zofka explores why the so-called "Transnistrian Moldovan

Republic" emerged and managed to secede from Moldova while the Autonomous Republic of Crimea failed to separate from the Ukrainian state, in the 1990s.

Zofka explains the difference in the trajectories of the two separatist movements with reference to diverging social backgrounds of the main autonomist actors.[4] This thesis is juxtaposed to alternative explanations, such as a putative determining impact of Moscow's help for or management of the separatist movements, or possible repercussions of the movements' drive by either nationalist or other ideological motivations. Zofka's argument about the importance of the socialization of the main protagonists as a determinant of separatism's success is based on a close reading of articles from local and factory newspapers and biographical literature and memoirs. It also relies on several dozen interviews with mid-level separatist leaders close to the movements' leaderships, as well as archival material.

Zofka points out that the eventually successful separation of the Dniester or, in Moldovan, Nistru valley did not begin as a separatist movement *per se*. The initial protests emerged as a challenge to new language policies in the then Soviet Moldovan Republic in 1989, which made Moldovan the official language. This obliged, among others, factory workers to learn Romanian within five years.

The initial impetus for the industrial protests was to maintain the Russian language as the main language of communication, and to preserve the workers' jobs. At that point, the goal was not to disrupt the inherited status quo. The movement only gradually transformed into a full-scale secession. After the protests failed to reverse the language policy, factory elites sought to take control of local municipalities tasked with implementing the policy. The conflict escalated into a full-scale autonomous movement when the

---

[4] For a recent paper on a related issue by another contributor to this special section, see: Ion Marandici, "Structural Bias, Polarized Mediation and Conflict Resolution Failure: A Comparative Examination of the Disputes in Transnistria and Donbas," *Southeast European and Black Sea Studies*, 13 July 2022, DOI: 10.1080/14683857.2022.2101188.

strikers' leadership won local elections in the industrial towns of the Nistru valley and a conflict over state symbols ensued.

Zofka argues that the factories came to serve as frameworks of mobilization for Transnistrian separatism because, via them, autonomist factory managers could organize workers. The general directors of big factories had considerable power, including over the distribution of social security and other public services, including pensions, housing, and access to holiday facilities. The enterprises ran canteens, shops, and agricultural entities to supply their employees with meals and food.

Another late Soviet peculiarity that empowered autonomist factory directors was that most of them held seats in local party structures and often ran for election for local, regional, and national parliaments (*sovety*). This also applied to factory directors in the Nistru valley who came to lead the Transnistrian separatist movement. Yet another enabling social feature was the fact that late Soviet factory managers were elected by their workers, whose main worry was possible unemployment, and that these elections legitimized the directors' power.

Initially, the separatist "Republican Party of Crimea" enjoyed wide political support on the Black Sea peninsula. Yet it was short-lived and less successful than the Transnistrian separatism. Pro-Russian parties won the presidential and parliamentary elections in 1994. While they opposed the status quo that Crimea belonged to newly independent Ukraine, they did, however, not achieve sovereignty beyond the limited autonomy already achieved in the late-Soviet period, in January 1991.

Zofka proposes that the social make-up and plural composition of the Crimean separatist movement accounted for its failure. The secessionist coalition consisted of intellectuals, small businessmen, and Afghan war veterans. It was a medley of single-issue groups, social assistance organization of former servicemen, and owners or managers of newly founded, mostly small enterprises in trade and services. Relations within this variegated coalition were guided by personal and career ambitions. Such individual interests in, for example, allocating government posts, proved fatal. The animosities between the pro-separatist factions even translated into institutional struggle between the presidency and parliament.

Zofka also argues that the small businessmen did not have the political resources and social infrastructure to organize sustained opposition to Ukrainian statehood. Unlike in Transnistria, the higher standing economic and political elites, who had vested interests in the manufacturing sector, made arrangements with Kyiv that benefited their materialist interests. Thus, they did not support the separatist movement. In conclusion, the Crimean and Transnistrian pro-Russian separatist movements had largely similar ideological and nationalist ambitions, yet had different political fates largely because of their different social make-ups.

In the final full-length research article in this special section, entitled "Loss Aversion, Neo-Imperial Frames and Territorial Expansion: Using Prospect Theory to Examine the Annexation of Crimea," Ion Marandici combines empirical analysis with theoretical interpretation. The paper makes its own contribution to understanding the Russian capture of Ukraine's peninsula, and serves as the basis for an ensuing debate. This controversy contains five scholarly replies to Marandici as well as his response to the critics.

Marandici's question is: "Why did Russia's authoritarian leader decide to annex Crimea in 2014?" The author constructs his answer around an argument based on prospect theory. Originally a psychological approach developed in economics, prospect theory is here used to understand foreign policy decisions. Prospect theory's core ideas are the prevalence of loss aversion and a dependence on reference points in the making of strategic decisions. According to it, decision-makers use certain salient reference points to determine whether they are in the domain of losses or gains. If they deem themselves to be in the domain of losses, they are inclined to accept more risks. If, in contrast, a decision-maker thinks that she or he is in the domain of gains, she or he will tend to avoid risks.

The author establishes the crucial reference points on the basis of, among others, a textual analysis of documents released by Ukraine's National Defense and Security Council and of participant accounts of the deliberations of key decision-makers. For Putin, for instance, the status quo entailed his being in indirect control of Ukraine as long as President Viktor Yanukovych was in office. A turning point occurred in Putin's calculus when, after Yanukovych postponed the signing of the Associated Agreement, the Euromaidan protests started. Yanukovych's flight from Kyiv was perceived as a major loss by Putin.

As he found himself in the domain of losses, Putin took the risk of initiating a hybrid war against Ukraine. One can thus explain Russia's decision to annex Crimea with reference to the changing status quo in Ukraine. Moreover, the article refers to aspirations, analogies, and emotions to elucidate the major protagonists' thoughts and behavior.

An application of prospect theory to this case can help answer such questions as whether Putin himself made the decision, whether the annexation was planned ahead of time, and whether it reflected Putin's perception of Kyiv's and the West's ability and willingness to resist. Marandici finds that the annexation was mostly an individual-level decision. Putin made it in an informal setting. Its discussion in the Security Council was inconsequential. Second, Marandici notes that the annexation involved more advanced planning than the Kremlin officials were admitting to in public, but that, ultimately, the takeover of Crimea was initiated in reaction to the success of the Euromaidan. Third, the author suggests that Putin was emboldened by a presentiment that Ukraine was too weak to put up resistance and that the West would be reluctant to impose sanctions.

Marandici complements his prospect theoretical considerations with deliberations from additional explanatory frameworks. The diversionary theory of war posits that leaders initiate armed conflicts to pursue domestic political goals. The theory of expected utility proposes that leaders are rational utility maximizers, weighting gains and losses equally, with the goal of gaining power. Personality-based theory propounds that some persons are less risk-averse than others.

Marandici's thesis is the starting point of a vivacious discussion of five respondents to his paper. Peter Rutland casts doubt on the utility of using prospect theory to explain Moscow's decision to annex the Black Sea Peninsula. That is because Rutland believes it is difficult to categorize events into losses and gains. He illustrates this point by arguing that while the annexation can be considered a gain, as Russia expanded its territory, it could be also considered a loss, because it led to the souring of Russia's relationship with Ukraine. It is not clear what weighted more heavily on Putin's mind.

In his response to Marandici's article, Tor Bukkvoll raises three empirical issues, questions Marandici's approach to sources, and offers two alternative interpretations. Bukvoll criticizes, for example, Marandici's assertion that Yanukovych by default defended Russian interests. The author points out that Yanukovych's party was split on its attitude to Moscow and that Yanukovych willingly started negotiations with the European Union on an Association Agreement. Bukvoll also suggests that in assessing whether the annexation was pre-planned, Marandici should distinguish between military planning, which is made regardless of political intentions, and political planning, which would be more indicative of prior intent on the part of Putin.

In his response to Marandici's article, Mykola Kapitonenko develops his own elaborate interpretation of Russia's attack on Ukraine, making his response a research contribution in its own right. He supports the application of prospect theory, arguing that, in his view, it explains the annexation better than rational choice theory. From a rational choice perspective, the annexation should have been perceived by Putin as more costly than such alternatives as non-interference or supporting Crimea's independence without annexing it. Then US President Barack Obama announced sanctions already before the 16 March 2014 pseudo-referendum to create a fake legitimacy for Russia's capture of the peninsula. Yet, Obama's announcement evidently did not have any effect on Putin's choice.

Kapitonenko believes that prospect theory offers a better explanation as to why Putin took on more risk as tensions in Ukraine intensified. Kapitonenko echoes Bukkvoll's point that Yanukovych had not always been pro-Russian. He still believes that Yanukovych's flight and the victory of the Euromaidan protests triggered enormous uncertainty in Moscow. It created a perception of a loss of control that, under the security dilemma, made annexation, in the Kremlin's terms, a less rather than more risky strategy.

Rumena Filipova advocates cross-fertilization of prospect theory with constructivism, so that an application of prospect theory can better account for the neo-imperial framing of the annexation narrative which included historical claims and references to a common identity. In addition, Filipova argues that a constructivist perspective could help to better distinguish different levels of analysis in prospect theory. Constructivism is also suited to account for the collective aspects of the Russian leadership's decision-making. Putin's position was affected by his close circle, the state-owned media, and other actors.

While Martin Malek sides, in his response, with Kapitonenko's thesis that for Putin the annexation was the least risky move, Malek does so for different reasons. Kapitonenko argues that annexing the peninsula was less risky because other options brought more uncertainty and loss of control. In contrast, Malek propounds that it was less risky because the interim government in Kyiv that took office after Yanukovych's fall was deadlocked. At no point did Moscow face the prospect of military resistance in Crimea, by Kyiv, Berlin, or Washington. The author disputes Marandici's assessment that the operation was not substantially pre-planned. He instead argues that a properly prepared deployment of tens of thousands of soldiers and several branches of the armed forces takes months, and possibly years.

The special issue ends with a response by Ion Marandici to the commentators of his paper. Marandici's second text is a useful attempt to integrate the remarks of his critics into his argument and is additionally interesting as it was written several weeks after the escalation of the Russian–Ukrainian War on 24 February 2022. Marandici thus not only answers the comments of Rutland, Bukvoll, Kapitonenko, Malek, and Filipova. He also compares the Russian attacks on Ukraine of 2014 and 2022 and points out the similarities as well as differences between these two events and their contexts.

In 2022, the historical and political salience of the various issues addressed in this series of special sections has risen sharply.

The start of Russia's covert special service and military operation to annex Ukraine's Crimea in February 2014 started the conflict that escalated almost exactly eight years later into the most important fighting in Europe since World War II. We hope that this collection of papers and comments, as well as the two previous special sections in this series, will be helpful for gaining a better understanding of the origins and nature of the fateful confrontation that the European continent is experiencing, as this *JSPPS* issue goes to print.

The Personal Stakes of Political Crisis: The 2014 Attempted Annexation of Crimea

Greta Lynn Uehling

Abstract: Based on ethnographic fieldwork carried out in Ukraine, this article explores how the 2014 attempted Russian annexation of Crimea not only upset the geopolitical balance in wider Europe, but also adversely affected interpersonal relationships. I demonstrate that intimate, parent–child, and friend relationships were all affected. Specifically, my interlocutors used the political and legal concept of treason from the Crimean and Second World Wars to reorder their personal relationships. This had significant consequences for the relationships themselves as well as triggering migration. My analysis shows how the haunting and warped mourning known to characterize post-Soviet cultural representations can be extended to interpersonal relations, expanding our understanding of the politics of memory in Ukraine. The article provides a unique window on the empirical processes through which Crimea was brought under Russian control.

Introduction: The Personal Stakes of Political Crisis

Based on ethnographic fieldwork carried out in Ukraine, this article explores how the occupation and attempted annexation of Crimea by Russian Federation in 2014 not only upset the geopolitical balance in wider Europe, but adversely affected interpersonal relations. Data collected between 2015 and 2017 suggest that as the Russian Federation was taking control of the Black Sea peninsula, people took up the political and legal concept of treason as salient for thinking about their romantic, friend, and family relations, resuscitating the trope of treason from the Crimean and Second World Wars. I argue this had significant consequences for the relationships themselves, and became a factor contributing to displacement. Given how the twin political and interpersonal "break-ups" drew upon the historic past, I utilize the concepts of haunting and warped mourning to elucidate what transpired, opening a new vantage point on the empirical processes through which Crimea was occupied and brought under the de facto control of Russian Federation. The article contributes to the existing literature on the 2014 events in Crimea by illuminating the profound personal stakes of the attempted annexation.

Seleme's[1] experience demonstrates the reconfiguration of social networks more concretely. She was a single mother of Crimean Tatar ethnicity living with her school-age son at the time the Black Sea peninsula was occupied by soldiers without insignia. Previously, she had enjoyed close friendships with ethnic Russians. An especially close bond had formed with a family living down her street who also had a son. But their relationship began to unravel as soon as the territory came under foreign control. As Seleme described it:

> My friends have stopped talking to me, the ones that slept at my house, ate there, drank there. Now we're "goddamn Tatars" to them, "crazies", and [they say] "we hate you." And when I see that on social networks among my friends, I say, "hey, lady! Did you hate us as much when you'd bring your child to us for the entire day?" I said, "he'd be here like at a kindergarten, we fed him, he slept here, ate here, we brought him up!" And suddenly we're traitors.
>
> [They said that] that we served Hitler. It's the same rhetoric all over again, from the Soviet times, that we served Hitler, that we're collaborationists, that we did this, that we did that. I said, "Guys! you're the collaborators!" (No. 60, current resident of Crimea, Crimean Tatar, female, age 40).

This statement exemplifies how the 2014 attempted annexation of Crimea not only altered the political order but reverberated through relationships, sometimes leading to their dissolution.[2] To accuse

---

[1] The names used throughout are pseudonyms.
[2] In some respects, this resembles how families and friendships were upset by the "Brexit" referendum. Similarly, the tense relationship between Hong Kong and mainland China profoundly affected personal relationships. See Chris Harris, "How Break-Ups and Lost Friendships have been Brexit's Hidden Casualty,"

Seleme of serving Hitler dredges up the allegations leveled at the Crimean Tatars after World War II, albeit in a distorted way. Whether based in reality or the imagination, accusations of collaborationism and treason had the effect of fracturing social bonds and reorganizing the ways that people related.³

The trope of the traitor circulating in conversation is anchored in writings such as the public announcement in *Izvestiia* ("News") explaining massive Stalin-era deportations and the published correspondence between Lavrenty Beria, the People's Commissar for Internal Affairs, and Joseph Stalin. In a communique dated 10 May 1944, for example, Beria wrote:

> Taking into account the treasonous activity of the Crimean Tatars against the Soviet people and considering the undesirability of the Crimean Tatars' continued residence in a border region of the Soviet Union, the NKVD of the SSSR submits for your consideration the proposal of the State Defense Committee on the exile of all Tatars from the territory of Crimea.⁴

Whether interacting with her neighbors, her son's teachers, or her supervisor at work, her pro-Ukrainian position was not treated as a mere difference of political opinion, but as a moral failure suggesting deeper, even essential character flaws. Based on these experiences, Seleme decided she could not reasonably stay in Crimea: her support for Ukraine was conflated with support for the Third Reich and this became a problem in virtually every dimension of her life. The conflict with her friends raises the question at the

---

Euronews, 23 June 2017, http://www.euronews.com/2017/06/23/how-break-ups-and-lost-friendships-have-been-the-hidden-casualty-of-brexit; Susan Hill, "My Sadness at the Friends I've Lost over Brexit," *The Spectator*, 12 February 2017; and Glosswitch, "My Brexit Christmas—or what I've Learnt about Family since 23 June 2016," *New Statesman*, 20 December 2017, https://www.newstatesman.com/politics/brexit/2017/12/my-brexit-christmas-or-what-i-ve-learnt-about-family-23-june-2016 (accessed 2 June 2021).

3   Eleonora Narvselius and Gelinada Grinchenko, "Introduction: 'Formulas of Betrayal'—Traitors, Collaborators and Deserters in Contemporary European Politics of Memory," *Traitors, Collaborators and Deserters in Contemporary European Politics of Memory*, ed. Gelinada Grinchenko and Eleonora Narvselius (Palgrave Macmillan, 2018), 1-30; here: 7.

4   N. F. Bugai, *Josef Stalin and Lavrenty Beria, "They Must Be Deported:" Documents, Facts, and Commentary* (Moscow: Friendship of Peoples, 1999).

center of this article: how and why were social memories of the Crimean past activated in this particular manner? In other words, how and why was the political idea of treason operationalized in decidedly private and personal contexts? I argue the trope of the traitor gained currency precisely because it could be harnessed in flexible ways to do the work of transforming Crimean society. My argument is consistent with scholarship on the politics of memory that argues accusations of treason are less about actual treason than a way to exploit collective memories in the pursuit of political or ideological objectives.[5] In Crimea, the objective appeared to be uniting public opinion on the rightness of Russian rule.

From the outset, it seems clear Seleme and her friends were operating with different interpretations of the Crimean past. I therefore examine the social tensions associated with the attempted annexation under the general rubric of politics of memory. If social memory refers to the representations and practices that constitute a collective and selective interpretation of the past, we can say there are politics of memory operating when these interpretations are used strategically to control what is "remembered," "forgotten" and commemorated in the interest of managing power and resources.[6] Politics of memory are central in Crimea due to the diametrically opposed and highly contested interpretations of what happened in the tumultuous eighteenth, nineteenth, and twentieth centuries.

Scholars interested in the politics of memory have turned to notions of haunting and warped mourning to understand the workings of the past in the present.[7] Jacques Derrida suggested that

---

[5] Narvselius and Grinchenko, "Introduction," 2.
[6] Ibid.
[7] Alexander Etkind, *Warped Mourning: Stories of the Undead in the Land of the Unburied* (Stanford University Press, 2013); Jacques Derrida, *Specters of Marx: The State of the Debt, the Work of Mourning and the New International*, Peggy Kamuf, trans., with "Introduction" by Bernd Magnus and Stephen Cullenberg (Routledge, 1994); Avery Gordon, *Ghostly Matters: Haunting and the Sociological Imagination* (University of Minnesota Press, 1997); Maria del Pilar Blanc, and Esther Peeren (eds.), *The Spectralities Reader: Ghosts and Haunting in Contemporary Cultural Theory* (Bloomsbury, 2013); Ann Laura Stoler, "Intimidations of Empire: Predicaments of the Tactile and Unseen," in *Haunted by Empire: Geographies of Intimacy in North American History*, ed. Ann Laura

history is not characterized by a smooth or regular progression. Rather, remnants from the past fracture and "haunt" the present. He conjoined "haunting" with "ontology" to form the word "hauntology" and to refer to these fractures, which he thought of as revealing the otherwise hard-to-describe traces of the past in the present and strange simultaneities. When Derrida developed the term, he was thinking about the fall of the Soviet Union and the promise of communism as well as Karl Marx's use of the metaphor of a ghost in *The Communist Manifesto*. With the term hauntology, Derrida aimed to capture the sense that time has been disrupted, and feels out of joint.[8] He wanted to show how historical figures that become spectral (e.g. heroes, victims, traitors) have a way of lingering and may even seem more real than their embodied counterparts. Put simply, haunting makes itself known in disruptive collective memories. In this article, I use the notions of haunting and warped mourning, discussed next, as concepts that help us flesh out the politics of memory in Crimea more specifically.

Alexander Etkind built upon these ideas when he called ineffective attempts to deal with the past "warped mourning." He maintained that in formerly Soviet areas, the past remains uncannily present as a result of incomplete mourning.[9] Etkind thinks about mourning through the lens of psychoanalysis, and its founder, Sigmund Freud, who made a distinction between mourning and melancholia. Societal mourning is a healthy process accomplished through processes of cultural representation in literature, film, and the arts. In mourning, the past is processed and integrated until it can be recognized as truly past and over. In "melancholia," by contrast, mourning also takes place, but without a conscious or clear understanding of the loss. As a result, the past "returns" or is acted out in ways that are chaotic or strange. Now, the extent to which mourning and melancholia are truly separate is debated. Tammy

---

Stoler (Duke University Press, 2006), 1–22; and Kashif Jerome Powell, "Making #BlackLivesMatter: Michael Brown, Eric Garner, and the Specters of Black Life-Toward a Hauntology of Blackness," *Cultural Studies-Critical Methodologies* 16, no. 3 (2016): 253–60.

8   Derrida, *Specters of Marx*, 49.
9   Etkind, *Warped Mourning*, 16.

Clewell proposes the two modalities of grieving operate together.[10] What is important for this analysis is to take advantage of the insight that the past has a way of troubling and "contaminating" the present.

Although Etkind focused primarily on cultural representations in literature, poetry, art, and film, I use his insights to interpret interview data concerned with interpersonal relationships. Further, whereas Etkind suggests the past is made present in a largely symbolic and detoxified way, I contend that raising the issue of past treason in the Crimean present was destructive for the people involved.[11] The everyday spaces of relationships illuminate the porousness of any boundary between the political and the personal or the past and the present demonstrating the vulnerability of intimate relationships to political forces.

My focus on interpersonal relationships fills a gap in knowledge about the 2014 events in Crimea. Scholarship has illuminated the profound implications for international law and relations[12] as well as repercussions for national identity formation.[13]

---

[10] Tammy Clewell, "Mourning Beyond Melancholia: Freud's Psychoanalysis of Loss," *Journal of American Psychoanalytic Association* 52, no. 1 (2004): 43–67, and Etkind, *Warped Mourning*, 245.

[11] Ibid., 2.

[12] Natalia Belitser, "The Status of the Crimean Tatars in Ukrainian and International Law," *Journal of Soviet and Post-Soviet Politics and Society* 6, no. 2 (2020): 155–82; Gergana Dimova and Andreas Umland, "Introduction: Russia's 2014 Annexation of Crimea in Historical Context: Discourses and Controversies," *Journal of Soviet and Post-Soviet Politics and Society* 6, no. 2 (2020): 145–54; Gergana Dimova, "Legal Loopholes and Judicial Debates: Essays on Russia's 2014 Annexation of Crimea and Its Consequences for International Law," *Journal of Soviet and Post-Soviet Politics and Society* 5, no. 1 (2019): 1–6; Andrew Wilson, "The Crimean Tatar Question: A Prism for Changing and Rival Versions of Eurasianism," *Journal of Soviet and Post-Soviet Politics and Society* 3, no. 2 (2017): 1–46; Nikolai Petrov, "Crimea: Transforming the Ukrainian Peninsula into a Russian Island" *Russian Politics and Law* 54, no. 1 (2019): 74–95; and Ted Hopf, "'Crimea is Ours': A Discursive History," *International Relations* 30, no. 2 (2016): 227–55.

[13] Marlene Laruelle, "Russia as a 'Divided Nation' from Compatriots to Crimea: A Contribution to the Discussion on Nationalism and Foreign Policy," *Problems of Post-Communism* 62, no. 2 (2015): 88–97; and Magdalena Leichtova, "Why Crimea Was Always Ours: Legitimacy Building in Russia in the Wake of the

The militarization of the peninsula, (which is significant for the security of Western Europe), has also received much needed attention.[14] The human rights situation has inspired both academic publications and intergovernmental organization reports.[15] When it comes to the humanitarian dimensions, scholarship on population displacement has argued convincingly that fear and safety concerns, together with issues of sheer survival (emerging from the sanctions and economic isolation of the peninsula) justify treating the Russia-related migration from Crimea as forced displacement.[16] Political repression, draconian economic policies, and social factors all impinged the ability to sustain one's life. While social networks have long been viewed as influential in determining where migrants eventually settle,[17] the Crimean case shows us that interpersonal friction, some of which was based on tropes of treason, was among the social factors influencing flight.

In what follows, I first provide the relevant historical background on events leading up to the 2014 annexation attempt. I then apply the theoretical framework of warped mourning and haunting to Crimea more specifically. After a discussion of my methodology, the main body of the article is devoted to a detailed analysis of interview transcripts utilizing this framework beginning with intimate relationships, progressing to parent-child relations,

---

Crisis in Ukraine and the Annexation of Crimea," *Russian Politics* 1, no. 3 (2016): 291–315.

[14] Andrii Klymenko, "The Militarization of Crimea under Russian Occupation," *Atlantic Council Issue Brief* (2018): 2. https://www.files.ethz.ch/isn/194724/The_Militarization_of_Crimea_under_Russian_Occupation.pdf (last accessed June 2020); and Nikolai Petrov, "Crimea: Transforming the Ukrainian Peninsula into a Russian Island," *Russian Politics and Law*, 54, no. 1 (2019): 74–95.

[15] Halya Coynash and Austin Charron, "Russian-Occupied Crimea and the State of Exception: Repression, Persecution, and Human Rights Violations," *Eurasian Geography and Economics* 60, no. 1 (2019): 28–53.

[16] Austin Charron, "'Somehow, We Cannot Accept It': Drivers of Internal Displacement from Crimea and the Forced/Voluntary Migration Binary," *Europe-Asia Studies* 72, no. 3 (2020): 432–54; and Coynash and Charron, "Russian-Occupied Crimea and the State of Exception."

[17] Khalid Koser, "The Smuggling of Asylum Seekers into Western Europe: Contradictions, Conundrums, and Dilemmas," in *Global Human Smuggling: Comparative Perspectives*, ed. David Kyle and Rey Koslowski (The Johns Hopkins University Press, 2001), 58–73.

and ending with friendship. I find that the resurrection of the traitor concept had a negative impact on many relationships, and was among the factors triggering displacement. I conclude that even though the occupation of Crimea was indeed bloodless, the political events evolving into what is often referred to as a "de facto" annexation had profound personal costs not yet acknowledged in the scholarship on the 2014 Crimean events. In other words, understanding the full significance of the attempted annexation requires integrating the personal experiences analyzed below with the existing literature on the political and humanitarian dimensions of the attempted annexation.

Historical Context

Crimea came under Russian control for the first time in 1783 when Empress Catherine II annexed the territory for geostrategic reasons. Before that, the territory had been controlled by the Crimean Khanate, a major power in eastern European politics. Distrust between Russian authorities (not to be conflated with the Russian people) and Crimean Tatars has followed.

In the nineteenth century, the Crimean War (1853–54) brought Russian colonial policy toward the Crimean Tatars to a new low. During the war, the Russian government charged the Crimean Tatars with a range of crimes including collaborating with the enemy, espionage, and betrayal. Mara Kozelsky argues that, "In an era of heightened religious tension, Russian officials believed their own propaganda: the Crimean War was a holy war and that they had an internal as well as external enemy."[18] Based on archival documents, Kozelsky describes how authorities in Crimea wrote a multitude of reports based primarily on rumor and speculation. She argues that the suspicion of Crimean Tatars was unfounded: a gross exaggeration was fabricated out of three mutinies.[19] In fact, the alleged existence of an extensive Crimean Tatar spy ring at this time

---

[18] Mara Kozelsky, "Casualties of Conflict: Crimean Tatars during the Crimean War," *Slavic Review* 67, no. 4 (Winter 2008): 866–91, here: 866.

[19] Ibid., 877.

was most likely the fantasy of Russian imperial authorities seeking to justify their impending defeat.[20] Immediately after the war, an estimated 200,000 Crimean Tatars emigrated to the Ottoman Empire, followed by years of slow exodus.[21]

The issue of treason became even more important during World War II. When Nazi and Romanian forces occupied Crimea, Crimean Tatars were recruited into support roles with a narrative that they would be liberated from Soviet repression.[22] The Crimean Tatars were prefigured as traitors to the Soviet project by Nazi propaganda aimed to inflate the Crimean Tatar collaboration and enhance an image of German strength.[23] Over the course of the war, the Germans occupiers are believed to have organized about 20,000 Crimea Tatars into self-defense battalions.[24] The primary purpose of the battalions was to protect Crimean residents from the Soviet partisans and they were comprised of people from a variety of ethnic groups. What has received less attention is the participation of some 20,000 Crimean Tatar men in Soviet military forces.[25] Ultimately, the Crimean Tatar cooperation with Nazi and Romanian forces that occupied the peninsula was emphasized, while their significant patriotic contribution to the Soviet effort was downplayed.[26]

Soviet policy played into this hand. Crimean Tatars were not allowed to join the Soviet partisans at the beginning of the war. When Crimean Tatars were admitted, commanders made false reports about their poor performance, tarnishing their reputation.

---

[20] Ibid., 880; and William Fuller, *The Foe Within: Fantasies of Treason and the End of Imperial Russia* (Cornell University Press 2006).
[21] Brian Williams, "A Homeland Lost: Migration, the Diaspora Experience and the Forging of Crimean Tatar National Identity" (Doctoral Dissertation: University of Wisconsin, 1999), 176–78; and Arsenii Markevich, "Pereseleniia krymskikh tatar v Turtsiiu v sviazi s dvizheniem naseleniia v Krymu," *Izvestiia Akademiia Nauk SSSR, gumanitarnykh nauk*, vol. 1 (1928): 375–405 and vol. 2 (1929): 1–16.
[22] Fisher, *Crimean Tatars* (Hoover Institution Press, 1978), 153.
[23] Greta Uehling, *Beyond Memory: The Crimean Tatars' Deportation and Return* (Palgrave Macmillan, 2004): 59–60. See also Alexander Statiev, "Soviet Ethnic Deportations: Intent Versus Outcome," *Journal of Genocide Research* 11, no. 2–3 (2009): 243–64.
[24] J. Otto Pohl, *Ethnic Cleansing in the USSR* (Greenwood 1999), 113.
[25] Ibid.
[26] Williams, "A Homeland Lost," 323; and Pohl, *Ethnic Cleansing in the USSR*.

Further complicating the situation was the shifting definition of treason. If at the beginning treason referred to those who chose to fight alongside the Germans, the notion expanded to encompass people who were forced to aid the occupational regime in any capacity.[27] An example given to me was housekeeping for officers of the German command after one's home was taken over. As Borovyk argues, it is far too gross a simplification to refer to this as "betrayal" or "treason" when it concerns an apolitical population primarily concerned with survival.[28] Whether we are discussing World War II or present times, stark moral dichotomies are ill-suited for understanding strategies of adaptation under occupation.[29]

Nevertheless, the Crimean Tatars were punished with deportation at the end of World War II. To be clear, the victims were not the main collaborators who retreated with defeated German forces, but rather the non-combatants comprised primarily of the elderly, women, and children. Those who were deported traveled in cattle cars that came to be called "crematoria on wheels" due to the high death toll. More perished from malnutrition, dehydration, and disease in the years after deportation. Although the exact number of victims remains disputed, the Ukrainian government has recognized the event as a genocide. It is important to note that the losses could not be mourned at the time: there was no mention of it in the public press and the survivors were forbidden from speaking about the matter. Although a 1967 decree acknowledged the deportation was wrongful, it did not grant Crimean Tatars permission to return, and enmity towards them has lingered.[30] Only

---

[27] Uehling, *Beyond Memory*, 51–52

[28] Mykola Borovyk, "Collaboration and Collaborators in Ukraine During the Second World War: Between Myth and Memory," in *Traitors, Collaborators and Deserters in Contemporary European Politics of Memory*, ed. Gelinada Grinchenko and Eleonara Narvselius (Palgrave Macmillan, 2018).

[29] J. W. Jones, "Every Family Has Its Freak: Perceptions of Collaboration in Occupied Soviet Russia, 1943–1948," *Slavic Review* 64, no. 4 (2005): 747–70.

[30] International Committee for Crimea, "Soviet Decree, 5 September 1967," http://www.iccrimea.org/surgun/sovietdecree1967.html. See also Greta Uehling, "The Crimean Tatars as Victims of Communism," Part II. Dissident (2015) http://blog.victimsofcommunism.org/the-crimean-tatars-as-victims-of-communism-part-ii/.

with the disintegration of the Soviet Union were the Crimean Tatars able to repatriate from places of former exile on a large scale. Their return to Crimea (then part of independent Ukraine) was among the events that Etkind refers to as uncanny. They were people who were strangely familiar and yet different, repressed and yet mysteriously returned.[31]

Fast forwarding to the attempted Russian annexation in 2014, Crimean Tatars were labeled potentially dangerous and traitorous political subjects with renewed vigor. Russian-backed Crimean authorities sought to associate Crimean Tatars with Islamic extremism, banning religious literature and carrying out mass arrests. The enforced disappearances, a contraction of civil liberties under Russian law, and the human rights violations documented by bodies like the OSCE became part of the picture.[32] As for politics of memory, under the new de facto administration, Crimean Tatars were banned from observing their annual day of mourning for the 1944 deportation, which they had publicly observed for over two decades when Crimea was part of independent Ukraine. At the same time the Crimean Tatars were banned from assembling, the de facto authorities arranged for public observances of a new-fangled holiday called "day of happiness." The superimposition of joyfulness on mourning in 2014 captures something of the dissonance in post-2014 memory politics.

The attempted annexation of Crimea prompted significant numbers of people to flee. The exact number, however, is difficult to estimate because not everyone who is displaced chooses to register and the Ministry of Social Policy does not disaggregate its statistics in a way that would assure a clear distinction between those fleeing Donbas and Crimea. While David Blair estimated 100,000 left Crimea as a direct result of the attempted Russian annexation,[33] and this was also the figure parliamentarian Mustafa

---

[31] Etkind, *Warped Mourning*, 36.
[32] OSCE HCNM, "Human Rights Assessment Mission in Ukraine. Human Rights and Minority Rights Situation," The Hague/Warsaw, May 12, 2014, www.osce.org/odihr/118476.
[33] David Blair, "100,000 Flee "Worsening Oppression" as Russia Tightens Grip on Crimea," *The Telegraph*, 11 June 2016, available at: http://www.telegraph.co.uk/

Djemilev cited to me, more conservative estimates like the Internal Displacement Monitoring Center placed the figure at 20,000.[34] The Office of the Prosecutor General in Crimea put the figure in between the two extremes at 48,000.[35]

Theorizing the Past in the Present

The process of reckoning with the totalitarian past has produced a rich literature examining both official discourse from the top down, and a plethora of collective memories from the bottom up. While the categories of victimhood and heroism, as Grinchenko and Narvselius point out, have received abundant attention, betrayal, collaboration, and treason have been relatively neglected.[36] This needs to be rectified considering how often Soviet authorities fabricated cases of "betrayal of the motherland" to quash dissent. Especially in times of accelerated change, betrayal was the leading ideologically charged trope, and the main tool of social and political control in the Soviet Union. As we shall see, the trope is really operative on at least two planes: public and private. That Soviet authorities cast the normative relationship between the state and its citizens as one of love, loyalty, and commitment laid important groundwork for the public and the private to intersect.

But how to account for the workings of the Soviet past in the Crimean present? Attempts to come to terms with the past in formerly Soviet eras, from Etkind's perspective, have been complicated by the lack of clarity with regard to who, exactly, is a perpetrator and who is a victim. As he points out, the perpetrators of human rights abuses in the Soviet Union often became victims

---

news/2016/06/11/100000-flee-crimea-as-russia-tightensgrip/ (accessed 31 July 2019).

[34] Ukraine IDP Figures Analysis', Internal Displacement Monitoring Centre, 2015, available at: http://www. internal-displacement.org/europe-the-caucasus-and-central-asia/ukraine/figures-analysis/ (accessed 13 March 2018).

[35] "'Deportatsiia povtoriaetsia': Okolo 48 tysiach chelovek vynuzhdenno pokinuli Krym za vremia anneksii—Mamedov," *Krym.Realii*, 18 March 2020, https://ru.krymr.com/a/news-krym-anneksija-vynujhdennyj-perejezd-ofis-genprokurora/30619035.html.

[36] Grinchenko and Narvselius, "Introduction," 3.

themselves, and in some cases survivors lived to become perpetrators. During the occupation of Crimea in 1941–44, residents were known to switch between Allied and Axis sides, sometimes multiple times in the course of a single day.[37] Mourning and moving on is therefore often foreclosed, interrupted, or "warped" in these regions, Etkind argues, because understandings of events have not yet stabilized.[38] In Crimea, the lack of a unified historical narrative about either the Crimean War or the occupation by Romanian and Nazi forces during World War II provides precisely this kind of unstable foundation. Rather than being acknowledged *as* past, the past remains present, manifesting in the vocabulary of treason, which is deployed a way that is disconcerting and inaccurate. Statements about betrayal and treason, long part of the Crimean social landscape, became even more polyvalent when the attempted annexation provided additional pretext.

Making matters worse, the 2014 Crimean operation brought back Soviet-era symbols and slogans as part of the larger strategy of influence.[39] Continually reiterating the glories that the Soviet Union presented as "friendship of peoples" is one example. We also see children dressed in Russian military uniforms trotting in Crimean parades, and the St. George's Ribbon, a Russian symbol commemorating World War II pinned ubiquitously to chests. Speaking of rallies and demonstrations, Soviet flags and placards with images of Stalin were held high after the attempted annexation. The lack of consensus then, is further exemplified by the way some people mourned the end of the Soviet Union whilst others mourned the lives that were lost as a result of it. This idea that the present is "oversaturated with the past"[40] goes part of the way to explaining

---

[37] Greta Lynn Uehling, "Having a Homeland: Recalling the Deportation, Exile, and Repatriation of Crimean Tatars to Their Historic Homeland" (Doctoral Dissertation, Ann Arbor, 2000).
[38] Etkind, *Warped Mourning*, 10.
[39] Jolanta Darczewska, "The Anatomy of Russian Information Warfare: The Crimean Operation, a Case Study," *Point of View* 42, available at https://www.osw.waw.pl/sites/default/files/the_anatomy_of_russian_informat ion_warfare.pdf (accessed 3 May 2021).
[40] Etkind, *Warped Mourning*, 11.

why labels like "traitor" (crude terminology when the legitimacy of the authorities is in dispute) were used in 2014.

To be clear, the point is less that links to the past are durable, which would be too broad, than that notions of treason and traitors proved to be remarkable tools for sorting Crimean society according to political objectives. Indeed, examining the ontology of haunting, or "haunt-ology," as Derrida describes, suggests that what societies grieve is perhaps not so much the past itself as the great future it was supposed contain. Hauntology proposes that unless the social memories of losses and traumas can be recognized, processed, and mastered, they may continue to be disruptive.[41] Talk of treason and Nazi collaboration after the 2014 events certainly demonstrates strange simultaneity.

Methodological Considerations

My argument is based on three periods of ethnographic fieldwork in Ukraine of two months duration each, carried out between May 2015 and July 2017. During this time, I taped 90 interviews devoted to the occupation of Crimea. Two types of interviewing were carried out: semi-structured interviewing with internally displaced persons according to an interview schedule, and open-ended interviewing with people who were best engaged with a tailored approach because of their expertise or unique experience. This includes ten interviews that were carried out with people who continue to live in Crimea while they were visiting Ukrainian government-controlled territory.

A random sample of the internally displaced was not possible because as a matter of policy, the Ministry of Social Policy did not disaggregate the displaced population by ethnicity. Another complicating factor is that not all internally displaced persons (IDPs) register as such. I used a combination of non-random sampling methods to obtain the perspectives of people from different ethnic, religious, and age groups. Respondents were selected with the assistance three NGOs that work with internally

---

[41] *Ibid.*, 16.

displaced persons. I also invited people I met at social, cultural, and political events over the three-year period to speak privately. All interviews were carried out face-to-face by myself. Respondents were welcomed to speak in Russian, Ukrainian, or English.[42] Since they were displaced from a predominantly Russian-speaking region, the majority chose Russian. The people who left Crimea as a result of the attempted annexation are dispersed across Ukraine, and I therefore distributed my interviewing across areas where they had settled. Specifically, I worked in Kyiv, Lviv, Kherson, Slavyansk, and a number of small villages and towns like Drohobych surrounding these urban hubs.

Interviewing was supplemented with various forms of participant observation including socializing with people I had previously lived with one and two decades earlier; attending concerts, political speeches, and cultural events, and two stays at the Crimean blockade in Ukrainian government-controlled territory. I also used a participatory methodology of photo journaling, in which participants were asked to provide a visual account of their daily life. Previous trips spanning two decades, especially one in 2013, just seven months prior to Russian occupation also inform this work. The interviews were transcribed, coded, and analyzed using software for qualitative data analysis. The coding was emergent and the structure refined over the three-year period leading to the findings presented below.

According to the terms of my funding, I was prohibited from going to Russian-controlled Crimea or non-Ukrainian-government-controlled territory in the eastern part of Ukraine, terms that I strictly adhered to. The methodological limitation here is also an epistemological one: this article cannot make any claims to representativeness. I will leave such claims to sociologists and demographers. Aiming for validity, this study is small, in-depth, qualitative, and ethnographic by design.

---

[42] Since the author understands but does not speak Ukrainian, the assistance of a native Ukrainian speaker was utilized in transcribing the interviews, which were carried out in a mixture of Russian and Ukrainian.

Findings on a Present Haunted by the Past—
Part One: Intimate Partner Relationships

Between 2015 and 2017, the people I spoke with used treason, a political concept integral to citizenship and statehood, to describe contexts that were unofficial, personal, and intimate. In fact, the theme of treason came up in discussions about relationships in over three quarters of the ninety Crimea interviews I carried out. The theme was germane for people of Russian, Ukrainian, and Crimean Tatar ethnicity alike. Only rarely did this topic arise in the interviews I carried out for a separate project with people displaced from the Donbas region of eastern Ukraine, suggesting the idea of treason is especially important in Crimea.

Being labeled a traitor or collaborator influenced decisions to leave Crimea. For example, asked why he left Crimea, a 38-year-old Crimean Tatar man I will call Edem replied primarily in terms of an interpersonal relationship:

> I got burned. Badly. My wife, with whom I was on friendly terms, basically refused to even converse with me anymore because I became Ukrainian and became, for the second time, a "traitor." The first time our people turned out to be traitorous was in 1944 and now we are again "traitors," because we did not go for union with Russia. That's why she doesn't want to associate with me now (Edem, No. 02, IDP, Crimean Tatar, male, age 38).

We might think of Edem as appearing to his wife like a ghost of traitors past: as Derrida and Etkind explain, a ghost is the body of someone, appearing as someone else.[43] In a nutshell, to haunt is to have an enduring force.[44] Although Edem was born in the 1980s, his ethnicity prefigures him as betraying his country twice. Thus the vocabulary left over from World War II was quite effective in socially

---

[43] Derrida, *Specters*, 7; and Etkind, *Warped Mourning*, 17.
[44] Yael Navaro-Yashin, *The Make-Believe Space: Affective Geography in a Postwar Polity* (Duke University Press, 2012), 17.

sorting people into categories, producing parallel and interconnected crises of loyalty.⁴⁵

Like Edem, Oksana recalled the circumstances of her flight from Crimea through relationality as much as nationality. A Ukrainian woman, she recounted how she ended her engagement to her ethnically-Russian fiancée after nine years of co-habitation.

> There was a personal reason for my departure. The father of my boyfriend was very pro-Russian and was of such a bent that I felt tension that intensified in our home. I did not feel comfortable. On the day of the referendum, when I saw how pleased he was with the unification with Russia I sensed a certain kind of condescension against me. These are my roots and it is not only that they are not accepted, but they are being laughed at in that house. I decided that that was the last straw, that I could not live like that (Oksana No. 01, IDP, Ukrainian, female, age 31).

In this example, the attempted annexation upset the previously harmonious personal relationship between the young woman and her future in-laws. Interactions like these bring "the weight of hundreds of past volitions and motivations into the present."⁴⁶ Talk of treason and betrayal thereby become foundational to both the political and the social terms in which annexation was being carried out at the most intimate levels. Oksana continued:

> So, we broke up. We haven't talked in over a year. My personal belongings remain there. He doesn't make contact because I am actually considered a "traitor." They alleged that my patriotism is useless and I will soon become convinced of that (Oksana, No. 01, IDP, Ukrainian, female, age 31).

Oksana watched as her Ukrainian loyalty made her a "traitor." From her perspective, the only path that made sense was to break off the engagement, and flee the peninsula.

---

45 Anne Murrell Taylor, *The Divided Family in Civil War America* (University of North Carolina Press, 2005): 9. Speaking of the American Civil War, Abraham Lincoln famously used the family as a metaphor for the nation.
46 William Reddy, *The Navigation of Feeling: A Framework for the History of Emotions* (Cambridge University Press, 2001), 120.

But that is not all. Oksana suspected that, had she stayed, her relationship with her (yet-to-be-born) children would have been undermined. She thought her in-laws and her children's teachers would work to alienate her from children on the basis of her political views. An abundance of stories about the re-socialization of children in school, as well as a mother-son example I relate below, make her concerns reasonable. A specific classroom exercise will illustrate the point. According to a parent with a primary school-aged child in Crimea, sheets of paper with an empty rectangle were distributed periodically. Pupils would be asked to draw the national flag. The children who filled in Ukrainian colors were sent to the principal's office, chastised, and threatened with bad marks. Stories like this one gave Oksana a basis to infer raising her child to share her love of Ukraine would create problems for them both.

Voting in the referendum of 2014 was a major impetus for accusations of treason, and decisions to flee, between intimate partners. This was the case even though the legitimacy of the referendum was in question. In one of the most extreme examples related to me, a husband threatened homicidal violence against his wife. Maria, a Russian woman who reported having been happily married for about five years, told me of the chilling call she received from her husband after the votes had been tallied:

> After the referendum, he called with the words, "now I have an automatic [rifle] and I am coming to kill you and the children. You are traitors—you didn't go to the referendum." (Maria, No. 113, IDP, Russian, female, age 30).

We can think of Maria's identity as a spectral one when she is labeled with the ultimate political crime. Maria is not only herself but, in a way, also standing in as a traitor to the motherland of 1944. And to a certain extent, those supposed traitors deported in 1944 were standing in, as ghostly hauntings if you will, of the Crimean Tatar mutineers during the 1853–54 Crimean War. Pervasive talk of treason makes Crimea into a space of haunting in Derrida's sense of "an obsession, fear, fixed idea, and nagging memory" that seeps into and overshadows the situation.[47] This is also a space of mourning in

---

[47] Derrida, *Specters*, 177.

the sense that it raises memories of losses and anxieties suffered long ago. After receiving this call, Maria immediately left the peninsula, not even pausing to pack any belongings other than her identity documents and a single change of clothes.

This "break up" transpired on the basis of a political loyalty that was new, supporting the idea that the tropes of treason and betrayal are deployed with considerable agility. Gaining importance in times of change, they have the ability to index both continuity and change. Maria explained that in the early days of the occupation, her husband had been surreptitiously defending Crimea *against* Russian forces as part of a civilian brigade. After the referendum, he swiftly repositioned himself to align with the acting authorities. Accusations of betrayal and treason, then, were part of the process of social and political transformation. Integral to establishing the new boundaries of moral community, they helped to delineate insiders and outsiders, and establish who is with "us" and who is not.

**Findings on a Present Haunted by the Past—
Part Two: Parents and Children**

A majority of the people I interviewed reported that their family relationships had been adversely affected and this too, figured in decisions about whether to remain in Crimea or leave. A young Russian man I met picking through used clothing at a humanitarian shelter in government-controlled Ukraine, Stepan, told me that his father became angry and told him "you are no longer my son" when he learned Stepan had not participated in the referendum. The shelter's director told me intense emotional reactions like this one were common. To protect his staff from the emotional fall-out, he had placed tall shelves between staff desks and the area where clients were allowed to select shoes and clothing from an enormous mound on the floor. Stepan told me he fled his parent's home—and Crimea—as a result of the squabble. Had this not occurred, Stepan would have been in a position to inherit a home and the family's business. His losses make the material as well as emotional stakes in the Crimean transformation more clear.

Relationships between parents and younger children further demonstrate how political changes came at a high personal cost. A Crimean Tatar woman, Elvira, recounted how her ten-year-old son, who usually took enormous pleasure in recounting the events of his day after being picked up from school, suddenly withdrew. She described the day when her son sat with his arms crossed in the back seat. For a little while, asking him what was wrong drew only a terse "nothing." Then:

> Finally, he told me that in school that day the teachers said that all Ukrainians are "traitors." He had seen me watching programs in Ukrainian on the Internet and even weeping at some of the content and concluded [that] therefore I am a traitor and he shouldn't associate with me (Elvira, No. 57, IDP, Crimean Tatar, female, age 45).

Elvira recalled in tears the silence that had suddenly come between herself and her young son. We have already considered how schools play a role in setting a pro-Russian patriotic tone. Here we see the toll on a family when patriotic emotions were officially prescribed.[48] For the boy, getting along with peers and authority figures at school required expressing positive emotions about the political order. This alignment simultaneously created tension with his pro-Ukrainian mother. These "schoolyard" politics are integral to what has been described as the redrawing "interior frontiers" within national communities.[49] In Crimea, it takes place in part along ethno-national lines: it was firstly the ethnic Crimean Tatar and Ukrainian children, presumed to be loyal to Ukraine, who were scrutinized. Observant Muslims were another target of interest as potentially disloyal subjects. But as Stepan and others show, the primary frontier was political loyalty: One either was or was not loyal to the Russian-backed authorities of Crimea. Like some kind of osmosis: the trope of treason could fill the classroom, the police station, or the intimate space in a private automobile.

---

48 Reddy, *Navigation of Feeling*, 114.
49 Stoler, *Race and the Education of Desire*, 7.

In contrast with the classic Soviet morality tale of Pavlik Morozov,[50] this story of Elvira and her son ends with reconciliation. Finding themselves in a hostile atmosphere, the entire family fled to government-controlled Ukraine, where Elvira and her son regained their closeness. I interacted with the family on numerous occasions and the son consistently spoke favorably about his new life in the capital city. A photo-journal he made in Kyiv dramatized the process: he selected Ukrainian national colors and symbols and his favorite Ukrainian language teacher to depict his life. What was most conducive to harmony, it seemed, was a categorical separation of people according to the political leanings.

Elvira and her son recovered, but the redrawing of interior frontiers could also divide nuclear families. Take Darina, a woman of mixed Russian and Ukrainian heritage. After deciding she identified most closely with Ukraine, she left Russian-occupied Crimea. Formerly a physician, she took a job as a nurse in a hospital. Darina's account of her disagreement with her mother dramatizes the workings of these internal frontiers because being pro-Ukrainian meant a significant split from her pro-Russian mother, who stayed in Crimea. In one texting thread, her mother asked her to bring her the grandchildren for a summer visit. Darina retorted "you betrayed us (Ukrainians) and now you are asking us to vacation on your stolen land? The only way I will come back is on top of a tank." The idea of returning "on top of a tank," used by many with whom I spoke between 2015 and 2017, conjures images that are iconic of the end of World War II. Darina's statement takes up the 1944 lexicon in a way that suggests strange simultaneity: time is out of joint. That Darina identifies as Ukrainian, not Crimean Tatar (the group traditionally assumed to be traitorous), further supports my point that treason and collaboration were being used as tropes for

---

[50] Soviet ideology rejected what was construed as a "bourgeois" value placed on family. The morality hero, Pavlik Morozov is fabled to have denounced his father to the authorities for hiding the family's grain during collectivization. In Soviet times, the boy's behavior was presented as a model of loyalty to nation. His story became the subject of plays, a symphonic poem, a full-length opera, and at least six biographies. It was also the basis for a number of films.

sorting people according to political positions, not factual historical referents.

Taken together, these exchanges show the conversational processes through which relationality was brought into alignment with politicality. Darina's mother attempted to persuade her to visit with statements like, "if you are a good mother, you will think of your children and come home." But not even this attempt to elicit maternal guilt softened Darina's resolve to reject all aspects of Russian control over Crimea. At the end of the text exchange, Darina and her mother called one another "traitor," superimposing the political and personal. The emotional intensity was obvious in the exclamation points and all-caps texts with which they communicated. Darina's mother closed the conversation hyperbolically with "Never write to me again." Mother and daughter had reconfigured their relationship using the vocabulary of treason in such a way that their personal relationship became analogous to the political one.

Having considered intimate and family relations, we turn now to friendship. Whereas the disruption of intimate and family relations were often explicitly described as triggers to flee the peninsula, the dissolution of friendships influenced migration less directly through broader fears and frustrations. As we shall see, it boiled down to what kind of society one wanted to live in.

Findings on a Present Haunted by the Past—
Part Three: Friendship

Questions of loyalty and betrayal had a major impact on friendship after the attempted Russian annexation. Some preserved friendships by avoiding all discussion of politics. This enabled friendships to continue even if political views diverged. Others were unable or unwilling to bracket the personal from the political, treating them, as feminist theorists have long argued, as inseparable. When political views differed, these friendships often ended. The majority of IDPs I spoke with reported having lost friends.[51]

A prevalent theme with regard to friendship was that the change in authorities revealed "who was who." As a man named Aider related:

> Of course, [my] circle of friends has changed. (...) A person shows himself for real when he says: "you're a traitor." Why am I a traitor? For what reason? How? How have I become a traitor?
>
> They say it directly, "you're a traitor." And at the same time the person can't explain why I'm a traitor and whom do I betray, it is just the way it is. (Aider, No. 91, IDP, Crimean Tatar, male, age 36).

The inability to explain how or why another person was a traitor points to the unhinged quality of warped mourning, in which the real historical referents are misplaced or missing altogether. This Crimean Tatar man felt that anti-Crimean Tatar statements became socially acceptable making the atmosphere inhospitable.

Labeling other people "traitors" became an effective way to signal one's own allegiance to current authorities. People who refused to make statements about respect for Stalin, love for Putin, or loyalty to Russian Federation were faced with the prospect of social ostracism and the potential of losing friends. Several university students who continue to reside in Crimea pointed out that their acquaintances not only took pains to express pro-Russian political opinions, but quickly switched their ethnicity when the new authorities took power. The rapid speed with which these changes were made conveys just how important articulating the "right" views and position must have seemed. Politics, identity, and friendship became thoroughly entangled.

A specific example of this entanglement is provided by Fatima. Her friend's rapid change of ethnic identification evoked strong feelings of betrayal:

---

[51] Women were more likely to talk about a loss of friends, with forty-eight mentions across the twenty-seven interviews with females and twenty-eight mentions across the twenty-three interviews with males.

> My Ukrainian friend registered herself as Russian as a result of the occupation. I want to live among people who do not betray you, and are not traitors to their country. The state, friends, husband: it turns out it is all linked together [interlacing her fingers and forming her hands into a ball] (Fatima, No. 59, IDP, Crimean Tatar, female, age 55).

The slide from betrayal as an act to traitor as an identity here awakens the ghosts of conflicts past. Even when people's choices may have had more to do with survival, the "overflow" of the past in the present contributed to strong moral judgements.

With regard to an over-abundance of the past in the present, both Derrida and Etkind advocated reflecting rather than reenacting.[52] This is easier said than done when personal and political are imbricated. Based on her expectation of unambiguous political fidelity, Russian identification made her friend a "traitor" to country, family, and friends. I spent time with Fatima each year that I returned to Ukraine between 2015 and 2017 and we continue our conversation. She was as definitive her friend betrayed her in 2020 as in the 2015 conversation related above. Like the fingers of two hands, then, political allegiance could be tightly interlaced with personal relationships in a way that necessitated leaving.

Throughout, people justified laminating the personal and political with parsimonious logic: if a person betrays his country by accepting a foreign power, he will sooner or later betray you as his friend or family member. Churchill was sometimes quoted as saying that a person who is capable of betraying you once will do it a second time. One way to understand how a single lexicon was used across personal and political is in terms of metonymy. Etkind suggested haunting could be metonymic in the sense that a part may come to stand for the whole. This parallels the idea that what metonymy does is create mental associations. Sara Ahmed gives the example of "Islamist" and "terrorist" that come to be used together habitually. As minds utilize these signs, they become durably linked to each other and people.[53] The fallacy is more difficult to discern with each iteration. But these associations across official and unofficial

---

[52] Gordon, *Ghostly Matters*, 202.
[53] Ahmed, *The Cultural Politics of Emotion* (Routledge, 2004), 15, 75, 76, 194.

interactions bring us only part of the way to understanding how, and with what consequences, the word "traitor" operated in this context: the conversational dynamics I have been discussing are so much more than metonymy, having consequences for who lives on the Black Sea peninsula.

The attempted annexation prompted between 20,000 and 100,000 people to leave the peninsula.[54] The material and demographic correlations are also evident in the migration of Russian subjects to Crimea. According to the Department of State Statistics under Russian Federation, more than 200,000 have relocated from places in Russia to Crimea. Andrei Klymenko and Tatyana Guchakova argue that figure could be as high as one million if unregistered Russian residents in Crimea are also included.[55] In the first year of occupation alone, Russian citizens purchased 10,000 apartments and another 21,000 new apartments were projected to be constructed for Russian military and their families.[56] Journalists and scholars have recorded many statements to the effect that "Russia is doing everything to rid itself of the unwanted population in Crimea."[57] According to Ridvan Bari Urcosta and Lev Abalkin, Russian authorities aim to rid the peninsula of opponents to Russian rule or "cow them to silence through increasingly repressive

---

[54] "'Deportatsiia povtoriaetsia': Okolo 48 tysiach chelovek vynuzhdenno pokinuli Krym za vremia anneksii—Mamedov," *Krym.Realii*, 18 March 2020, https://ru.krymr.com/a/news-krym-anneksija-vynujhdennyj-perejezd-ofis-gen prokurora/30619035.html; "Ukraine IDP Figures Analysis," Internal Displacement Monitoring Centre (2015), http://www.internal-displacement. org/europe-the-caucasus-and-central-asia/ukraine/figures-analysis/ (accessed 13 March 2018); and David Blair, "100,000 Flee 'Worsening Oppression' as Russia Tightens Grip on Crimea," *The Telegraph*, 11 June 2016, http://www.telegraph. co.uk/news/2016/06/11/100000-flee-crimea-as-russia-tightensgrip/ (accessed 31 July 2019).

[55] Andrii Klymenko and Tatiana Guchakova, "Sotsial'no-ekonomichne stanovyshche na okupovaniy Krymu 2014–2020," *Listopad*, 3.

[56] Andrii Klymenko, "The Militarization of Crimea under Russian Occupation," *Atlantic Council Issue Brief* (2018), 2, available at: https://www.files.ethz.ch/isn/194724/The_Militarization_of_Crimea_under_Russian_Occupation.pdf.

[57] "'Rossiia delaet vse, chtoby izbavit'sia ot neugodnogo naseleniia v Krymu'— Eskender Bariev," *Krym.Realii*, 6 August 2019, https://ru.krymr.com/a/esken der-bariev-o-zameschenii-krymchan-rossiyanami/30095186.html (accessed 10 January 2021).

measures and militarization of the peninsula, which in turn serves the paramount goal of establishing Crimea as a Russian military asset."[58] Talk of treason, then, is one piece of a larger, more complex puzzle that includes migration and demographic change in the interest of the solidification of Russian-backed rule.

Portraits of Stalin: A Hauntological Understanding

The lack of consensus about the past, and the way it remains "hot and liquid" rather than "cool and crystalized," to use Etkind's words, is perhaps most clearly articulated in responses to portraits of Stalin I collected about seven months before the Russian occupation.[59] Participants in my study were presented with a copy of a popular image of Stalin and asked what came to mind when they looked at the portrait. Many respondents made clear that what they grieved was Stalin, rather than his millions of victims. Responses included statements like "pride for the activities he carried out," and normative appraisals that "this is the image of a good person." Pro-Stalin sentiments were right at the surface and easy to find. As Andrei, a veteran of World War II (which he referred to emphatically as the Great Patriotic War) stated: "How to put it into words? Empathy that he may have overplayed his leadership somewhat."[60] Rather than extend his empathy to the victims, then, Andrei offers it to a genocidal leader. Although ideas about Stalin are admittedly multifaceted,[61] Andrei's statement points to a repetition of the past, rather than repair. The statement points to the unfinished quality of mourning because it fails to acknowledge the losses and suffering that were also a part of his rule. Just as it is crude to equate loyalty to Ukraine today with "fascism," it is

---

[58] Ridvan Bari Urcosta and Lev Abalkin, "Crimea: Russia's Stronghold in the Black Sea," *European Council on Foreign Relations*, 1, https://www.ecfr.eu/article/essay_crimea_russias_stronghold_in_the_black_sea.

[59] Etkind, *Warped Mourning*, 176.

[60] Uehling. "Having a Homeland."

[61] Maria Lipman, Lev Gudkov, Lasha Bakradze, and Thomas de Waal (eds.), *The Stalin Puzzle: Deciphering Post-Soviet Public Opinion* (Carnegie Endowment, 2012). Polls have showed approval for Stalin has increased since the end of the Soviet Union.

grotesque to empathize with Stalin, whose reign unleashed terror for the Soviet people.

In Crimea, the failure to come to terms with the Nazi occupation is evident in the way the whole question of treason is taken as part of the present. When people speak of treason in contemporary Crimea (with explicit reference to Hitler and the Nazi forces that had previously occupied Crimea) they are effectively conjuring the specter of World War II or Great Patriotic War traitors. This can be profitably viewed as a haunting because the past is "lurking" within the present: the ostensible traitors are dead and yet continue to trouble the living. The concept of treason has been let loose in a way that obfuscates what actually happened then and, in particularly unhelpful ways, reanimates an exclusionary logic. Practices run the gamut from ostracism in schools and hate speech at bus stops to denial of services in health clinics and harsh treatment at police stations. Russian-occupied Crimea is therefore characterized by what Derrida would call a failure of social imagination: people still imagine Crimea as it was under Stalin.[62] With Natalia Khanenko-Friesen, then, I think the continual reliance on the tropes of betrayal and treason demonstrates both the fluidity of the construct, which can be easily borrowed from one political context to the next, and its abiding centrality.[63]

Every region of the world has been through war, and virtually every country interprets its present with recourse to its past. In Crimea, these processes reveal a palimpsest of treasons and "traitors." The hauntological aspect is particularly evident in the suspicion towards Crimean Tatars who were not actively or openly pro-Ukrainian. A Crimean Tatar man living and working in government-controlled Ukraine who I will call Alim told me that after his son returned to Crimea from visiting him, school

---

[62] Gordon, *Ghostly Matters*; and Maria Del Pilar Blanco and Esther Peeren, "Introduction: Conceptualizing Spectralities," in *Ghosts of Memory: Essays on Remembrance and Relatedness*, ed. Janet Carsten (Blackwell, 2007).

[63] Natalia Khanenko-Friesen, "Betrayal and Public Memory: 'The Myroslav Irchan Affair' in the Diaspora-Homeland Disjuncture," in *Traitors, Collaborators and Deserters in Contemporary European Politics of Memory*, ed. Gelinada Grinchenko and Eleonora Narvselius (Palgrave Macmillan, 2018), 361–82.

administrators brought the young man in for questioning. At the end of the questioning, he stated, school authorities threatened his son that if he leaves Russian-controlled territory to visit his Crimean Tatar father again, they would block him from going to college. Alim, who frequently traveled back and forth, reflected:

> There are no centuries there. Maybe it's like the nineteenth, maybe the twentieth century. Honestly. Old Soviet music is pounding at the bus stations that wasn't heard before (Alim, No. 131, IDP, Crimean Tatar, male, age 39).

Centuries are extraneous in the sense that the present is organized to resemble what was at least imagined as the Soviet past. A hauntological understanding of the statement that there are no centuries in Crimea (and the 2014 Russian occupation more broadly) points to how events are being reenacted rather than repaired. One such reenactment without reflection is that Crimean Tatars reported their Slavic neighbors standing in front of their homes discussing how they would divide up the appropriated property of Crimean Tatars after President Putin orders the next, 21st century deportation of the Crimean Tatars. The rhetoric about treason may also represent an attempt to conjure away the specter of a multi-ethnic, politically plural Crimean society. Instead, a schizochronic concatenation of future-oriented economic development and Russian militarization coupled with deep longing for Soviet days propels Crimea into a very uncertain future.

The literature on haunting is agnostic about the potential for mourning to result in the resolution of social tensions. Etkind argues that integrating the repressed and forgotten content into a coherent narrative gives a voice to victims and ends the ineffective kind of mourning that is locked in repetition. Derrida is more interested in learning to live better *with* ghosts, where specters and ghosts are metaphors for the inherent disjointedness of history, inheritance, and ideology.[64] In his view, the ghosts and remains from the past inevitably return and provide a powerful tool for

---

[64] Maria Del Pilar Blanco and Esther Peeren, "Introduction: Conceptualizing Spectralities," 7.

reflection, if we can only become more fully conscious of these processes.

Derrida also advocated for "hauntological justice," meaning recognition for the un-mourned victims of nationalist, racist, colonialist, sexist, or totalitarian violence as the basis for ethical politics.[65] As Etkind corrects, however, "justice" is perhaps not the best term.[66] Fallen victims don't benefit from posthumous recognition of their suffering or sacrifice. Rather, it is learning that is most important to breaking cycles of repetition. This idea was echoed throughout my fieldwork in statements like:

> In my opinion, we need to remember our past, but live in the present and plan for the future. Right now, what we need is to understand. It's necessary to learn history so we don't make the same mistakes in the future (Servir, No. 79b, resident of Crimea, male, Crimean Tatar, 20).

Treason Writ Large

As a qualitative study, the focus of this article has been the politics of memory within interpersonal relationships. As such, it has concerned itself with what could be called the micropolitics memory. Similar politics are evident at other analytic and discursive levels from Presidential speeches, to legislation, and the press and commentary about both. For example, politicians used #zrada (betrayal) to help followers in Ukraine find and categorize their posts.[67] In both Ukrainian and Russian courts of law there have been numerous efforts to legislate and prosecute treason. In Russia, there has been severe repression of "traitors."[68] Two examples of the former include the case of the ex-Crimean health minister who was

---

[65] Derrida, *Specters*, xix.
[66] Etkind, *Warped Mourning*, 219.
[67] Tanya Zaharchenko, "In the Ninth Circle: Intellectuals as Traitors in the Russo-Ukraine War," in *Traitors, Collaborators and Deserters in Contemporary European Politics of Memory*, ed. Gelinada Grinchenko and Eleonora Narvselius (Palgrave Macmillan, 2018), 197–212; here: 198.
[68] Marlene Laruelle, "The Three Colors of Novorossiya, or the Russian Nationalist Mythmaking of the Ukrainian Crisis," *Post-Soviet Affairs* 32 (2015): 55–74.

sentenced to ten years in prison,[69] and the decision to impose sanctions on 10 former Crimean law enforcement officers for high treason.[70] Members of the Crimean government who found new positions among the Russian-backed authorities, and military and police officers who took a new oath were in general excoriated. On the Russian side, President Vladimir Putin's "etymological ammunition" includes calling anyone who publically questions the need to fight Ukraine a "traitor."[71] It is no mere coincidence, then, that World War II is at the forefront of Crimean consciousness: Zaharchenko argues that Russian elites' meticulous fusion of the present day struggle with the anti-fascist struggle of World War II has created a "mnemonic stronghold." World War II and the present fight are conflated in a way that raises strong fears and sentiments.

On the Ukrainian side, the Ukrainian government has made a plethora of attempts to make up for past injustices by including the Crimean Tatars in the Ukrainian historical narrative.[72] More broadly and paradoxically, however, the Ukrainian government's decision to not take action when Russian-backed forces entered Ukraine's Crimean territory has also been characterized as traitorous to the people of Crimea. While attempts to mourn the unmourned dead and to find ways to reckon with the past are laudable, then, the processes of recognition and reconciliation are only beginning.

---

[69] "Ex-Crimean Health Minister given 10-Year Prison Term in Ukraine for Treason," *Interfax: Russia & CIS Military Newswire*; Moscow, 13 July 2020 (accessed 3 May 2021).
[70] "Zelensky enacts NSDC decision on indefinite sanctions to 10 former law enforcement officers for high treason" Interfax: Ukraine General Newswire; Kiev [Kiev], 1 March 2021.
[71] Zaharchenko, "In the Ninth Circle," 198.
[72] In March 2014, the Ukrainian Verkhovna Rada or parliament recognized the Crimean Tatars as indigenous or at least "rooted," and recognized the Crimean Tatar political body as this people's highest political organ. In November 2015, the *Rada* named the 1944 deportation a genocide.

Conclusion

This article has demonstrated how the 2014 occupation and attempted annexation of Crimea by Russian Federation profoundly disrupted interpersonal relationships. My interlocutors between 2015 and 2017 utilized the vocabulary of betrayal and treason from the Crimean War and World War II to talk about damaged friend, family, and intimate relationships in the wake of the 2014 political events. Given how the political and interpersonal "break-ups" mobilized the politics of memory, concepts of haunting and warped mourning were used to elucidate how the past was contaminating the present.

The central question was why the trope of treason was activated in private and personal contexts. The literature on notions of betrayal, collaboration, and treason suggests that in reckoning with the totalitarian past, treason becomes a trope that is highly effective in utilizing collective memories to achieve political or ideological objectives. In the wake of the 2014 Russian annexation attempt, treason was a tool for delineating the boundaries of a pro-Russian society. The specific objective of invoking betrayal in Crimea, then, was to redraw the internal frontiers between those loyal to Russia and those loyal to Ukraine. Put slightly differently, in Crimea after the annexation attempt, loyalty to Ukraine was deemed "betrayal" because it endangered social cohesion around Russian-backed authority. In a time of rapid social and political change, then, the trope of treason was not only a remnant of the past, but a tool for crafting the future.

All was not lost for those stigmatized as having "betrayed" Russian rule in Crimea, however. In leaving for government-controlled Ukraine, they sought out a civil society with like-minded individuals. We are accustomed to thinking about the politics of memory and migration separately, but in Crimea they come together. The tropes of betrayal, collaboration, and treason acted as more than metaphors when they influenced, together with other factors of course, the decision to flee the Black Sea peninsula. Deciding to stay in Crimea and support an occupying Russian regime or oppose this regime and leave are high stakes positions that reflect moral as well as political convictions. The choice, as some respondents understood it, was between a return to a Soviet-like authoritarian state where what to say and do is proscribed, and casting one's lot with the somewhat beleaguered state of Ukraine. These values go to the heart of what kind of a society one would like to live in.

Understanding of the attempted annexation will be incomplete if it is confined to the political, legal, and humanitarian repercussions of 2014. Only by acknowledging the disruptions to intimate, friend, and family relationships can we fully appreciate the nature and kind of suffering for those who objected to annexation. I have therefore argued that the trope of treason reveals the personal costs of political upheaval in Crimea.

"Dark" and "Golden" Times: Crimean Tatars under Tsarist and Soviet rule (1783–1941)

Kerstin S. Jobst

Abstract: In this article, Jobst examines the Crimean Tatar history under Russian and Soviet rule up to the deportation in 1944. She asks whether the attributions of a "golden" or "dark age" evident in Crimean Tatar discourse are tenable. Instead of looking at Tatar-Russian history only from the vanishing point of 1944, she argues for a differentiated view that considers phases of confrontation and cohabitation between Tatars and Slavs as well.

One hundred years after the Russian annexation of the Crimean Khanate, the Crimean Tatar reformer Ismail Gasprinskii (İsmail Gaspıralı; 1851–1914)[1] praised this act with great enthusiasm in the bilingual journal *Terjiman/Perevodchik* ("The Translator"): "On 8 April 1783, a small Khanate, exhausted by disorder and bloodshed, became part of one of the world's greatest empires and received peace and the protection of just laws under the auspices of a formidable power." So for Crimean Muslims, he said, this anniversary is a cause for celebration.[2] Despite all the fractures and ambivalences in Gasprinskii's relationship with the tsarist empire and Russianness[3] and the not unlikely deference to tsarist censorship that might also speak from these words, he was fundamentally convinced that not only the Crimean Tatar

---

[1] On Gasprinskii's biography and the significance of the journal *Terjiman/Perevodchik*, and further reading, see Ulrich Hofmeister, "Ein Krimtatare in Zentralasien: Ismail Gasprinskij, der Orientalismus und das Zarenreich," *Österreichische Zeitschrift für Geschichtswissenschaft/Austrian Journal for Historical Studies* 28, no. 1 (2017): 114–41.
[2] "Stoletie," *Terjiman/Perevodchik*, no. 1, 10 April 1883, 1.

population but Russian Muslims in general benefited from Russian rule.[4] Only with the help of this European power, was the mantra at least in his Russian-language publications,[5] could the backwardness of Muslim society that he had identified be overcome.

Contrary to this positive assessment of Russian imperial rule, in retrospect the first century after 1783 marked a dark period for historians with Tatar nationalist viewpoints.[6] In contrast, Soviet rule before World War II—especially the years 1923 to 1928—is often described as a golden era by both Russian authors and representatives of the Crimean Tatar diaspora.[7] At the same time, however, the greatest collective trauma of the Crimean Tatar community is associated with Soviet rule of the Crimea: the deportation of almost all Crimean Muslims on the Black Sea peninsula in May 1944 by armed NKVD units. Under the pretext that this population group had collaborated en masse with the Wehrmacht during the German occupation, the approximately 200,000 Crimean Tatars were deported to Central Asia under terrible, and for many even deadly, conditions. They were denied the opportunity to return home for the decades to come. The Crimean Autonomous Soviet Socialist Republic (ASSR), which had existed since the 1920s, was dissolved in 1945 and—until the so-called Khrushchev gift of 1954, which made Crimea part of the

---

[4] On this, in principle, Sue Curry Jansen, *Censorship: The Knot that Binds Power and Knowledge* (Oxford University Press, 1988), and Charles A. Ruud, *Fighting Words: Imperial Censorship and the Russian Press 1804-1906* (University of Toronto Press, 1982).

[5] A systematic comparison of Gasprinskii's Tatar and Russian-language writings is lacking so far.

[6] Sirri H. Kirimli, *National Movements and National Identity Among the Crimean Tatars 1905-1916* (PhD diss., The University of Wisconsin, 1990), 43, for example, refers to the years between 1783 and 1883 as the "dark century of the Crimean Tatars."

[7] This is the assessment of the author of the standard work on the history of the Crimean Tatars; Alan W. Fisher, *The Crimean Tatars* (Hoover Institution Press, 1978), 136. See also Vladimir Poliakov, *Krym: Sud'by narodov i liudei* (Tavrida, 1998), 51. See also Kerstin S. Jobst, *Geschichte der Krim: Iphigenie und Putin auf Tauris* (de Gruyter/Oldenburg, 2020).

Ukrainian Soviet Socialist Republic—became part of Soviet Russia.[8] The 1944 deportation—*sürgün* (expulsion) in Crimean Tatar—can be compared to other national/ethnic traumas in its lasting significance for the Crimean Tatar collective, such as the Ukrainian *Holodomor* or the genocide of the European Roma (*porajmos*).[9] Unlike the latter two cases (not to mention the singular Shoah), however, world public opinion has paid very little attention to this event. In any case—and this is one of the central theses of this article—both positive and negative developments are associated with the history of Crimea under Russian and Soviet rule. It is not possible to assess the fate of the Crimean Tatars under the dominance of St Petersburg or Moscow solely from the perspective of 1944,[10] since the Russian–Crimean *encounter*,[11] as is common in colonial and imperial contexts, varied between phases of (spatially and locally varying) cohabitation and confrontation. In order to substantiate this thesis, the following is a concise description of the

---

[8] Swetlana Czerwonna and Martin Malek, "Literarische Verarbeitungen der Deportation der krimtatarischen Bevölkerung: Eine 'vergessene' Quelle der Geschichtsforschung," *Österreichische Zeitschrift für Geschichtswissenschaft/ Austrian Journal for Historical Studies* 28, no. 1 (2017): 218–28; Otto Pohl, *Ethnic Cleansing in the USSR, 1937–1949* (Greenwood Press, 1999); Alexander Nekrich, *The Punished Peoples: The Deportation and Fate of Soviet Minorities at the End of the Second World War* (Norton, 1978); and Norman Naimark, *Fires of Hatred: Ethnic Cleansing in Twentieth-Century Europe* (Harvard University Press, 2001), here especially 85–107.

[9] Cf. Greta Lynn Uehling, *Beyond Memory: The Crimean Tatars' Deportation and Return* (Palgrave Macmillan, 2004).

[10] This is especially true since the Crimean Tatar–Russian history continues to be written, as the Black Sea peninsula was once again annexed by a Russian power in 2014, this time by the Russian Federation. Under the auspices of international law the overwhelming majority of Crimean Tatars reject the secession from Ukraine, as do the majority of international experts. They are very critical of Russia's actions. See, among others, Otto Luchterhand, "Die Krim-Krise von 2014: Staats- und völkerrechtliche Aspekte," *Osteuropa*, no. 5–6 (2014): 61–86. At present (winter 2021/2022), the Russian–Ukrainian conflict is reaching another, international dimension.

[11] It is not without reason that I use the term *encounter*, which is often used in postcolonial studies, to refer to the encounter between colonial power and colonial object, but decidedly without assuming the passivity of the latter. See, for example, John J. Clarke, *Oriental Enlightenment: The Encounter between Asian and Western Thought* (Routledge, 1997).

history of the Crimean Tatars under Russian (i.e. from 1783 until the First World War) and Soviet (until the invasion of Nazi Germany in 1941) aegis; it is asked to what extent the ex post attributions—"dark" and "golden times"—reflect these findings and how any ambivalences in the Russian–Crimean Tatar relationship, which are to be expected, are to be evaluated.

In the case of Crimea, it is also assumed that the colonial *encounter* was not a one-way street, i.e., the imperial (primarily Russian/Slavic) culture by no means exerted a one-sided influence on the Muslim one. Rather, at least in the daily interactions between Crimean Tatars and non-Muslim new settlers of various origins who moved to the peninsula in the years after the annexation, it can be assumed that there was a lived reciprocity: One side at least partially assimilated the other, one group learned something from the other, and both parties often made quite pragmatic efforts to shape their lifeworlds *("Lebenswelten")* in a consensual manner.[12] This aspect of intercultural contacts on the peninsula has so far been investigated by historians only in rudimentary fashion and not systematically, despite numerous references in contemporary reports.[13] The

[12] Historically, until the Second World War, the peninsula was a multi-ethnic area. This was to change in the long term only after the *Shoah*, which was also carried out in the Crimea by the Nazis, and the deportations of 1944, to which not only Crimean Tatars, but also Crimean Greeks and Armenians, among others, fell victim. After the German invasion of the USSR, the Soviet authorities had already resettled the descendants of the Germans recruited by Catherine II, for the most part, in inner-Soviet territories. On German colonists as a whole, see Hans Auerbach, *Die Besiedlung der Südukraine in den Jahren 1774–1787* (Harrassowitz Verlag, 1965); and Detlef Brandes, *Von den Zaren adoptiert: Die deutschen Kolonisten und die Balkansiedler in Neurußland und Bessarabien 1751–1914*, Schriften des Bundesinstituts für ostdeutsche Kultur und Geschichte, vol. 2 (Oldenburg, 1993). On the Crimean Germans in the context of National Socialism, see Meir Buchsweiler, *Volksdeutsche in der Ukraine am Vorabend und Beginn des Zweiten Weltkrieges – ein Fall doppelter Loyalität?* (Bleicher, 1984), esp. 280.

[13] See, for example, the memoirs of the St. Gallen merchant Daniel Schlatter, who repeatedly traveled to the Crimea in the 1820s, *Bruchstücke aus einigen Reisen nach dem südlichen Russland in den Jahren 1822 bis 1828: Mit besonderer Rücksicht auf die Nogayen-Tataren am Asowschen Meer* (Huber, 1830), 65, where Schlatter reports on the offer made to him by a Crimean Tatar to give him a Tatar woman as a wife, since he was virtually taken for one of their own. On the Schlatter family, see also Ursula Kälin, "Die St. Galler Kaufleute Daniel

research situation is more satisfactory with regard to the opportunities for participation of the Crimean Tatar population under tsar and Soviet rule.[14]

On the basis of previous research on Russian Crimean politics in the tsarist and Soviet periods, the following aspects are particularly noteworthy: In both regimes, a not inconsiderable discrepancy between (legal) norm-setting and (lived) practices can be assumed, which could situationally be to the advantage or disadvantage of the Crimean Tatar population. In addition, the Muslim Crimean population "was subjected to a thoroughly dialectical modernization process in cultural contact with both Russian and Soviet power," as a result of which they underwent profound, irreversible social and economic change.[15] Moreover, the relationship between Russian/Soviet power and Crimean Tatars, whose Khanate had after all been an important actor, political balancer and power factor in the region and in Eastern Europe in the early modern period, as the Polish historian Dariusz Kołodziejczyk convincingly points out, can basically be described as

---

und Abdullah Schlatter in Südrussland," in *Fakten und Fabeln: Schweizerisch-Slavische Reisebegegnungen vom 18. bis zum 20. Jahrhundert*, eds. Monika Bankowski *et al.* (Helbing & Lichtenhahn, 1991), 335–63, especially 337: Elsewhere Schlatter praised the good relationship between Tatars and the inhabitants of the colony Zürichtal. The reason for this was, among other things, the fact that the Swiss living there had an excellent command of Crimean Tatar. Cf. initial findings and reflections in Kerstin S. Jobst, "Die Wahrnehmung von Assimilations- und Akkulturationsprozessen im russischen Krim-Diskurs vor dem Ersten Weltkrieg," in *Gemeinsam getrennt: Lebenswelten der multiethnischen bäuerlichen Bevölkerung im Schwarzmeer- und Wolgagebiet vor 1917*, eds. Victor Herdt and Dietmar Neutatz (Harrassowitz Verlag, 2010), 181–94.

[14] Stefan B. Kirmse, "Law and Empire in Late Tsarist Russia: Muslim Tatars Go to Court," *Slavic Review* 72, no. 4 (2013): 778–80; and Kerstin S. Jobst, "Gefährliche Fremde und Titularnation? Partizipation der Krimtataren im. Zarenreich und in der frühen Sowjetunion," in *Staatsbürgerschaft und Teilhabe: Bürgerliche, politische und soziale Rechte in Osteuropa*, eds. Katrin Boeckh *et al.* (De Gruyter Oldenbourg, 2014), 179–98.

[15] Jobst, "Gefährliche Fremde," 179.

colonial, even if—as is usual in colonial contexts—there was certainly room for maneuver for the latter.[16]

The 1783 Annexation and Its Consequences for the Crimean Tatar Population

Almost two decades ago, E. L. Lazzerini, undoubtedly one of the most important experts on the history of Muslims under Russian rule and, moreover, Ismail Gasprinskii's biographer, rightly stated that the consequences of the Russian annexation of 1783 had been "substantial and fundamental" for Crimean Tatars. Unlike Gasprinskii, however, Lazzerini was much more critical in his assessment of Russian rule: Although some social groups, in particular the Islamic clergy, had benefited from tsarist rule, the consequences for the Muslim community had been demographically (because of the Crimean Tatar exodus, to which we will return later) and economically (above all because of the changed situation of the peasantry) devastating. He made a particularly drastic judgment, however, about the spiritual and material condition of Crimean Tatar society itself, which, at least until the first decades after the Crimean War, was extremely poor: "Culturally, Tatar society appears to have become a wasteland unable to sustain even a modicum of intellectual, literary, or artistic activity."[17] Whether such a drastic finding about an "indigenous"[18]— or subaltern—society influenced by colonial conditions would still

---

[16] Dariusz Kołodziejczyk, "Krymskoe khanstvo kak faktor stabilizatsii na geopoliticheskoi karte Vostochnoi Evropy," in *Ukraina i sosednie gosudarstva v XVII veke: Materialy mezhdunarodnoi konferentsii*, ed. T. Yakovleva (Skif, 2004), 83–89.

[17] Edward L. Lazzerini, "The Crimea under Russian Rule: 1783 to the Great Reforms," in *Russian Colonial Expansion to 1917*, ed. Michael Rywkin (Mansell Publishing Limited, 1987), 123–38, here 136.

[18] In the case of the Crimean Tatars in particular, the term "indigenous" in the literal sense of the word is not very appropriate, even though it was repeatedly used by the community itself as well as by the tsarist and Soviet administrations. The peninsula, like the northern Black Sea shore as a whole, has historically always been a highly divergent transit area of different population conglomerates and ethnic groups.

be formulated in the same way[19] in times of Postcolonial Studies or the Subaltern Studies Group, which have meanwhile also been applied in Eastern European history, is more than questionable.[20] Nevertheless, the parameters mentioned by Lazzerini are undoubtedly relevant for assessing the living conditions of the Crimean Tatar population under Russian (and Soviet) rule. These are: Population development, economy, and culture, so that these, as well as the general political participation opportunities of the Crimean Tatar population, will be examined in more detail below.

The Crimean Khanate, which had been under a privileged relationship of suzerainty with the Ottoman Empire since the late 15th century, had been a very serious threat to the security of the southern borders of Moscow and also to Poland-Lithuania for several centuries.[21] Again and again its cavalry army, sometimes alongside the Ottomans, had invaded the north, above all to take prisoners, who either found good sales on the slave markets around the Black Sea, or whose redemption they let themselves pay dearly. Sometimes, however, they also cooperated with the Russians, for example when it came to defeating the Polish or other opponents.[22] At the latest since the end of the 17th century, however, the

---

[19] A representative example is Gayatri Chakravorty Spivak, *Can the Subaltern Speak? Postkolonialität und subalterne Artikulation*, trans. Alexander Joskowicz and Stefan Nowotny, with an introduction by Hito Steyerl (Turia + Kant, 2007).
[20] All the more so, since Lazzerini ("Crimea," 136) assigns to Russian power quite patriarchally the role of educator: "While the Russian government was hardly solely responsible for the grim condition in which Tatar society found itself by the middle of the nineteenth century, it certainly did little to ease the transformation which it had a hand in fostering of a once vital culture."
[21] Cf. Kerstin S. Jobst, "Das Krimchanat in der frühen Neuzeit: Eine historische Einführung," in *Im Auftrag des Königs: Ein Gesandtenbericht aus dem Land der Krimtataren: Die Tartariae descriptio des Martinus Bronovius*, eds. Stefan Albrecht, Michael Herdick and Falko Daim (Schnell und Steiner, 2011), 17–24. For the history of the Crimea from ancient times to the present see Kerstin S. Jobst, *Geschichte der Krim: Iphigenie und Putin auf Tauris* (De Gruyter Oldenbourg, 2020).
[22] Cf. Anna L. Khoroshkevich, *Rus'i Krym: Ot soiuza k protivostoianiiu. Konets XV – nachalo XVI vv.* (Editorial URSS, 2001); and Dariusz Kołodziejczyk, *The Crimean Khanates and Poland-Lithuania: International Diplomacy on the European Periphery (15th-18th Century): A Study of Peace Treaties Followed by Annotated Documents* (Brill, 2011).

elimination of the Khanate, which over time had fallen behind Russia technologically, was on the foreign policy agenda of the tsars. The desire to extend the tsarist empire to the northern shore of the Black Sea and thus (in geopolitical terms) bring it to its "natural borders" was one reason for this, as the Russian historian V. O. Kliuchevskii a century later explained the Russian Crimean policy of the 18th century.[23] The aim was to expel the Ottomans, who had a whole series of bases there, and possibly even to capture Constantinople/Istanbul and dissolve the Crimean Khanate.[24] The latter was finally achieved in 1783, after the Khanate had gone through a brief period of sham independence (1774–83).[25] This short decade had been marked by civil war-like conflicts and several Russian military interventions, leaving Crimea to face widespread destruction and general chaos. In order to convey to the majority Muslim population of Crimea that the general situation would change for the better as a result of the Russian takeover, Russian officials, most notably the confidant of Tsarina Catherine II, Prince Grigory Potemkin (1739–91), pursued a policy of small steps. Confidence-building measures included giving the impression that the old Muslim elites would continue to have some say. The previous Crimean Tatar officials in the administration were not completely disempowered, especially since they were needed: Because the peninsula was terra incognita for the Russian military,[26]

---

[23] Vasily O. Kliuchevsky, *Russian History from Peter the Great to Nicholas I* (Artemis Verlag, 1945), 167.
[24] This plan is most often referred to as the so-called Greek Project; Edgar Hösch, "Das sog. 'Griechische Projekt' Katharinas II," in *Jahrbücher für Geschichte Osteuropas* 12 (1964): 168–206; and Nadezhda Korshunova, "Vostochnyi vektor geopolitiki Ekateriny II: 'Grecheskii proekt,' *Library of the Chelyabinsk State University website*, http://www.lib.csu.ru/vch/10/2003_01/006.pdf (accessed 21 January 2016).
[25] Alan W. Fisher, *The Russian Annexation of the Crimea 1772–1783* (Cambridge University Press, 1970).
[26] Cf. the chapter "Die russischen Krim-Debatten im 18. Jahrhundert: Von der Terra Incognita zur Perle des Imperiums" ("The Russian Crimean Debates in the 18th Century: From Terra Incognita to Pearl of the Empire," in Kerstin S. Jobst, *Die Perle des Imperiums: Der russische Krim-Diskurs im Zarenreich* (UVK Verlag, 2007), 85–130. On Russia's Crimean policy in this phase, see Alan W. Fisher, *The Crimean Tatars* (Hoover Institution Press, 1978), 70-78; and Kelly

essential tasks of the polity (such as that of tax collection) remained in Tatar hands for a brief transitional phase.[27] After only a few months, however, a radical change of course took place, as the creation of the greatest possible "structural uniformity between these new territories and the core areas of Russia" was strived for[28] —and largely implemented. The Crimea was administratively, politically, and economically firmly integrated into the existing imperial structure;[29] it was hardly ever referred to as a colony in Russian discourse,[30] and it held a special position among many Russians simply because of its charming climate, its lush nature and beauty (at least in the South) or its historical charge.[31]

In this process, there were Crimean Tatar winners and losers—and both groups were often not recognizable at first glance, since, for example, legal guarantees granted to certain social groups de jure were by no means always implemented de facto, so that there were sometimes considerable discrepancies between written and actually granted rights. One example of this is the Crimean Tatar upper classes, the *murza*: In many empires, including the Russian Empire, the co-option of indigenous elites was part of the policy in newly acquired territories, as it was an important means of generating loyalty and thus effective colonial rule. This was also the case in the Crimea with the Statute of Nobility promulgated in 1785. In it, the secular Tatar elites were placed on an equal footing with the Russian *dvorianstvo*. Among the rights granted were, for

---

O'Neill, *Claiming Crimea: A History of Catherine the Great's Southern Empire* (Yale University Press, 2017).

[27] Lazzerini, "Crimea," 125, describes the policy of the new rulers in the first months after annexation as a combination of Russian military administration and "a native civil government."

[28] Stephan Conermann, "Expansionspolitik im Zeichen des Aufgeklärten Absolutismus? Katharina II. und die Krimtataren," in *Russland zur Zeit Katharinas II: Absolutismus - Aufklärung - Pragmatismus*, eds. Eckhard Hübner, Jan Kusber and Peter Nitsche (Böhlau Verlag, 1998), 337–59, here 355.

[29] This distinguished Crimea, for example, from the Muslim territories in Central Asia that were conquered in the course of the 19th century.

[30] Cf. Jobst, *Perle*, 225f.

[31] On this in detail *ibid*. as well as Jobst, "Über den russischen Südländer: Zur Funktion der Krim als russischer Süden und des južanin (Südländers) im russischen Krim-Diskurs des Zarenreichs," *Comparativ* 19, no. 5 (2009): 34–49.

example, exemption from compulsory service and taxes, as well as the guarantee of noble land ownership by the crown.[32] On the level of law, the *murza* thus possessed the same privileges as Russian nobles in Moscow or Saratov. In practice, however, it turned out that the Crimean Tatars were by no means always able to implement this right, since, in contrast to the Russian nobility, they rarely possessed documents certifying ownership, which had striking economic consequences for the people concerned. The discrepancy between (Tatar) customary and Russian written law thus often led to an actual disadvantage for the actually co-opted indigenous elite, whose property was confiscated in favor of the crown in quite a few cases. In addition to this partial economic expropriation, there was also a political expropriation,[33] since the indigenous administration was gradually eliminated, a situation that was to change only in the course of the gradual introduction of empire-wide landscape representations (Russian *zemstva*) beginning in the 1870s. Only then did Crimean Tatar local politicians gain greater influence over municipal affairs such as worship or infrastructure.[34] At the same time, a partial assimilation into Russian (upper-class) worlds could be observed, as some *murza* had begun to adapt the lifestyle and social outlook of the Russian nobility and to move closer to their social counterparts.[35]

Similarly ambiguous must be judged the consequences of Russian rule for the Crimean Tatar peasantry, who at first glance appear privileged compared to Slav peasants in the central Russian territories. Tatar peasants remained personally free after 1783, even though the proportion of serf peasants in the newly acquired territories in the south, including the peninsula, was to increase to over six percent until immediately before the peasant liberation of

---

[32] Cf. Paul Robert Magosci, *This Blessed Land: Crimea and the Crimean Tatars* (University of Toronto Press, 2014), 55.
[33] Cf. Fisher, *Crimean Tatars*, 75–77.
[34] Exceptions were the Tatar centers such as Karasubazar and Bakhchisarai.
[35] Magocsi, *This Blessed Land*, 55. This aspect of Russian–Crimean Tatar cultural contact also still awaits fundamental scholarly study.

1861 due to the influx of Russian or Ukrainian serfs.[36] Their influx and St. Petersburg's peupling policy, which was pursued quite consistently until the first third of the 19th century, with the help of German colonists, among others,[37] expanded the labor supply on the peninsula. This was to the disadvantage of the Crimean Tatar peasants and contributed to the deterioration of their economic situation. In addition, many large landowners—whether of Tatar or other origin—tried to undermine the traditional rights confirmed to the Tatar peasants by Catherine II. Although state actors occasionally acted as protectors of the Tatar peasant classes, the latter fell into a profound economic crisis in the course of the 19th century.[38]

The Muslim clergy *(ulema)*, on the other hand, was clearly one of the winners and—as was to be seen—also one of the Romanovs' loyal supporters until the end of the tsarist empire. The Muslim "clerical assembly," formed in 1794, was presided over by a mufti appointed by the respective ruler, who—in accordance with the Russian system—received a title of nobility and was responsible for the religious concerns of the Muslims for the province or Governorate of Taurida, which extended beyond the actual peninsula.[39] He was paid by the state, as were the other Muslim clergy, thus creating a special bond between the crown and Islam dignitaries. The mobile and immobile (real) property of the Muslim community was also exempt from state taxes, and the *ulema* retained supervision over religious and ritual matters as well as over the keeping of birth and death registers.[40]

With regard to the parameters of "economic development" and "opportunities for participation," the tsarist period was "rather dark" for the Crimean Tatar population, especially if another of the

---

[36] Patricia Herlihy, *Odessa: A History 1794–1914* (Harvard University Press, 1986), 79f.
[37] See also the recent work by V. E. Vozgrin, *Nemetskie kolonisty i korennoi narod Kryma v natsional'noi politike rossiiskoi imperii* (RKhGA, 2015).
[38] For an overview, see Jobst, *Perle*, 220–25.
[39] *Tavricheskaia oblast'* (Taurian Province), formed in 1784, became *Tavricheskaia guberniia* (Taurian Governorate) in 1802.
[40] Lazzerini, "Crimea," 131f.

abovementioned assessment criteria is added, namely that of Tatar population development. This was lastingly influenced by own and foreign migrations, much less by natural changes in the birth or death rate.[41] This shows that the Russian–Tatar cultural contact was already characterized by the factor of Muslim emigration, above all to the Ottoman Empire, long before the violent exodus of the Tatar Crimean population in 1944. Even though the first reliable census in the Russian Empire was conducted only in 1897, which, moreover, in the case of southern Russia, did not distinguish between the peninsula proper and the *Tavricheskaia guberniia* beyond it, it is indisputable that the Crimean Tatars, who constituted the majority of the population until 1783, were marginalized in the course of the 19th century, even though exact estimates of the Crimean Tatar share of the peninsula's population before the first Russia-wide census of 1897 are not very valid. Generally, the following figures are assumed: At the time of annexation, an estimated 300,000 people had inhabited the peninsula, a majority of them Crimean Tatars (i.e., over 150,000). By 1790, their number is said to have been only 140,000, so that a first wave of emigration of over 10,000 people can be assumed.[42] After the Ottoman–Russian Peace of Jassy in 1791, another 20,000 to 30,000 of those Tatars left the peninsula who did not want to accept the "foreign," i.e., Christian-Orthodox tsarist rule, as this treaty destroyed all Muslim hopes for the re-establishment of the political supremacy of the Sultan. Emigration never completely dried up until the end of the Crimean War, and then peaked in the early 1860s before largely coming to a halt in the early 20th century. During the great emigration after the Crimean War, in which two-thirds of the Crimean Tatars are said to have participated according to estimates that are admittedly open to

---

[41] Crimean Tatar emigration during the tsarist period can be considered well studied. The following works are representative: Gulnara Bekirova, "Problema emigratsii krymskikh tatar v rossiiskoi istoricheskoi literature 1800-1930 godov," *Krymskie Studii* 7, no. 1 (2001): 186–200; Mark Pinson, "Russian Policy and the Emigration of the Crimean Tatars," *Güney-Doğu Avrupa Araştırmaları Derigisi* 1 (1972): 37–56; and the seminal work by Brian Glyn Williams, *The Crimean Tatars: The Diaspora Experience and the Forging of a Nation* (Brill, 2001).
[42] V. D. Yaremchuk and V. B. Bezverkhyi, "Tatary v Ukraine. Istoriko-politologichnyi aspekt," in *Ukrains'kyi istorichnyi zhurnal* 5 (1994): 18–29, here 20f.

debate, it was predominantly the Tatars settling in the steppe areas who left the peninsula, less so those in the coastal and mountain regions.⁴³ Due to the continued colonization with mainly Slavic (Russian, Ukrainian, and Bulgarian) settlers, the number of Crimean inhabitants increased to more than half a million by the end of the century.⁴⁴

The great exodus of Crimean Tatar inhabitants after the Crimean War was fiercely discussed in Russian circles, its causes sought and debated as to whether it was beneficial for Crimea and the empire. As it turned out, public opinion was by no means unanimous, as a contemporary aptly stated in 1860, i.e., at the height of the emigration wave: There were representatives of a "bold" position who saw the Crimean Tatar exodus as one of the "happiest events of recent times," since these Muslims had proved to be disloyal and, moreover, economically ineffective during the Crimean War. Representatives of the "cautious" position, on the other hand, would have lamented above all the loss of the Crimean Tatar labor force.⁴⁵ This "cautious" position had quite famous and respected supporters, such as the general engineer E.I. Totleben (1818–84), one of the heroes of the Crimean War.⁴⁶ He spoke out strongly against the Tatar exodus, deplored the bad state policy

---

43 Cf. Brian G. Williams, "*Hirja* and Forced Migration from Nineteenth-Century Russia to the Ottoman Empire. A Critical Analysis of the Great Crimean Tatar Emigration of 1860-1861," *Cahiers du Monde Russe* 41 (2000): 79–108, here 79. In the first half of the 19th century, according to his estimate, the Crimean Tatar population had grown, due to a high birth surplus and a long period of peace, to about 300,000, of which, according to this author's estimates, up to 200,000 left the Crimea in the 1860s. Andrii Kozyts'kyi arrives at somewhat different figures and assumes just over 140,000 exiles; Andrii Kozyts'kyi, *Henotsyd ta polityka masovoho vynyshchennia cyvil'noho naselennia u XX st.* (Litopis, 2012), 363f.,

44 For this, see fundamentally Henning Bauer *et al.* (eds.), *Die Nationalitäten des russischen Reiches in der Volkszählung von 1897*, 2 vols. (Steiner, 1991).

45 N. Shcherban', "Pereselenie krymskikh tatar," in *Zabveniiu ne podlezhit: Iz istorii krymsko-tatarskoi gosudarstvennosti i Kryma: Nauchno-populiarnye ocherki* (Tatarskoe Knizhnoe Izdatel'stvo, 1992), 36–54, here 36 (originally *Russkii Vestnik* 5 [1860], issues 11–12).

46 Another "proto-Tatar" actor was Alexander Herzen (1812–70), who also took a stand against the Tatar exodus in his London exile journal *Kolokol* (The Bell). On this and the debates mentioned above, see Jobst, *Perle*, 232–42.

towards this useful population group—and at the same time attested them a rather low intellectual development potential.⁴⁷ Despite this advocacy, for Totleben, just as for other imperial "defenders" of the Crimean Tatars, there was no doubt whatsoever about Russian superiority over Muslims or even about the legitimacy of tsarist rule over the peninsula; at least, however, individual political measures were criticized.⁴⁸

There is no doubt that economic reasons played a major role in the emigration of a partly pauperized peasant population, but there were also two other factors: On the one hand, the former titular nation was met with mistrust from the very beginning, certainly also due to a diffuse, historically internalized "Tatar fear."⁴⁹ The Crimean Tatars' religious differences were taken into account, as was their special, cultural proximity to the Ottoman Empire, which in any case represented a decisive variable in Russian foreign and security policy. It was no coincidence that Crimean Tatars were considered notoriously disloyal to Russia, whether in the Crimean War or in the two world wars. The military and ideological strategist of the Russian annexation of Crimea, Prince Potemkin, was neither the first nor the last Russian politician to desire a peninsula "liberated" from the Crimean Tatar population.⁵⁰ In fact, Russian administrations more or less sublimely encouraged Crimean Tatar emigration, for example by issuing passports unusually generously

---

47 E. I. Totleben, "O vyselenii tatar iz Kryma v 1860 godu: Zapiska generaladiudanta E. I. Totlebena," *Russkaia Starina* 24, vol. 78, no. 4–6 (1893): 531–50, here 534.
48 Totleben, too, can thus be described as an ethnic imperialist. Cf. Robert H. MacDonald, *The Language of Empire: Myths and Metaphors of Popular Imperialism 1880–1918* (Manchester University Press, 1994), 6f.
49 On learned, collective fears, see Johannes Feichtinger and Johann Heiss (eds.), *Geschichtspolitik und "Türkenbelagerung," Kritische Studien zur "Türkenbelagerung,"* 1 (Mandelbaum, 2013); and Feichtinger and Heiss, *Der erinnerte Feind, Kritische Studien zur "Türkenbelagerung,"* 2 (Mandelbaum, 2013).
50 Potemkin to Catherine II, 29 July 1783, in *Ekaterina II i G. A. Potemkin: Lichnaia perepiska 1769-1791*, ed. V. S. Lopatin (Nauka, 1997), Letter 672, 178; "Sei poluostrov eshche budet luchshe vo vsem, ezheli my izbavimsia tatar na vykhod ikh von."

in times of strict population regimes.[51] All in all, however, Russian policy toward Crimean Tatars in the tsarist period was characterized by structural rather than direct physical violence (unlike under Stalinism).[52]

On the other hand, certain conditions within the Crimean Tatar community itself led to emigration. For example, the obligation of Muslims to leave the domain of "infidels" and to move to a "prepared second homeland [...] in the bloc of non-subjugated Muslims"—in the case of the Crimean Tatars, that is, to the Ottoman Empire—which has been judged differently in research.[53] The extent to which this religiously motivated emigration, known as *hirja*, was preached as doctrine by the local mullahs and thus influenced the believers cannot be conclusively assessed, but it may have played a role in some villages.[54] Another motive for emigration seems plausible, which is generally associated with the so-called

---

[51] See also Mara Kozelsky, "Casualties of Conflict. Crimean Tatars during the Crimean War," *Slavic Review* 67, no. 4 (2008): 866–89.

[52] Mara Kozelsky (University of South Alabama) referred to the forcible resettlement of Tatars from the Evpatoria region (northeastern Crimea) and the burning of their villages by Cossack units in the course of the Crimean War in her presentation given at ASEEES 2015 in Philadelphia in November. The background to this is likely to have been the evacuation from the front of groups considered disloyal, which was also common in the context of other acts of war. On the Caucasus, for example, Seteney Shami, *Ethnicity and Leadership: The Circassians in Jordan* (PhD diss. University of California, 1989). On the Crimean War, see Orlando Figes, *The Crimean War: A History* (Metropolitan Books, 2012), 332. On World War I, Kerstin S. Jobst, "Im Spiel mit großen Mächten? Nationale Konflikte nach dem Zerfall des Zarenreichs bis zum Beginn des Russischen Bürgerkriegs 1918/19 auf der Halbinsel Krim," in *Nationalitätenkonflikte im 20. Jahrhundert: Ursachen von inter-ethnischer Gewalt im Vergleich*, eds. Philipp Ther and Holm Sundhaussen (Harrassowitz Verlag, 2001), 83–107. On the question of collaboration of the Crimean Tatar population with the Wehrmacht: Norbert Kunz, *Die Krim unter deutscher Herrschaft 1941-1944: Germanisierungsutopie und Besatzungsrealität*, Veröffentlichungen der Forschungsstelle Ludwigsburg der Universität Stuttgart, 5 (WBG, 2005), 208–10.

[53] Fritz Meier, "On the Controversial Duty of the Muslim to Emigrate in the Event of Non-Muslim Occupation of His Land," *Der Islam* 68 (1991): 65–86, here 68.

[54] Williams, *Crimean Tatars*, 167, also makes out a so-called stock effect, a chain migration triggered by communication between emigrants and the home community, which is often observed in migration contexts.

crisis of the Russian Muslims in the second half of the 19th century.⁵⁵ According to this, emigration was an attempt to stabilize the Muslim identity construction, which was endangered by increasing pressure to modernize. This is supported, for example, by the wave of emigration after 1874, when several thousand Crimean Tatars went into exile to escape the compulsory military service introduced shortly before in the tsarist empire; the fact that this service could be "a Russifying stimulant" was recognized by the Tatar community.⁵⁶

This is an example of an unintended effect that can often be observed in modernization processes, as a measure intended to promote integration sometimes leads to the opposite results. As is well known, the introduction of compulsory military service was part of the so-called Great Reforms, which were successively introduced after the Crimean War, which ended ingloriously for Russia.⁵⁷ So while conscription was not accepted, or only partially accepted, by the Muslim community, the latter certainly benefited from other parts of the reform package. These were a whole series of measures that had varying degrees of success throughout the empire. One of the most important reforms was the abolition of serfdom in 1861, which by its nature did not have a major impact on the personally free Crimean Tatars. The situation was different with reforms in education (1863 and 1871), judicial reform (1864) and the introduction of local self-government units (1864 and 1870).⁵⁸ For this reason alone, it is difficult to assess the tsarist period as "dark," since the scope of action and organization of the Crimean Muslims

---

55 Christian Noack, *Muslimischer Nationalismus im Russischen Reich: Nationsbildung und Nationalbewegung bei Tataren und Baschkiren, 1861–1917*, Quellen und Studien zur Geschichte des östlichen Europas, 56 (Steiner, 2000), 152.
56 Cf. Jobst, "Gefährliche Fremde," 187f. Until then, only Crimean Tatars who served voluntarily served in the Russian army.
57 For the developments in the Crimea after the war see Mara Kozelsky, *Crimea in War and Transformation* (Oxford University Press, 2018).
58 On the targeted exploitation of the leeway granted by Tatars in the Crimea and the Volga-Kazan region, see Kirmse, "Law and Empire in Late Tsarist Russia," and Stefan Kirmse, *The Lawful Empire: Legal Change and Cultural Diversity in Late Tsarist Russia* (Cambridge University Press, 2019).

expanded from the last third of the 19th century onward to a similar extent as that of other nationalities in the empire. It is not without reason that the reform movement of the Russian Muslims that emerged in this phase, so-called Jadidism, originated in the Crimea and is inseparably linked with the name of Gasprinskii, mentioned at the beginning of this article.[59]

The point of departure for Gasprinskii,[60] who was educated both in the West (in Moscow and Paris) and in the East (in Istanbul), was the desolate state of the Muslim school system in Russia, which had traditionally been dominated by religious instruction. Initially, there was no alternative to these schools for Muslims, especially since the Russian educational system had also been underdeveloped for a long time and, moreover, was so little adapted to the needs of Muslim believers that these institutions were often avoided.[61] Gasprinskii was convinced that without a modern (=Western) education system, the Tatars would be excluded from technical and cultural progress and thus susceptible to Russification tendencies. In 1884, therefore, he opened a reform school in the Tatar center of Crimea, in the former capital of Bakhchisarai, where reading and writing Tatar was taught according to an effective method and secular education (including learning Russian) played a greater role in general. After initial skepticism, Muslims from other parts of the empire were convinced by Gasprinskii's educational institutions in Crimea, which had become model schools—and exported his ideas,[62] including the use of a standardized language understandable to all Turkic peoples in Russia, in which, incidentally, the *Terjiman/Perevodchik* was also written. In the long term, Gasprinskii and his comrades-in-arms were concerned with

---

[59] This also had significance beyond the Russian Empire, as pan-Muslim networks emerged; cf. Franziska Davies, "Muslime im Russischen Reich und in der Sowjetunion in globaler Perspektive," in *Globalisierung imperial und sozialistisch. Russland und die Sowjetunion in der Globalgeschichte 1851-1991*, ed. Martin Aust (Campus-Verlag, 2013), 253–73.

[60] On Gasprinskii's biography, see Edward L. Lazzerini, *Ismail Bey Gasprinskii and Muslim Modernism in Russia 1878–1914* (PhD diss., University of Washington, 1973).

[61] See Kirimli, *National Movements*, especially 29–39.

[62] Noack, *Muslimischer Nationalismus*, 147f.

"the creation of a modern, secular Muslim society shaped by men and women *together* (...), in which Islam should only provide a moral guideline."[63] The "Djadidist (...) discourse thus created (...) a community of Muslim elites from all parts of Russia as a communication network,"[64] which, however, did not remain uncontroversial, especially after the empire-wide caesura of the Russian Revolution of 1905: Jadidism was criticized by the Young Tatar movement, which strongly propagated a "three-dimensional" (i.e., Crimean Tatar, ethnic Turkic, and Islamic) national identity construction. For them, this concept was not far-reaching enough. For the traditional Muslim clergy, who were closely tied to the Romanovs, it went much too far.[65]

The fact that such a Muslim reform movement could emerge at all in Crimea, which was ruled by the Russian Empire, and that its "central organ"—the *Terjiman Perevodchik*—could appear, speaks for the fact that Crimean Tatars were by no means merely an object of tsarist imperial rule. Also, the fact that they used this room for maneuver in local self-government or in court, that their indigenous elites were co-opted and that these could become collaborating profiteers, shows that despite all the distortions and notorious distrust of the Crimean Tatars, tsarist rule could not have been only "dark." Nevertheless, the Crimean Tatar elites were indisputably deprived of the primacy of independent political action and their autonomous competence to shape society was at least limited, as is common in colonial contexts.

The Soviet Crimea until 1941

The transition from religious to national collective identification models, which was typical of this part of Europe at the turn of the 19th and 20th centuries, had also taken place among parts of the Crimean Tatar population, as became apparent in the course of the

---

[63] Jobst, *Perle*, 204.
[64] Noack, *Muslimischer Nationalismus*, 150.
[65] Hakan Kirimli, "The 'Young' Tatar Movement in the Crimea 1905–1909," *Cahiers du monde russe et soviétique* 34, no. 4 (1993): 529–60, here 534.

First World War and the revolutions of 1917. The *Milliy Fırqa* (Party of the People), which saw itself as their national mouthpiece before its rapprochement with the Bolsheviks, came into being in the same year. It modified its political goals in the course of the upheaval, which was marked by revolutionary unrest (especially in Sevastopol, which was dominated by soldiers and sailors), repeated invasions of the peninsula by the Red Army and White Guards, and the German occupation (February to November 1918): While in the spring of 1917 one could still imagine cultural autonomy within a democratic, federal Russian state, by the end of the year an independent Crimean state was already on the agenda. In the end, however, this did not come to pass, as the Bolsheviks finally prevailed and took over an extremely exhausted region marked by hunger and destruction at the end of 1920.[66]

Despite the great ideological distance between the "white" (tsarist) and the "red" (Soviet) empires, there were continuities in the political and discursive treatment of non-Russian nationalities in general and the Crimean Tatars and Crimea in particular. Two aspects seem especially important: 1. the Soviet Crimea was once again not a *corpus separatum* endowed with special rights, but participated for better or for worse in the general development of the state as a whole; and 2. even in Soviet times—and this became clear not only in connection with the deportation of 1944—the Russian side distrusted the "foreign" Tatars on principle, which may explain the discrepancy between legal norms and implemented practice that can also be observed in the interwar period.

In any case, the period of Bolshevik rule, later called "golden," began violently in November 1920. This had already been apparent in the various previous interim seizures of power since the end of 1918, which, however, had been directed primarily against exponents of the old regime, not specifically against the Crimean Tatar population. This was in contrast to the regime of the "white" general Anton I. Denikin, who in the summer of 1919 had preferentially persecuted non-Russian Crimeans.[67] No ethnic distinctions were

---

[66] On this extremely confusing period of Crimean history, see Jobst, "Spiel."
[67] Ibid., 103.

then made by the so-called Revolutionary Committee, which was finally established this time, and which was led from late autumn 1920 by the former leader of the Hungarian Soviet Republic, Béla Kun, and Rozalia S. Zemliachka (1876—1947). Actual and supposed opponents of the new regime—captured soldiers of the Volunteer Army, members of the so-called bourgeoisie, Crimean Tatar partisans fighting for an independent Crimean state, called "Greens"—were fought indiscriminately. There are said to have been several tens of thousands of victims,[68] and contemporary authors were already using the term Red Terror in Crimea in their literary works.[69] Due to the important geostrategic position of the peninsula, Moscow was particularly concerned about the never-ending resistance of Crimean Tatar residents to the new regime. Finally, a communist of Volga Tatar origin, the later regime victim Mirsaid Sultan-Galiev (1892–1940[?]), was sent to the south to investigate and possibly calibrate the situation. In April 1921, he submitted to the Kremlin the memorandum "On the Situation in the Crimea" which was so momentous for the further history of the Crimea. In it, he sharply criticized Kun's and Zemliachka's actions toward the indigenous population, who were actually, according to Sultan-Galiev, natural supporters of the Bolsheviks. To win them over to the good cause, he suggested a whole series of measures: The experiment, unloved by Crimean Tatar peasants, of introducing large-scale state-owned farms (*sovkhozy*) should be suspended, at least for a while, and land should be allocated directly to Muslim peasants instead. Crimea would also have to be instituted as a

---

[68] Exiled Russian historians such as Sergei Mel'gunov in his pioneering 1924 study spoke of "red" violent excesses, in which the numbers were set particularly high, if only for propaganda reasons; Mel'gunov assumed more than 100,000 victims of the so-called Red Terror in Crimea; S. P.Mel'gunov, *"Krasnyi terror" v Rossii 1918–1923*, available at http://www.lib.ru/POLITOLOG/MELGUNOW/terror.txt, accessed 10 February 2016).

[69] For example, the later Stalin Prize winner (for the Crimean War novel *Sevastopol'skaia strada*) Sergei Sergeev-Tsenskii (1875–1958), in his story "Liniia ubiitsy" published as early as 1922, which, however, was reprinted after its first publication only in 1996; cf. on this Dmitrii Sokolov, *Kartiny krasnogo terrora v Krymu v proizvedeniiakh sovetskoi literatury*, available at http://beloedelo.com/researches/article/?410; (accessed 10 February 2016).

separate territorial entity and given autonomous rights, and the Communist Party would have to be made attractive to Crimean Tatar intellectuals.[70] "[A]bsent pragmatic considerations[71]"— including the propaganda character of a positive Crimean Tatar policy toward national minorities as a whole and toward the Ottoman Empire (until 1923) and Turkey, respectively, the need to generate calm and loyalty after a destructive civil war—Moscow went along. On 18 October 1921, the decree on the formation of an Autonomous Soviet Socialist Republic (ASSR) came into effect, which was still quite general in nature[72] and was supplemented in February 1922 by the much more concrete "Resolution on the Tatarization of State Agencies and on the Use of the Tatar Language in the Institutions of the Republic."[73]

Until the dissolution of the Soviet Union in 1991, there was a whole series of Autonomous Soviet Socialist Republics within the USSR; these possessed a constitutional status that guaranteed certain autonomous rights to some nationalities that were often minorities on their ancestral territory. These territorial entities were always part of a Union Republic—the Crimean ASSR, for example, belonged to the Russian Soviet Federative Socialist Republic (RSFSR),[74] which was responsible for monitoring compliance with

---

[70] Mirsaid Sultan-Galiev, *O polozhenii v Krymu. Dokladnaia zapiska*, 14 April 1921, Tatarstan State Archive Committee website, http://www.archive.gov.tatarstan.ru/magazine/go/anonymous/main/?path=mg:/numbers/1997_3_4/03/03_2/, (accessed 19 February 2016).

[71] Jobst, "Gefährliche Fremde," 191.

[72] "Dekret vserossiiskogo tsentral'nogo ispolnitel'nogo komiteta i soveta narodnykh komissarov RSFSR ob avtonomnoi krymskoi sovetskoi sotsialisticheskoi respubliki, 18.10.1918," in *Krymskotatarskoe natsional'noe dvizhenie*, vol. 2, *Dokumenty, materialy, khronika*, eds. Mikhail N. Guboglo and Svetlana M. Chervonnaia (IEA RAN, 1992), 37–39.

[73] "Postanovlenie tsentral'nogo ispolnitel'nogo komiteta i soveta narodnykh komissarov Kryma o tatarizatsii i tatarskogo iazyka v uchrezhdeniakh respubliki, 10.2.1922," in *ibid.*, 40–41.

[74] After the dissolution of the Crimean ASSR in 1945, Crimea initially became an *oblast'* (administrative region) within the RSFSR without any special rights, before it became part of the Ukrainian Soviet Socialist Republic after the so-called Khrushchev gift of 1954. An exception was Sevastopol, which since 1948 had received a special constitutional status comparable only to Moscow and Leningrad in the structure of the Union.

Union laws or foreign policy, among other things, and also influenced key local personnel decisions. Unlike the Union Republics, autonomous republics did not have the right to withdraw from the Soviet Union, but this right was more of an empty phrase than a serious option. Unlike in the tsarist empire, where the territory of the Tauridan Governorate (*Tavricheskaia Guberniia*, from 1802) extended beyond the peninsula proper, Soviet Russia or the Soviet Union (from 1922) created nationally-denominated administrative units, even if, at least in the case of the Crimean Tatars, this ethnonym did not become part of the official republic designation.[75] The notion that a nationality must[76] necessarily possess not only a common language, culture, and "physical essence," but also a territory, was implemented by Iosif Stalin as a guiding principle of nationality policy in the early Soviet Union. The coupling of nationality and territory had not been his idea, but had already played some role in Austro-Marxist circles in the Habsburg Monarchy.[77] In the Soviet context, however, this idea developed a great impact and was linked to the so-called policy of rooting

---

[75] Thus, the Crimean ASSR, like the Nakhichevan Autonomous Soviet Socialist Republic and the Autonomous Mountain Socialist Republic (a short-lived autonomous republic within the Russian SFSR in the Northern Caucasus, existing between 1921 and 1924) was rather exceptional among the more than twenty autonomous republics before World War II. There were at least two other "non-ethnic" ASSRs besides the examples mentioned: Turkestan until 1924 and Dagestan until 1991. Nevertheless, as Brian Glyn Williams (*Crimean Tatars*, 370) points out, this territorial entity played a major role in the formation of a national consciousness as a collectively appropriated homeland for the Crimean Tatar population.

[76] Iosif Stalin wrote his paper "Marxism and the National Question" in 1913 in exile in Vienna; it was actually intended as a critique of the nationality theories of Austrian socialists such as Otto Bauer; http://www.stalinwerke.de/bando2/bo2-050.html (accessed 10 February 2016): "A nation is a historically created stable community of people, created on the basis of the community of language, territory, economic life and the psychic nature revealed in the community of culture." "Thus we have exhausted all the characteristics of the nation," he concluded.

[77] For Stefan Scheuzger (*Der Andere in der ideologischen Vorstellungskraft: Die Linke und die indigene Frage in Mexiko* (Vervuert Verlagsgesellschaft, 2009), 67), "Stalin's intellectual contribution to the (sic!) Marxist theory of nationality is quite modest."

(*korenizatsiia*) or indigenization: Non-Russian nationalities formerly "oppressed" by the tsarist empire, such as the Crimean Tatars, were to be tied to the new regime, trained as pro-Soviet elites, and "preferentially integrated into local administrative and party structures."[78] The targeted granting of advantages to non-Russian nationalities in the early Soviet Union,[79] described in detail by Terry Martin—and in places uncritically evaluated too positively—actually produced results in Crimea until the end of the 1920s that make the verdict of a golden age for Crimean Tatars at least somewhat comprehensible. Nevertheless, the Crimea and its inhabitants were severely affected by negative events affecting the state as a whole, such as the famine of 1921/22, which was caused by drought and exacerbated by a distribution policy that gave priority to the cities.[80] This was also true of the Great Famine of 1932/33, which was even more severe for the whole Crimea.

The aforementioned "resolution" of February 1922 had announced the consistent promotion of the Crimean Tatars,[81] who made up a quarter of the peninsula's population, their language, education, and culture, and the integration of the elites into state structures. This was in fact largely implemented: Henceforth, Tatar played a greater role in public life than it had in tsarist times. The

---

[78] Jobst, "Gefährliche Fremde," 181f. See also fundamentally: Terry D. Martin, *The Affirmative Action Empire: Nations and Nationalism in the Soviet Union, 1923-1939* (Cornell University Press, 2001); and Yuri Slezkine, "The USSR as a Communal Apartment: Or How a Socialist State Promoted Ethnic Particularism," *Slavic Review* 53, no. 2 (1994): 414–52.

[79] Martin, *Affirmative Action*: "By encouraging the growth of national identity and resolutely opposing assimilation, the Soviet government showed an ostentatious and unthreatening respect for the national identity of all non-Russians" (183).

[80] Williams, *Crimean Tatars*, 348–50. See also the 1931 article by Cafer Seydahamet (1889–1960), one of the most important Crimean Tatar exile politicians of his time: *Famine in Crimea, 1931*, International Committee for Crimea website, http://www.iccrimea.org/historical/famine1931.html (accessed 10 February 2016).

[81] According to Fisher, *Crimean Tatars*, 138, Russians and Ukrainians made up almost fifty percent of the population, followed by Crimean Tatars with 25 percent; the fourth largest group with eight percent were the Jews, who were considered a separate nationality in the Soviet Union, and the rest were recruited from Germans, Bulgarians, and Armenians, among others.

school system, which despite the existence of the Gasprinskii reform schools was predominantly in the hands of the Muslim clergy at the time, was consistently secularized. Education became, to borrow a Stalin quote, "national in form and socialist in content."[82] Crimean Tatars were disproportionately represented among Crimean party cadres and in other representative bodies.[83]

On Stalin's part, the Union-wide policy of indigenization was understood from the outset as catch-up modernization. A nation-building process, if not initiated from above, then at least encouraged, was seen as part of this modernization and was to be completed within a few years.[84] After the Soviet Union and Stalin's rule consolidated at the end of the 1920s, a far-reaching, if not complete, abandonment of *korenizatsiia* can be noted. In Crimea, the turnaround in nationalities policy became apparent early on, in 1928: Veli Ibrahimov, a Crimean Tatar party leader who had been involved in the *Milliy Firqa* in 1917 and later defected to the Bolsheviks, was tried and executed in 1928 on charges of conspiring with Turkey. He may thus have been one early victim—Sultan-Galiev, arrested in 1924 for the first time, was probably the first—of the campaign directed against alleged national communists in the Soviet Union. The actual cause, however, was probably different: Ibrahimov had vehemently opposed the so-called productivization campaign of Soviet Jews planned in Moscow and the associated land allocation in the Crimea.[85] Although Ibrahimov also pursued the

---

[82] Until the 1930s, however, there was still a functioning Islamic school system, although it was hampered in some phases: Alexander Bogomolov et al., "Islamic Education in Ukraine," in *Islamic Education in the Soviet Union and Its Successor States*, eds. Michael Kemper, Raoul Motika, Stefan Reichmuth (Routledge, 2010), 67–106, esp. 77–88.
[83] I follow Jobst here, "Gefährliche Fremde," 192.
[84] On Stalin's ideas, see Martin, *Affirmative Action*, 5f.
[85] The diaspora politician Edige Kirimals (*Der nationale Kampf der Krimtürken mit besonderer Berücksichtigung der Jahre 1917-1918* (Verlag Lechte, 1952), 29) emphasized that this attitude of Ibrahimov could by no means be interpreted as anti-Semitic, since Jews and Tatars had a long common history. As is well known, the project of a Jewish territory within the Soviet Union is connected with the Birobidzhan Autonomous District in the Amur region. Also on corresponding projects in the Crimea Antje Kuchenbecker, *Zionismus ohne Zion: Birobidžan: Idee und Geschichte eines jüdischen Staates in Sowjet-Fernost*

goal of replenishing the Crimean population, which had been decimated by war, revolution, civil war, and hunger, this was to be done preferably with exiled Crimean Tatars from the former territories of the Ottoman Empire, such as the Dobruja between the lower Danube River and the Black Sea; between 1925 and 1927, two dozen new Crimean Tatar settlements had already been established in this way.[86] After Ibrahimov's execution, this immigration came to an abrupt end, and further arrests of Crimean Tatar party members followed.

In Crimea, therefore, a kind of prelude took place to what was to be carried out throughout the Soviet Union in the years to come—the persecution and "purges" of party cadres on the charge of national communism, their replacement with preferably Russian and Ukrainian comrades or even with Tatars who were less self-confident than Ibrahimov. The embedding of Crimean history in the overall state context is also evident in other events: The persecution of the kulaks, which began in 1929 in connection with the sometimes massive peasant resistance to collectivization, also had results in the Crimea.[87] The Kremlin now regarded the Islamic clergy, which had hitherto been relatively spared in comparison with the Orthodox Church, as supporters of the alleged kulaks, and their members, who were in any case dubious as religious exponents, were repressed.[88] According to estimates, between 30,000 and 40,000 Crimean Tatars became victims in one form or another of the various waves of purges.[89] Thus, by the mid-1930s at the latest, the supposed golden era of the Crimean Tatars was definitely over. Nevertheless, and this is one of the manifold ambivalences in the Russian–Crimean Tatar *encounter*, the indigenization policy was not completely abandoned, and concessions were also made to the Crimean Tatar population

---

(Metropol Verlag, 2000), especially 91–112; in 1931 and 1935, however, two Jewish rayons were established on the peninsula, Fraydorf and Larindorf.

[86] Fisher, *Crimean Tatars*, 141.
[87] *Ibid.*, 143, reports on at least one uprising in Alakat on the south coast, which could only be put down after the massive deployment of the army and police.
[88] Bogomolov *et al.*, "Islamic Education," 88: The climax was the arrest of a hundred Muslim clerics in 1937, 99 of whom were reportedly executed.
[89] Williams, *Crimean Tatars*, 368.

on the symbolic level. For example, in 1934 the ASSR was awarded the Order of Lenin, the highest Soviet award, for its services in the field of culture.[90] Overall, the basic recognition of a Crimean Tatar nationality could be seen not only in identity papers, where—as was customary in the Soviet Union—the nationality was also entered. The curricula, for example, stipulated the treatment of Crimean Tatar topics, and Crimean Tatar folklore was promoted. All these measures fostered a secular national consciousness among Crimean Tatars despite persecution,[91] which is also a legacy of the Soviet Union. Soviet nationality policy promoted, albeit in a different way than the Kremlin intended, national identity constructions, which also took on a life of their own in the Crimean Tatar case.[92]

Conclusion and Outlook

In the course of 1941, the German Wehrmacht and the Einsatzgruppe D (the death squad of SS and SD), which gained terrible notoriety for the so-called Simferopol Massacre, among other things, captured parts of the Crimea, and finally, in 1942, after a long and bloody defensive struggle against the Soviet troops massed in Sevastopol, captured the entire Crimea.[93] The occupiers were received more warmly by parts of the Crimean Tatars remaining on the peninsula and not serving in the Soviet army than in some other places of the USSR. The persecution suffered at the hands of Soviet power during the preceding years, which also claimed the lives of widely known exponents of the Crimean Tatar culture previously promoted by the Soviet Union, such as the Turkologist and writer Bekir Çoban-zade (1893–1937),[94] was as much a reason for this as the German policy, which was occasionally

---

[90] Fisher, *Crimean Tatars*, 148.
[91] On this subject Williams, *Crimean Tatars*, 368f.
[92] Martin (*Affirmative Action*, 13), points to the often aggressive promotion of "symbolic markers of national identity."
[93] Cf. Andrej Angrick, *Besatzungspolitik und Massenmord: Die Einsatzgruppe D in der südlichen Sowjetunion 1941–1943* (Hamburger Edition, 2003).
[94] Cf. Inci Bowman, *Çobanzade: A Crimean Tatar Poet and Turkish Scholar*, International Committee for Crimea website, http://www.iccrimea.org/literature/cobanzade.html (accessed 15 February 2016).

conciliatory toward some non-Russian nationalities for pragmatic reasons. In the case of dealing with the Crimean Tatars, the "concession" of Berlin was due to the fact that the beautiful, war-economically important and strategically valuable peninsula was of value in the context of the "General Plan East" of the Reich Security Main Office (RSHA) and also Hitler himself as a so-called Gothic Gau. The less restrictive policy toward the Crimean Tatar population in individual cases and on the part of individual National Socialist actors (for example, through the partial promotion of Tatar cultural activities or through certain concessions in self-administration) is to be located as part of an offer of cooperation necessary in occupation regimes, not as a positive Tatar policy. Ultimately, in the National Socialist resettlement plans, these Muslims were destined to suffer a fate similar to that of other "non-Aryan" groups in the medium term.

This soon became apparent, as the German policy, as Norbert Kunz has pointed out,[95] soon turned into a brutal occupation. Jews, Soviet partisans, including Crimean Tatars, as well as the civilian population, who were brought to the German Reich as so-called Eastern workers, were their victims. At the same time, as in other parts of the occupied Soviet Union, there were also collaborators; in the Crimean Tatar case, research is not entirely unanimous as to how many, for example, placed themselves in the service of the so-called self-defense units and thus of the Nazi regime. Estimates range from about 6000[96] to 15,000 or even recently 20,000.[97] In any case, it is impossible to speak of a mass collaboration of "the" Crimean Tatar population, which Moscow then finally cited as the reason for the deportations in the spring of 1944, especially since several tens of thousands of Crimean Tatar soldiers served in the Soviet army and some of them received highest honors.[98] However,

---

[95] Kunz, *Die Krim*, esp. 133–54.
[96] Magosci, *This Blessed Land*, 111.
[97] Isabelle Kreindler, "The Soviet Deported Nationalities: A Summary and an Update," *Soviet Studies* 38, no. 3 (1986): 387–405, here 391.
[98] According to an article published by the Russian newspaper *Kommersant"* after the 2014 annexation, 35,000 Crimean Tatars are believed to have served in the Soviet army between 1941 and 1944: "Krymskotatarskoe ego. "ь" v techenie goda

this did not save the Crimean Tatars from expulsion in 1944 and the loss of their homeland for decades.

But how is the Russian rule over Crimea to be evaluated from the point of view of the Crimean Tatar population—was it "dark" (in tsarist) or "golden" (in Soviet times)? Can the history of this nationality under Russian aegis since 1783 be presented in a linear fashion, as, for example, the late Russian historian Valerii Vozgrin repeatedly presented it, as a long road "to genocide" of the Crimean Tatars?[99] This, by the way, is an approach that brought the respected historian major problems in the Russian Federation. Neither one nor the other can be held in the unambiguity stated above. However, it is undisputed that the Russian–Tatar *encounter* was and is a changeable and historically burdened one. Religious differences, historically "learned" enmity, collective attitudes, and a kind of competition over who "owns" Crimea play just as much a role as the fact that Russian Crimean policy had severe colonial connotations.

---

sledili za tem, kak krymskie tatary privykaiut k rossiiskoi deistvitel'nosti," *Kommersant.ru*, http://kommersant.ru/projects/crimeantatars (accessed 16 February 2016).

[99] V. E. Vozgrin, *Imperiia i Krym: Dolgii put' k genotsidu* (Bakhchisarai: n.p., 1994).

Agents of Separatism: The Social Background to the Pro-Russian Movements in Crimea and the Moldovan Dniester Valley in Comparative Perspective (1989–95)

Jan Zofka

Abstract: This article compares the social composition of two pro-Russian separatist movements during and after the Soviet collapse, in Crimea and Transnistria. It unfolds a collective biography of the top and mid-range leaderships and identifies the social contexts in which these networks developed and became active. On the one hand, the Transnistrian "factory corporatism" was able to capitalize the industrial assets of the region, as it was led by the management of the most important factories; on the other, the Crimean movement, a loose coalition of Russia-linked businessmen, Afghan-veterans and academics, was not able to control local power resources. The sharp contrast between the two movements highlights the significance of local agency in territorial conflicts during and immediately after the Soviet break-up.

Introduction

In December 1991 Igor Smirnov was elected first president of the "Moldovan Dniester Republic" (Russian: Pridnestrovskaia Moldavskaia Respublika, hereafter PMR). This republic in Moldova's East was still in the process of seceding from the Republic of Moldova, which itself had become independent only a few months before, in August 1991. Smirnov had arrived in Eastern Moldova only four years earlier, in 1987. He had been sent by the Soviet Ministry for the Electrotechnical Industry. The central ministry in Moscow had assigned him the post of director of a factory for electrical machines, Elektromash, in Tiraspol. During the process of secession this provincial town became the capital of the newly formed republic and the Siberian-born Smirnov, who until then had been pursuing a career as an engineer and manager in the electrical machinery industry, became the new republic's president—for more than twenty years.

Yurii Meshkov was voted president of the Autonomous Republic of Crimea in 1994. He was a lawyer from Simferopol, where he had lived most of his life, except for the period of his military service and his university studies in Moscow. During perestroika he had been active in the non-governmental movement and was involved for instance with the local branch of Memorial, before he became Chairman of the Republican Movement of Crimea—the Russian nationalist movement which made him candidate for the Crimean presidency. After Meshkov won the presidency, the movement fell into factional struggles, which paralyzed the institutions of the Autonomous Republic. Meshkov was ousted by the Ukrainian president, and the institution of a Crimean presidency was abolished after just a few months of existence.

These antithetical biographies exemplify the two pro-Russian separatisms in Crimea and in the Dniester valley in the years after 1989: on the one hand, Smirnov, a factory director, with the resources of the regional industry and the might of the networks of his Union-wide career behind him, and on the other, Meshkov, an academic, politicized in the "informal movement" of the perestroika era. Parallel to the social composition, the course of events also differed in the two cases: Dniester separatism was able to use its entanglement with the local industry and Soviet power apparatuses to found a state-like formation, whose de-facto independence from Moldova has lasted for three decades now. In contrast, the organizations of the pro-Russian movement in Crimea, based on personal networks of academics, small businessmen, and Afghan war veterans, fell into obscurity after 1995 until certain individual protagonists were able to profit from the 2014 Russian takeover of

Crimea.¹ The two movements were completely different in social background and this background determined their capability to form stable social power structures, or even state-like institutions.

This comparison suggests that the local actors and local structures in these late-/and post-Soviet territorial conflicts may have had an important impact on the course of the spatial reordering of the peripheries of the disintegrating Union. These movements were not simply steered from Russia, all support from and entanglements with Moscow notwithstanding. The comparison also suggests more broadly the need to look at the social (micro-)structures of secessionist movements, conflict actors, and armed groups, and not to be "blinded by"² their ideologies and discourses of ethnicity and nationhood. To understand these conflicts we need a "Sociology of Violence"³ or an "Economy of Civil War."⁴ The comparison of the social composition of the Transnistrian and Crimean separatist movements undertaken here sets out to make a contribution in this direction. Key questions for investigating the sociology of war include the following: which coalitions form to act as parties to the conflict? Which (or players from which) social groups, organizations, and institutions participate in the mobilization, and which ones oppose it? This article argues that behind the movements/conflict actors examined here stand

---

1 Most prominently, Sergei Tsekov, in 1994/1995 the pro-Russian movement's number two and chairman of the Crimean parliament, in the following years head of the "Russian Community" (Russkaia Obshchina) in Simferopol, was named representative of Crimea in the Russian Federation's federative assembly. Most of the persons now figuring prominently as representatives of Russian Crimea, such as prime minister Sergei Aksenov, had not played a significant role in the early 1990s.
2 Rogers Brubaker and David Laitin, "Ethnic and Nationalist Violence," *Annual Review of Sociology* 24 (1998), 423–52.
3 Trutz von Trotha (ed.), *Soziologie der Gewalt* (Westdeutscher Verlag, 1997); for an operationalization in respect of civil wars after 1989, see Klaus Schlichte, *In the Shadow of Violence: The Politics of Armed Groups* (Campus-Verlag, 2009).
4 François Jean and Jean-Christophe Rufin (eds.), *Ökonomie der Bürgerkriege* (Hamburger Ed.: 1999).

fragmentary coalitions of participants with political ambitions and economic or social interests.[5]

We still lack systematic findings and results about the protagonists and collective actors of "internal" territorial conflict in the decaying Soviet Union. To be sure, secessionist movements and civil war conflict parties do not have membership lists with registers of the social background of participants, and if they did, they would not be willing to hand them over to researchers. A sociology of war thus needs to resort to a mosaic of studies and methods to approach the task of investigating the fundamental character of these collective actors.

For the Yugoslav civil wars, such a mosaic partly exists and allows us to recognize the contours of the complicated processes of coalition-building in these conflicts. From the Belgrade suburb Zemun being a place of recruitment and the Crvena Zvezda Beograd football fan club Delije forming the fascist "Serbian volunteer guard"[6] to the relative absence of war in the provincial town of Tuzla with its hegemonic social-democratic milieus, and the foundation of an Autonomous Province in North-West Bosnia led by the Agrokomerc manager Fikret Abdić, studies on the micro-level allow for initial interpretations.[7]

---

[5] This article is based on the study I undertook for my PhD (the main field research having been undertaken in 2008), and later published as a book, *Postsowjetischer Separatismus. Die pro-russländischen Bewegungen im moldauischen Dnjester-Tal und auf der Krim 1989-1995* (Wallstein-Verlag, 2015). The article was completed before Russia's 2022 attack on Ukraine. Parts of this material have been published in my Hungarian-language chapter, "Kik voltak a szeparatisták? A krími és a dnyeszter-völgyi oroszbarát mozgalmak összehasonlítása (1989–1995)" (Who were the separatists? A comparison of the pro-Russian movements in Crimea and the Dniester valley), in *Politikai krízisek Európa peremén. A Kaukázustól a Brit-szigetekig* (Political Crises on the Outskirts of Europe: From the Caucasus to the British Isles), eds. Bálint Kovács and Hakob Matevosyan (Magyar Napló, 2014), 309–26.

[6] In their own propaganda "Arkan's Tigers," the sexist and war-breeding self-image which unfortunately is often transmitted and reproduced by observers and analysts—and thus many more people know this term.

[7] E.g. Xavier Bougarel, "Zur Ökonomie des Bosnien-Konflikts: zwischen Raub und Produktion," in *Ökonomie der Bürgerkriege*, Jean and Jean- Rufin, 191–218; Marie-Janine Calic, *Der Krieg in Bosnien-Hercegovina. Ursachen – Konfliktstrukturen – Internationale Lösungsversuche* (Surhkamp, 1998); Ivan

The post-Soviet conflicts, in comparison, are still understudied in this respect. We do not know much about the actors and there are just a few studies examining these. Many studies approach the conflicts through an ethnicity-bias or use abstract models seeking an "explanation" for the violence. In respect of the actors, there is not more than the beginnings of a picture of top leadership protagonists. The Georgian civil wars have been seen as being dominated by academics, intellectuals, or even artists at the top, from the ancient historian Vladislav Ardzinba on the Abkhazian side, to the sculptor and National Guard leader Tengiz Kitovani, the playwright Dzhaba Ioseliani as leader of the paramilitary "Mchedrioni," and Georgia's first president Zviad Gamsakhurdia, who was a philologist, on the Georgian side.[8] In the Azerbaijani civil war, among others, the textile factory manager Surət Hüseynov acted as a warlord, intervening as well in Nagorno-Karabakh,[9] and past and current publications analyze networks in the civil war in

---

Čolović, "Fussball, Hooligans und Krieg," in *Serbiens Weg in den Krieg. Kollektive Erinnerung, nationale Formierung und ideologische Aufrüstung*, ed. Thomas Bremer (Berlin-Verlag Spitz, 1998), 261–76; Valère P. Gagnon, *The Myth of Ethnic War: Serbia and Croatia in the 1990s* (Cornell University Press, 2004); Wolfgang Höpken, "Das Dickicht der Kriege. Ethnischer Konflikt und militärische Gewalt im früheren Jugoslawien 1991-1995," in *Wie Kriege entstehen. Zum historischen Hintergrund von Staatenkonflikten*, ed. Bernd Wegner (Schöningh, 2000); Mary Kaldor, *New and Old Wars: Organized Violence in a Global Era* (Stanford University Press, 1999); Mary Kaldor, "Bosnien-Herzegovina: Fallstudie eines neuen Krieges," in Mary Kaldor, *Neue und alte Kriege. Organisierte Gewalt im Zeitalter der Globalisierung* (Suhrkamp, 2000), 52–92, 83; Nenad Stefanov and Michael Werz, *Bosnien und Europa. Die Ethnisierung der Gesellschaft* (Fischer Taschenbuch-Verlag, 1994); Brendan O'Shea, *Bosnia's Forgotten Battlefield: Bihać* (The History Press, 2011); Christia Fotini, "Following the Money: Muslim versus Muslim in Bosnia's Civil War," *Comparative Politics* 40, no. 4 (2008): 461–80, 469; and Admir Mulaosmanović, "The Identity Factory. Agrokomerc and the Population of the Bihaćka Krajina," in *The Ambiguous Nation: Case Studies from Southeastern Europe in the 20th Century*, eds. Ulf Brunnbauer and Hannes Grandits (Oldenbourg, 2013).

8   Christoph Zürcher, *The Post-Soviet Wars: Rebellion, Ethnic Conflict, and Nationhood in the Caucasus* (New York University Press, 2007), 118–32, 137–39; and Schlichte, *In The Shadow of Violence*, 47–48. See also Georgi M. Derluguian, *Bourdieu's Secret Admirer in the Caucasus* (University of Chicago Press, 2005).

9   Zürcher, *Post-Soviet Wars*, 171.

Tajikistan.¹⁰ "Patriot-businessmen" and "ethnic entrepreneurs" are terms that have been proposed to characterize the motives and roles of central protagonists in these civil wars and nationalist/separatist movements.¹¹ Thus, there might be something like a first sketch of "why leaders lead," but we have much less of an idea "why followers follow."¹² Jan Koehler's analysis of civil war participants in Georgia, which includes an examination of the background of mass participation in post-Soviet civil wars, is one exception here.¹³

Concerning the conflicts under examination here, research has likewise tended to focus on elaborating the leadership. For the Transnistrian case, factory directors have been highlighted as part of the leading clique in Eastern Moldova.¹⁴ Klemens Büscher detects entangled "clan-structures" from party, Soviet, administration, and factory leaderships in the context of strategically significant heavy

---

10   Iraj Bashiri, *The History of the Civil War in Tajikistan* (Academic Studies Press, 2020); and İdil Tunçer Kılavuz, "The Role of Networks in Tajikistan's Civil War: Network Activation and Violence Specialists," *Nationalities Papers* 37, no. 5 (2009): 693–717.
11   Zürcher, *Post-Soviet Wars*, 3; Jan Zofka, "Politische Unternehmer. Fabrikdirektoren als Akteure postsozialistischer Bürgerkriege," in *Leipziger Zugänge zur rechtlichen, politischen und kulturellen Verflechtungsgeschichte Ostmitteleuropas*, eds. Adam Skordos and Dietmar Müller (Leipziger Universitätsverlag, 2015), 313–31.
12   David D. Laitin, "Secessionist Rebellion in the Former Soviet Union," *Comparative Political Studies* 34, no. 8 (2001): 839–61; here: 844. For a more general account of post-Soviet internal territorial conflicts and a focus on actors in the case of nationalist violence in Osh (Kyrgyzstan), see also Valery Tishkov, *Ethnicity, Nationalism and Conflict in and after the Soviet Union: The Mind Aflame* (SAGE Publications, 1996).
13   Jan Koehler, *Die Zeit der Jungs. Zur Organisation von Gewalt und der Austragung von Konflikten in Georgien* (Lit-Verlag, 2000).
14   S. J. Kaufman, "Spiraling to Ethnic War: Elites, Masses, and Moscow in Moldova's Civil War," *International Security* 21, no. 2 (1996): 108–38; Charles King, "The Benefits of Ethnic War. Understanding Eurasia's Unrecognized States," *World Politics* 53, no. 4 (2001): 524–52; Stefan Troebst, "Separatistischer Regionalismus als Besitzstandswahrungsstrategie (post-)sowjetischer Eliten. Transnistrien 1989–2002," in *Regionale Bewegungen und Regionalismen in europäischen Zwischenräumen seit der Mitte des 19. Jahrhunderts*, eds. Philip Ther and Holm Sundhaussen (Verlag Herder-Institut, 2003), 185–214; and John A. Mason, "Internationalist Mobilization during the Collapse of the Soviet Union: The Moldovan Elections of 1990," *Nationalities Papers* 37, no. 2 (2009): 159–76.

and defense industries as initiators of the separation.[15] For the Crimean mobilizations in the immediate post-1989 period, Gwendolyn Sasse postulates in her important book on the topic that "Crimean elites" led this movement—but these are not really specified.[16] There is a handful of further studies which point to the role of elites in the Crimean pro-Russian movement after 1989 in different ways, without undertaking a comprehensive analysis of the protagonists' social background.[17] These are the gaps which I have attempted to fill with my study, upon which this article is based.

Four types of sources have helped me to trace the socialization of the protagonists and their pathways into the separatist movements. First, articles from local and factory newspapers reveal the positioning of local powerholders. While Soviet newspapers at first glance make for a poor source, in the context of a public struggle between pro-autonomy and pro-status quo factions within local power structures, their role as mere organ of the local party apparatus, the local Soviet or enterprise directorate, respectively, makes them a useful primary source for analyzing which sides local elites took. Additionally, newspapers are valuable for their detailed reproduction of speeches at the local party and Soviet plena, factory assemblies, and street rallies.

Second, biographical literature and memoirs of movement protagonists reveal parts of the life stories of participants—their adherence to important organizations associated with the movement, their networks and milieux of contacts. An outstandingly useful source in this respect is the book *Defenders of Transnistria*, which contains short biographical notes on 457 deceased militants collected by the Dniester Valley separatists.

---

[15] Klemens Büscher, "Die 'Staatlichkeit' Transnistriens—ein Unfall der Geschichte?," in *Nationalismus im spät- und postkommunistischen Europa. Bd. 3 – Nationalismus in den nationalen Gebietseinheiten*, ed. Egbert Jahn (Nomos-Verlag, 2008), 227–52.

[16] Gwendolyn Sasse, *The Crimea Question: Identity, Transition and Conflict* (Harvard Ukrainian Research Institute, 2007), 167.

[17] Andrei Mal'gin, *Krymskii uzel. Ocherki politicheskoi istorii Krymskogo poluostrova* (Novyi Krym, 2000); and Boris Zazhigaev, *Evoliutsiia politicheskogo ustroistva v Respublike Krym v period 1989–1998* (kandidatskaia dissertation in Political Science, Moscow 2003), see 61–62, 84.

Third, several dozen interviews with mid-level protagonists, who were involved in the organizations close to the leadership but not the leaders themselves, have also shed light on the paths of the protagonists into the movement, into activism. The role of life experiences, socialization, and personal connections can be brought into focus through these interviews.

Fourth, archival material has been used to support my findings in several ways. Documents from informal archives, the State Archive of the Russian Federation, and the State Archive of the Autonomous Republic of Crimea (2012) helped me to gain additional insight into the social background of participants of the pro-Russian organizations, the legislative activities of the Meshkov government, and the correspondence and thus the relations of pro-Russian organizations in Crimea with the Duma bureaucracy in Moscow.

The article starts by looking at these latter relations, examining Moscow's policies and the influence of decaying Soviet state structures. In the following two sections, I examine each of the two movements in turn, before setting out a comparison in the conclusion.

Russian Policies and Soviet Legacies

With the takeover of Crimea in 2014, Moscow's exclusive decisive role in territorial conflict and shifts in post-Soviet space seems to have become clear. Nevertheless, as will be argued below, it is worth looking at local actors, especially during and directly after the fall of the Soviet Union. In 1989 and the early 1990s the situation was rather different from what it appears to be today—not least, when it comes to the Russian state and its institutions. These were still in the process of being built, and the context of the genesis of the conflicts during this period was the decay of Soviet structures. Even after the foundation of the Russian Federation, the position and the foreign policy structure of the new "Moscow" was not at all unitary. Before the shelling of the White House in October 1993, when Yeltsin crushed the power of the parliament, it was the partly nationalist factions around Vice-President Aleksandr Rutskoi and in the parliament, much less the Presidential Administration, which openly supported the protagonists of Dniester valley and Crimean pro-Russian separatism.[18] The activists in Crimea and the Dniester valley hated Yeltsin (and, of course, even more so Gorbachev). Indeed, Yeltsin's policies, or at least his rhetoric, avoided a clear commitment to the projects of these movements. For example, Yeltsin repudiated a decision of the Russian parliament that demanded the incorporation of Sevastopol into the Russian Federation.[19] Furthermore, in correspondence between organizations of the Crimean pro-Russian movement, the Russian parliamentary administration appears a cautious rather than staunch supporter of Crimean independence.[20]

One could even say the Russian government has changed sides on the issue of relations between the (post-)Soviet republics and their subordinated units. In 1991 Yeltsin, representing the RSFSR republican-structures, stood in a power competition with the Soviet, that is Union-wide, structures—personified by Gorbachev. Yeltsin thus was the leading voice of the cause of the Soviet republics. When Gorbachev suggested enhancing the status of the Autonomous Soviet republics (including Abkhazia, Crimea, and Nagorno-Karabakh, but also Tatarstan and Bashkiria in the RSFSR, for example), Yeltsin took the side of the Union republics like Moldova, Georgia, and Ukraine.[21] Only after the break-up of the Soviet Union did the Yeltsin administration effectively inherit the

---

[18] For press reports on Rutskoi's visits to Transnistria where he expressed his support: Vera Kuznetsova, "Otchet Vitse-Prem'era," *Nezavisimaia gazeta*, 7 April 1992, 3; and S. Frunze, "Rossiia—nasha Nadezhda," *Trudovoi Tiraspol*, 8 April 1992, 1.

[19] "Oborona Sevastopolia. Reshenie Rossiiskogo Parlamenta o vozvrashchenii Sevastopolia pod iurisdiktsiiu Rossii sozdaet novuiu politicheskuiu situatsiiu i v Kieve, i v Moskve," *Nezavisimaia gazeta*, 13 July 1993, 1.

[20] Correspondence between RDK and Supreme Soviet administration officials, containing a request for support and an exchange among the officials on the topic, July/August 1992, *Gosurdarstvennyi Arkhiv Rossiiskoi Federatsii (GARF)*, f. 10026, op. 1, d. 2767, ll. 195-98. For more detail, see Zofka, *Postsowjetischer Separatismus*, 134.

[21] Stuart J. Kaufman and Stephen R. Bowers, "Transnational Dimensions of the Transnistrian Conflict," *Nationalities Papers* 26, no. 1 (1998): 129-46; here: 130-33; and Sasse, *Crimea Question*, 133-37.

Soviet interest in maintaining influence in the by then *post*-Soviet space.

Furthermore, in the early 1990s, the situation around military forces, too, differed from today. The Baltic Sea Fleet could not have been taken into operation in the way it was in 2014. At this point it was still a bone of contention between the new Ukrainian and Russian governments until the partition agreement was concluded in 1997. In the critical years after 1991 the ships of the fleet themselves became sites of political mobilization. Most of these seem to have been pro-Russian, and the fleet's sailors joined the ranks of pro-Russian organizations, but the fleet as a whole remained under bilateral Russian–Ukrainian command until 1997 and was not able to act openly for any kind of territorial shift of Crimea.[22]

Like Crimea, Transnistria also has a history of disputed army units that then became Russian during the post-Soviet transformation. The history and the involvement of the 14th Soviet army in the foundation of the Transnistrian republic is also more complicated than being a matter of simply following orders from Moscow. This army is often seen as the Russian institution ensuring Transnistrian statehood, and the name of Aleksandr Lebed' is stereotypically repeated in explanations of the Transnistrian secession project. When he came to the region in July 1992, however, the eastern region of Moldova had already been de-facto independent for almost two years and the separatists had already built up or transformed local power structures and institutions—the bulk of the work was already done. In December 1991 a lack of clarity dominated the situation of institutions in the Soviet periphery. "It

---

[22] Mal'gin, *Krymskii uzel*, 35. For press reports on confrontation and mobilization inside the Black Sea Fleet, see *Nezavisimaia gazeta*, 29 April 1992, 3; 5 June 1992, 3; 23 July 1992, 1; V. Kuznetsova, "Chernomorskii Flot posle Ialtinskogo soglasheniia," *Nezavisimaia gazeta*, 8 August 1992, 1; E. Iurzditskaia, "Protsess deleniia flota budet trudnym, muchitel'nym, dolgim. Sokhranit' moratorii, ne dopustit' konfrontatsii," *Slava Sevastopolia*, 4 April 1992, 1; *Slava Sevastopolia*, 22 August 1992, 1. For marines hoisting the Russian St Andrew's flag on Black Sea Fleet ships, see e.g. *Nezavisimaia gazeta*, 25 May 1993, 1.

was a shock ... the army suddenly was no one's,"[23] is how one local commander described the situation around the army. Its former headquarters in Odessa were suddenly in a foreign country and the army was split in three parts—Ukraine got the units on Ukrainian territory, Moldova the right-bank divisions, and the left-bank divisions were taken over by the CIS command in Moscow. This happened only after long negotiations where the local embeddedness of the army was an argument brought up by the CIS representatives[24]—that is, not only did the Russian army help to establish the Dniester republic, but the Dniester republic also helped to bring the 14th army under Russian control in the end. That this was not clear from the beginning can be seen not only in the Moldovan–Ukrainian–Russian negotiations, but also in the attempts of the Dniester separatists to put the army under their own jurisdiction. The army commander Gennadii Yakovlev even was made "Defense Minister" of the PMR in December 1991. This was too much for the CIS command in Moscow —he was ousted and replaced.[25] Several assemblies of soldiers and officers complained about the army command's official stance of neutrality and demanded an intervention in the conflict.[26]

The army thus was in a process of unravelling when Lebed' came in summer 1992. The new army commander sent from Moscow made himself a part of this process, too, and became involved in multiple conflicts. At certain points he acted autonomously from

---

[23] "Eto byl shok. (...) Armiia okazalas' nichei"; Mikhail Bergman, *Na ringe epokhi. Neobychainye prikliucheniia polkovnika Rossiiskoj Armii, rasskazannye im samim* (self-published, Moscow, 2001), 164–65.
[24] Harold Elletson, *The General against the Kremlin: Alexander Lebed: Power and Illusion* (Little, Brown and Co., 1998), 159–61; and Aleksandr Lebed', *Za derzhavu obidno...* (Chest' i Rodina, 2004), 459–60.
[25] Bergman, *Na ringe epokhi*, 166–68; and Pål Kolstø and Andrei Malgin, "The Transnistrian Republic: A Case of Politicized Regionalism," *Nationalities Papers* 26, no. 1 (1998): 103–27; here: 110–12.
[26] E g. "Obrashchenie uchastnikov ofitserskogo sobraniia N-skoi voiskovoi chasti k ofitseram chastei Tiraspolskogo garnizona," *Dnestrovskaia pravda*, 14 September 1991. A unit in Bendery even declared its transfer to Trasnistrian command: "Obrashchenie ofitserov i praporshchikov v/ch 48414 k voennomu sovetu 14 gv. Armii i k lichnomu sostavu chastei i podrazdelenii, dislotsiruiushchikhsia na territorii PMR," *Trudovoi Tiraspol*, 27 May 1992, 1.

the Ministry of Defense in Moscow, participated in local politics in the Dniester republic, and protested against plans for a large-scale withdrawal of soldiers.[27] But he also came into conflict with the Transnistrian leadership, reproaching it for corruption and for its betrayal of workers' interests. It was his officer Mikhail Bergman who revealed the real identity of the Transnistrian minister of state security Vladimir Antiufeev (alias Vadim Shevtsov).[28]

This quarrel and Antiufeev's biography are another example of the chaotic reshuffling of state structures. Antiufeev was a former OMON officer who had fled Latvia to avoid prosecution for his role in the violent repression of street protests. By his own account, it was the nationalist Duma member Viktor Alksnis who recommended to him that he go to Tiraspol.[29] The infighting that followed, with the Russian army officers attacking him and revealing his real identity, suggests that his presence was not part of a Russian master plan—it was part of the decay of the Soviet state apparatus and the movements and regroupings it caused.

That is, these movements, rather than being a phenomenon incited or steered from Russia, were coined by the decay of Soviet state structures, by their characteristics and their transformation. The processes of Soviet state decay and of the erection of local state structures and Moldovan, Ukrainian, and Russian ones overlapped. Alongside the Soviet security and (para-)military structures, regional and local elite recruitment and rotation and power relations in Soviet factories were at the base of Dniester valley separatism and of the formation of state-like structures. Ironically,

---

[27] Elletson, *General against the Kremlin*, 170, 186–87; *Nezavisimaia gazeta*, 30 July 1992, 1, 3; and *Nezavisimaia gazeta*, 19 August 1992, 2.

[28] Mikhail Zorin, "Aleksandr Lebed protiv Igoria Smirnova?" *Nezavisimaia gazeta*, 3 November 1992, 3; *Nezavisimaia gazeta*, 2 December 1992, 3; and Nataliia Prikhodko, "Rossiiskie ofitsery razoblachaiut rukovoditelei Pridnestrov'ia," *Nezavisimaia gazeta*, 9 December 1992, 1, 3.

[29] Cited Gennadii Kodrianu, *Dnestrovskii razlom. Pridnestrovskii krizis i rozhdenie PMR: rol' i mesto spetssluzhb* (GIPP Tipar, 2002), 202. Antiufeev remained minister of state security for 20 years until Smirnov's fall in 2012. In 2014 he reappeared for a short intermezzo as vice-premier in the Donetsk republic; "Byvshii shef gozbesopasnosti Pridnestrov'ia stal vitse-prem'erom DNR," *Lenta.ru*, 10 July 2014, http://lenta.ru/news/2014/07/10/antufeev/.

perestroika reforms exacerbated the power asymmetries in the Soviet factories, thus enabling the factory directors to mobilize their workers, as we shall see in the next section.

One last crucial Soviet state structure that supported the development of the separatist movements was the Soviet nationalities policy. Starting from the Leninist idea of freeing the oppressed peoples from Russian colonialism and imperialism and fighting against Great Russian chauvinism, the Soviets had erected an administrative system that was governed by ethnicity.[30] Every (non-Russian) nationality in the Union was to have a right to its own territorial entity, from a Soviet republic down to an autonomous district Soviet. Only the Russians were different: even the RSFSR itself was not a territory defined nationally as homestead of the Russians. It contained many nationally marked autonomous entities, and a vast unmarked remainder. The Russian element was effectively supra-republican and imperial, because, as Rogers Brubaker puts it,

> what was Russian about the Soviet Union was diffused throughout its entire territory and (to a certain extent) its entire population. "Russianness" could not be adequately expressed in or contained by a delimited national territory or a distinct personal nationality. "Russianness" suffused the entire state; it was too big, too general to be encoded in the system of institutionalized nationality as one among many. Russianness, like "whiteness" in the US, was in a sense invisible; it was experienced not as a particular nationality but as the general norm, the zero-value, the universal condition against which other nationalities existed as particular ... "deviations."[31]

It was this discursive setting, and not that of a simple Russian nationalism, that the pro-Russian separatist movements were operating within, and which they were using. Certainly, the Transnistrian movement was more a Soviet conservative movement than a Russian nationalist one. The Soviet invisible norm of

---

[30] Terry Martin, *The Affirmative Action Empire: Nations and Nationalism in the Soviet Union, 1923-1939* (Cornell University Press, 2001); and Yuri Slezkine, "The USSR as a Communal Apartment. Or How a Socialist State Promoted Ethnic Particularism," *Slavic Review* 53, no. 2 (1994): 414–52.

[31] Rogers Brubaker, *Nationalism Reframed: Nationhood and the National Question in the New Europe* (Cambridge University Press, 1996), 48–49.

Russianness helps to explain the capability of the separatists to form broad coalitions, and their readiness to embrace—in the Transnistrian case—the symbols of the former central government. The PMR uses the flag of the former Moldovan Soviet Republic, has three official state languages—Russian, Ukrainian, and Moldovan (with the use of the Cyrillic alphabet)—and bears the word "Moldovan" in its name—something one might expect separatists to avoid usually.

Dniester Valley: Geography of the Movement and Conflict

The mobilizations in Moldova leading to the separation of the Dniester valley were not a secessionist movement from the start. In summer 1989, mobilizations in factories, enterprises, and public institutions turned against the language policy of the Moldovan Republican leadership, which wanted to make Moldovan the single state language in the republic and replace the Cyrillic alphabet with the Latin one. The initial protests, from which emerged the networks that would come to found the PMR, took place in cities and towns across the whole of the Moldovan Soviet Republic (hereafter MSSR), and did not pursue a goal of territorial autonomy or secession.

The language law passed on 31 August 1989 obliged officials in state and economic functions who were not speakers of the new state language to learn it in five years. The cadres in industrial enterprises—the directors, engineers, trade union and party secretaries—interpreted this law as an attack on their social position.[32] Their response was to mobilize for protest at the location of their socialization and power basis: the factory/enterprise. In most cases it was the management of enterprises and factories that

---

[32] Indeed the language law can be seen as a revocation of the Soviet elite rotation system by the MSSR party cadres coming from the agricultural and agro-industrial sector whose careers hitherto ended at the republican borders; Charles King, *The Moldovans: Romania, Russia, and the Politics of Culture* (Hoover Institute Press, 2000), 137–42.

organized the strikes.³³ Nevertheless, workers in these factories seem to have supported the mobilization to a certain extent. At least some industrial workers agreed with the goals of the movement—maintaining the Soviet Union and its social *status quo* and preserving Russian as the main language of communication. This was the case not only in the factories in the Dniester valley, in Rybnitsa, Tiraspol, and Bendery, but also in Chișinău and Bălți—the industrial centers in Bessarabia. The later so-called "Transnistrian movement" was initially a Soviet-conservative movement dominated by industrial milieus across the whole territory of the MSSR.

Territorialization: Local Power Competition and Autonomy

It was only when it became clear that the Republican leadership would not alter its plans, that the movement leadership changed its strategy. The movement now aimed to take power in local municipalities and to prevent the new language rules from being implemented in these towns. The territorialization of the conflict was an almost obvious step at the time: The concept of autonomy was ubiquitous across the Soviet Union in this phase when perestroika turned towards the "Parade of Sovereignties." In this context, activists of the movement first proposed an Autonomy for "Enterprises" before in September 1989 the first territorial concept of autonomy was published naming nine towns (including Bălți, a town west of the Dniester which never joined the separatist republic) to counter the language laws.³⁴

The idea of the Dniester valley as a territorial unit was by no means a given at the time. It was neither present as a political entity nor clearly defined in territory from the beginning. The initial point

---

33   There were a few cases where engineers and specialized workers organized strikes against the will of the director, for example at the main textile factory in Tiraspol.
34   "'Trudiashchimsia gorodov i raionov – Tiraspol', Bendery, Rybnitsa, Slobodzeia, Kamenka, Bel'tsy, Grigoriopol', Dubossary,' Resheniia XIII vneocherednoi sessii gorsoveta," *Dnestrovskaia pravda*, 16 September 1989, 1; and Anna Volkova, *Goriachee leto 1989* (Tipar, Tiraspol', 2004), 67.

of reference were towns and cities and not the region as a whole. In these towns the leaderships of the strike movement organized referenda for an autonomy project between winter 1989 and summer 1990, including the question of an adhesion to a potential autonomous Dniester republic, "in the event of its foundation."[35]

After local and republican elections in spring 1990 the conflict escalated and to an increasing degree followed territorial lines, i.e., it started to emerge as a conflict between different administrative entities. On the one hand, the coalition around the Romano-nationalist People's Front of Moldova (*Frontul Popular din Moldova*) won the elections for the Republican parliament in Chișinău. On the other, representatives of the strike and autonomy movement won majorities in the industrial towns in the Dniester valley. In some of these towns the management of important factories virtually took over the municipal administration. In Tiraspol the director of the factory Elektromash and later president of the PMR, Igor Smirnov, was voted "mayor" (Chairman of the city Soviet) and thus outcompeted the First secretary of the town CPSU committee. Further managers and engineers from the same factory took over posts in the city's administration.[36] In the northern provincial town of Rybnitsa the chief engineer of the local steelworks *(Moldavskii Metallurgicheskii Zavod—MMZ)* became mayor with the support of the general director Anatolii Belitchenko, and with the first party secretary being the main opponent as in Tiraspol.

Thus, at the local level, one can see that the Soviet power structures broke up and did not unitarily support the autonomy course. The most important local power apparatus of the Soviet

---

[35] For the conflict's territorialization and the introduction of the concept of autonomy to it: Gottfried Hanne, *Der Transnistrien-Konflikt. Ursachen, Entwicklungsbedingungen und Perspektiven einer Regulierung* (BiOST Köln, 1998), 14–17.

[36] "Itogi sessii—v tsentre vnimaniia," *Dnestrovskaia pravda*, 12 April 1990, 3; V. Grutsenko, "Stol' zhe reshitel'no," *Dnestrovskaia pravda*, 12 April 1990, 3; "Na sessii gorsoveta," *Dnestrovskaia pravda*, 29 March 1990, 1; "Soobshchenie gorodskoi izbiratel'noi komissii ob itogach vyborov deputatov gor. Soveta," *Leninskoe znamia*, 3 March 1990, 2–3. For the elections in general, see John A. Mason, "Internationalist Mobilization during the Collapse of the Soviet Union: The Moldovan Elections of 1990," *Nationalities Papers* 37, no. 2 (2009): 159–76.

system, the local party leadership, did not support the autonomist project. These officials defended the hierarchies they worked in—they were part of the republican organization of the CP *(Partidul Communist din Moldova—PCM)* and stood up against the factory directors when it came to the question of forming an autonomous republic.[37] In these times of perestroika however, their word was no longer the most potent one. The party had prescribed itself a democratization process and a withdrawal from complete control over enterprises. Local newspapers were contested as well. After the local elections, the local Soviets, then controlled by the autonomy movement, declared the newspapers, as in Tiraspol for example *Dnestrovskaia pravda*, to be under their jurisdiction, and pushed the party out of the editorship (previously they had been edited by party and Soviet together). The local party organizations had to found their own newspapers—which did not acquire the same dominant role as the former central organs.

While in Soviet times, elite members in industrial towns moved between the three columns of local elite institutions—party, Soviet and industry—this Soviet elite recruitment pattern now was defunct.[38] A party post became the worst position—its power eroded quickly, which is why party secretaries now aimed to be elected chairman of the parliament (Soviet). In many other places throughout the Soviet Union this strategy worked and Communist Party leaders stayed in power as presidents, provincial governors, or mayors—but in the Dniester valley they were outcompeted by the industrialists, or the autonomist movement respectively.

Wherever its members had conquered the municipal power positions, the autonomist movement used this to counter and undermine the increasingly nationalist policies of government and parliament in Chișinău. The conflict around the new state symbols in June 1990 highlighted this opposition between the local and republican authorities. Only a few weeks after being elected the

---

[37] See, for example, E. P. Berdnikov, "Internatsionalizm—ne na slovakh, a na dele. Pozitsiia gorkoma partii po otnosheniiu k sozdaniiu Pridnestrovskoi ASSR," *Leninskoe znamia*, 2 December 1989, 1.
[38] On Soviet elite rotation in Tiraspol, see Ronald J. Hill, *Soviet Political Elites: The Case of Tiraspol* (Martin Robertson, 1977).

FPM government introduced new state symbols for the Moldovan Soviet republic, which strongly resembled the Romanian ones. The Romanian tricolor, with slight changes, became the new flag of Moldova. In the East Moldovan towns governed by the autonomists local municipalities refused to hoist the new flag and kept the old red-green-red flag of the MSSR. In some places like Bendery and Grigoriopol the struggle around the flag escalated, leading to conflict between various state organs and protesters.[39]

Contested Spaces: Conflict in Rural Areas, Provincial Towns, and Bendery

While in Rybnitsa and Tiraspol the situation was clearly dominated by the autonomists, it was, with the exception of Bendery, the provincial towns and rural areas where the flag question escalated to open conflict. In provincial Grigoriopol FPM activists painted the main square and the town administration building in red-yellow-blue and flew the tricolor, before autonomists took the flags down.[40] In these more rural areas the power distribution after the elections was more complicated—the party stayed in power for longer, and the front lines ran, for example, between town council and town administration, or between the town administration and the district administration located in the same town. The government in Chișinău had lost control over a large part of the state apparatus in the Dniester valley but still controlled part of the local administrations, judiciary, and police forces in Dubossary and Grigoriopol. This is where violent conflict erupted in autumn 1990 and developed into low-intensity warfare until spring 1992.[41]

---

[39] For reports on these events, see V. Chudiakov, "Trevozhnoe voskresen'e. Slukhi i fakty," *Sovetskaia Moldaviia*, 22 May 1990, 3; Gimn Pologov, "Opravdannye deistviia," *Dnestrovskaia pravda*, 31 May 1990, 1; and D. Kondratovich, "Glazami ochevidtsa. Varnitsa i Bender, 20 maia," *Dnestrovskaia pravda*, 24 May 1990, 1.

[40] A. Alekseev, "K sobytiiam v Grigoriopole," *Dnestrovskaia pravda*, 6 May 1991, 3.

[41] See for example, N. P. Rudenko, *Dubossary—gorod zashchitnikov PMR* (Poligrafist Dubossary, 1995); and Zofka, *Postsowjetischer Separatismus*, 190–99.

The main and final escalation of the Transnistrian war happened in the industrial city of Bendery, which is located on the right (that is, the Bessarabian) bank of the Dniester, in June 1992. The city is comparable to Tiraspol in size and industrial profile, but it differed in that light industries, in Soviet times under Republican control, were more important than heavy industries, under Union-wide ministries in the Soviet system, and the labor force was recruited mainly on a regional basis. The Chișinău government tried to take it back with its embryonic army and special police forces, built on the Soviet OMON units. With the support of units of the former Soviet 14th army, now under Russian jurisdiction, the Transnistrian paramilitary groups and the newly established "Republican Guard" were able to hold the city and integrate it into the PMR-territory.[42]

Factories as Sites of Mobilization: Leadership, Engineers, and Workers in War

Factories were crucial sites for mobilization of the Transnistrian movement, from early protests against the Moldovan language laws in 1989 to the conflict escalation in 1992. Factory directors, engineers, and workers were dominant in the strike committees, in the paramilitary units of the war, and in the first governments of the PMR. What happened in these factories that they could become the site of secessionist mobilization? How were factory managers able to mobilize "their" workers for their political project?

To be sure, there were various ways events developed in different factories. There are various examples of light industrial factories in Tiraspol, Bendery, and Rybnitsa, where engineers participated in the autonomy movement from the beginning, while directors were reluctant or even resisted the separation project.[43] In

---

[42] Hanne, *Der Transnistrien-Konflikt*; Troebst, *Separatistischer Regionalismus als Besitzstandswahrungsstrategie (post-)sowjetischer Eliten*; and Zofka, *Postsowjetischer Separatismus*, 182–90.

[43] For example, in the textile factory "40ᵗʰ anniversary of the Komsomol" in Tiraspol: "S kem vy, Valentina Sergeevna?" *Bastuiushchii Tiraspol*, 28 August 1989, 1; Dmitrii Feodos'evich Kondratovich, "'Ne mogu stoiat' zatylkom k

contrast, three heavy industry enterprises were especially distinguished centers of the strike movement—Elektromash, Tiraspol; Kirov Works for moulding machines in Tiraspol; and the Steelworks in Rybnitsa. Their directors, Igor Smirnov, Anatolii Bol'shakov, and Anatolii Belichenko, were among the leading figures of the strike and autonomy movement. How were these figures able to transfer their power from the economic to the political sphere?

One reason for this ability was the typical Soviet factory power relations. The Soviet regulation system with its principle of giving all responsibility to one chairman *(edinonachalie)* rendered directors a position as strongman in the factory.[44] In the Soviet conception of corporate governance the general director of a big factory or a combine was conceived of as a general with ultimate decision-making power on the one hand, and a backslapping face-to-face manager, walking around the factory attentive to the concerns of employees at all hierarchy levels, on the other. Leading protagonists of the Dniester movement, such as the MMZ director Anatolii Belitchenko, played this role perfectly, at least for media staging.[45] The Trade Union and Party Committees did not function as a balancing or even a counter power but took over additional administrative functions.

The power position of the factory management was additionally strengthened by a material basis. The workers depended on the social welfare allocation by the enterprises, as large combines and enterprises took over a great extent of social security measures and public services. Pensions, housing, holiday facilities, and partly food were provided by the enterprise. The enterprise ran

---

boiu.'...", in L. Alfer'eva (ed.), *Slavy ne iskali. Sbornik vospominanii uchastnikov sozdaniia i stanovleniia PMR* (Poligrafist, Bendery, 2000), 196–99; G. Shargorodskaia, "Glavnoe - sluzhenie pravde," in L. Alfer'eva (ed.), *On zhizn' respublike otdal. Sbornik statej D. F. Kondratovicha i vospominanii o nem* (Poligrafist, Bendery 2003), 565–69.

[44] Paul R. Gregory, *Restructuring the Soviet Economic Bureaucravy* (Cambridge University Press, 1990), esp. 129; Paul R. Lawrence and Charalambos Vlachoutsicos, *Behind the Factory Walls: Decision Making in Soviet and US Enterprises* (Harvard Business School Press, 1990), 65–80.

[45] E.g. "Chelovek Dela," *Rybnitskii metallurg*, 29 January 1988, 1.

canteens, shops, and in the late 1980s even agricultural entities to supply their employees with meals and food.[46] The MMZ Steelworks in Rybnitsa had just completed building the most modern housing area on Val'chenko Street—being in or out of such a comprehensive organization did matter in a town like Rybnitsa in the late 1980s. The room for opposition thus was scarce.

Furthermore, the political careers of the factory directors meant that they had been part of the Soviet elite recruitment system. As mentioned above, local elites moved between posts in the party, the state (on the local level, the Town Soviet and its Executive Committee), and the economic realm. Important factory directors virtually automatically held seats in the town party committee, one of the most decisive political bodies, and they were usually elected to local or higher-level Soviets. The factory directors in the Dniester republic who became leading protagonists of the Transnistrian movement were already acting as local politicians in 1989. Holding seats on the local party committee and the town Soviets of Rybnitsa and Tiraspol, they also ran for higher level Soviets. For example, Anatolii Belitchenko ran as a candidate for the Union-wide Soviet elections in 1989, and enterprise resources were used for his campaign. The factory gazette *Rybnitskii Metallurg* banged the drum for the director, and at the campaign's public rallies Belitchenko promised to use the enterprise's resources for ensuring food and gas supplies for the town and the villages of the district.[47]

Thus, we see that the Soviet industrial relations had already created benevolent conditions for a political take-over by factory directors. These conditions, however, were further shaped by perestroika and market transformation. The power of management positions was strengthened massively by the crucial perestroika projects: market elements, autonomous accounting and financing at

---

[46] Josef Dietmar Aigner, *Reformbestrebungen und Zerfall des sozio-ökonomischen Systems der Sowjetunion (1980-1994): Analyse und Kritik des Transformationsprozesses unter besonderer Berücksichtigung des Sektors der Eisen- und Stahlindustrie* (Universitätsverlag Linz, 1999), esp. 79–80.

[47] "Vremia vpered!" *Rybnitskii metallurg*, 3 March 1989, 1–2; and "Nashi kandidaty v narodnye deputaty SSSR," *Leninskoe znamia*, 16 March 1989, 2.

the enterprise level, and the self-decreed withdrawal of the party left the management with uncontested power inside the factories.

In an ironic twist, even the perestroika reformers' attempt to democratize the economy ended up as a measure strengthening the management. According to the new enterprise law from 1987 all posts in the factory were to be elected by the working collective directly. In practice this did not lead to a democratic competition, however, but to an acclamation of the incumbent by the assembled workers, which gave the directors additional legitimacy and independence vis-à-vis the economic bureaucracy (which had appointed them as enterprise leader). The Council of the Work Collective *(Sovet Trudogovo Kollektiva—STK)* that had to be formed in all factories remained under control of the management nearly everywhere.[48] It was precisely these perestroika-born STK that were used by the Dniester factory directors for forming a United STK *(Ob"edinennyi Sovet Trudovykh Kollektivov – OSTK)* at the local and regional levels as the basic organization for mobilization of the autonomist movement.[49]

Last but not least, the increase in the factory directors' power was further boosted by the economic crisis entangled with the marketization process. Unemployment was a new and existential threat to the workers and as the state's consumer goods supply broke down or vanished in the early 1990s the workers depended directly on supplies through the combines. In 1991/1992 factories in the Dniester valley introduced a sort of corporate martial law that introduced paramilitary units in the factories and gave the management far-reaching control over the workforce. This was the direct basis for mobilizing hundreds of workers in each factory to fight for Transnistrian statehood in spring and summer 1992. Post-Soviet factory corporatism was thus the economic backbone of Dniester separatism.[50]

---

[48] Paul Thomas Christensen, *Russia's Workers in Transition: Labor, Management, and the State under Gorbachev and Yeltsin* (Northern Illinois University Press, 1999), 37–54, 67–72.
[49] Volkova, *Goriachee leto*, 21–55.
[50] Jan Zofka, "The Transformation of Soviet Industrial Relations and the Foundation of the Moldovan Dniester Republic," *Europe-Asia Studies* 68, no. 5

Crimea: Geography and Collective Biography

In respect of its social composition, pro-Russian separatism in Crimea was completely different from the Transnistrian movement. Here it was not the heavy industry directors of Sevastopol or Kerch who were the leading protagonists of the movement, but intellectuals, small businessmen, and Afghan war veterans, who had been politicized in the small groupings of the perestroika "informal movement." This movement, which was based on personal networks, was nowhere near as successful as the Dniester separatism in the years after 1989. The pro-Russian "Republican Party of Crimea," in coalition with several other like-minded parties, did win presidential and parliamentary elections in 1994, but the governing bloc fell apart through factional strife in the following months. The party and the parliamentary faction were dissolved and the Ukrainian government was able to dismiss the institution of the Crimean presidency completely.

The Beginning: Territory—Autonomy—Russian Nationalism— Decay

The administrative status of Crimea was under discussion already in the 1980s. Crimea had been downgraded from an autonomous republic to a simple district ("oblast'") in 1945 and in 1954 had been transferred from the Russian to the Ukrainian Soviet republic. With the advent of change during perestroika the idea of declaring Crimea a "Union-wide sanatorium" (Vsesoiuznaia zdravnitsa) was discussed in assemblies of regional and Union-wide politicians.[51] A remarkable event in this respect was a conference in Simferopol in October 1989 about the "Dialectics of the development of inter-

---

(2016): 826–46; "Rezhim osobogo polozheniia," *Rybnitskii metallurg*, 29 August 1991, 1; and "Etogo trebuet obstanovka," *Kirovets*, 14 August 1992, 2.

[51] "USSR legislative proposal for a recognition of Crimea as a health resort of Union-wide significance," GA RF, f. 9654, op. 7, d. 628, ll. 7-15; "Protocols of the Supreme Soviet health committee sessions", GA RF, f. 9654, op. 7, d. 628, ll. 16-98; and letter from executive committee chairman of the Crimean Soviet to the Supreme Soviet health committee, GA RF, f. R-9654, op. 7, d. 136, ll. 22-23.

national relations in the USSR under the current conditions," where regional CPSU party officials, scholars, and NGO activists discussed the current state of Crimea. While the party officials saw it as an occasion for discussing organizational questions related to the return of the Crimean Tatars, and the scholars reconsidered theoretical questions like Crimea's meta-historical multi-nationality and the ethnogenesis of the Karaites, the future activists of the pro-Russian movement, present at the conference as scholars or NGO activists, were already at this point coming up with suggestions for a renewed status of autonomy. One of them proposed a "Republic of Tavrida," using a term referring to tsarist times rather than "Crimea" with its Tatar origins. Another scholar stated more clearly than others at this early point in time that "Crimea cannot remain in the territory of Ukraine."[52]

Still under the auspices and leadership of the regional party a referendum for an autonomy of Crimea "in the USSR" was held in January 1991. Ninety percent of the voters agreed to this, and Crimea received autonomy status, which was recognized by the Ukrainian government after independence a few months later.[53]

The central organizations of the pro-Russian movement in Crimea were formed after the failed coup d'état in August 1991 in Moscow and the subsequent declaration of independence of Ukraine. In autumn 1991 activists from small groupings of the "informal movement" gathered to found the Republican Movement of Crimea (*Respublikanskoe Dvizhenie Kryma*—RDK), which opposed the status quo whereby Crimea belonged to newly independent Ukraine. The RDK launched a signature collection in spring 1992 as part of its campaign for a new referendum on Crimean independence from Ukraine. The activists claimed to have collected 250,000 signatures. No referendum was held because the Crimean parliament declared a moratorium over the referendum demand

---

[52] "Mezhnatsional'nye otnosheniia: Puti sovershenstvovaniia. V poiskakh vernykh reshenii," *Krymskaia pravda*, 5 October 1989, 1–3.

[53] "Oblastnaia (tsentral'naia) komissiia po referendumu v Krymskoi oblasti: O rezul'tatakh referenduma o gosudarstvennom i pravovom statuse Kryma," *Krymskaia pravda*, 22 January 1991, 1. For the debates in Crimea around the referendum, see Sasse, *Crimea Question*, 138.

pending the conclusion of negotiations with the Ukrainian government. The pro-Russian movement's activists were nevertheless able to use these signatures as a moral and argumentative resource.[54]

Elections in spring 1994 indeed did show that the movement was able to gain popular support. The candidate of the "Republican Party of Crimea" (the newly-founded RDK-party) Iurii Meshkov beat Nikolai Bagrov, who as Party Secretary and then Soviet/Parliament Chairman had been the strongman of Crimean politics for almost a decade, with a two-third majority. Two months later, the candidates of the RPK also won a majority in the parliament of the Autonomous Republic of Crimea by a similar margin.[55]

The pro-Russian movement was not able to form a stable government, however. The movement disintegrated in struggles between various factions, which translated into an institutional struggle between the presidency under Meshkov and the parliament under its chairman Sergei Tsekov, who had been a close co-worker of Meshkov until the elections. Meshkov had angered his party colleagues and co-militants because he allocated the government posts to a team around the liberal economist Evgenii Saburov from Moscow. Furthermore, the movement disintegrated along the lines of former cleavages, along which the RDK had split in 1992, before re-uniting for the electoral campaign as "Bloc Russia" (Blok Rossiia) in 1994.[56]

In autumn 1994 Meshkov locked himself up in the common building of the presidency and the Crimean Soviet with his security guard, and shut the parliament members out. This shutout was a desperate attempt to regain power. He was already politically isolated, and lost most of his competences after this escalation. Both conflict parties tried to win over the Ukrainian government for their

---

54   Mal'gin, *Krymskii uzel*, 69–70, 84–85.
55   Denis J. Shaw, "Crimea: Background and Aftermath of its 1994 Election," *Post-Soviet Geography* 35, no. 4 (1994): 221–34; and Andrew Wilson, "Presidential and Parliamentary Elections in Ukraine. The Issue of Crimea," in *Crimea: Dynamics, Challenges, and Prospects*, ed. Maria Drohobycky (Rowman and Littlefield, 1995), 107–31.
56   Mal'gin, *Krymskii uzel*, 84–96.

cause to win in the local power competition. This rendered Kyiv the opportunity to become the decisive body for the Crimean issues, to negotiate a constitution for Crimean autonomy in line with the Ukrainian one, and eventually to abolish the institution of the Crimean presidency.[57]

Social Composition of the Movement

The networks which formed the bases of the organizational cores of the pro-Russian movement did not derive from Soviet power apparatuses, but rather from political groupings and business networks outside the CPSU and large industrial state enterprises. The movement was dominated by academics and intellectuals, small businessmen and Afghan war veterans politicized in the "informal movement" of the perestroika period. Before gathering in the Republican Movement of Crimea after Ukrainian independence most of the leading protagonists had been active in groups like the anti-Stalinist historical memory organization "Memorial," the "Ecology and Peace" environmental association, the autonomist circle of intellectuals "20th January" (its name referring to the date of the 1991 autonomy referendum), and the autonomist "Demokraticheskaia Tavrida" or the "Electoral Club of Crimea," which was rather a recruitment organization for new political elites. These organizations were not necessarily democratic, anti-Soviet, or oppositional. They rather acted in a low-profile framework and limited their work to single political issues. Many of their members were at the same time members of the CPSU.

The role of the party apparatus and nomenklatura structures is a topic in the literature. Boris Zazhigaev ascribes an important role to the old nomenklatura, but the highest party officials among the leaders of the pro-Russian movement he names are Sergei Tsekov, who had been party secretary in a district hospital, and Valerii Averkin, who had been the driver of the oblast' committee secretary. From 1990, Meshkov and Tsekov held posts in the Supreme Soviet of Crimea and were party members but they did not

---

[57] Ibid., 84–96; and Sasse, *Crimea Question*, 175–79.

represent the party apparatus there. To be sure, there is no clean split between nomenklatura and non-nomenklatura, but nor can a systematic transfer of structures or networks from the party into the movement be detected. Rather, one could say that the pro-Russian movement was a means to compete for power with the old nomenklatura, in the person of the former Crimean party chief Nikolai Bagrov who lost the 1994 elections against Meshkov.[58]

A distinctive role was played by the "Union of Afghanistan-Veterans 'Bagram'" in Simferopol and its Crimean-wide organization. The organization's activities were a mixture of social assistance, including business operations, and political advocacy for veterans. Like the groupings mentioned above, it was part of the informal movement, and it acted in competition with the official Union for Afghanistan-Veterans run by the Komsomol. Its clubhouse "Klub Bagram" became a meeting point for a political milieu standing outside the Communist Party apparatus, and the leading activists of many groups met here. In 1991 the veterans' Union collectively entered the RDK. However, one year later, the important Union left the RDK again, and founded the "Russian-speaking Movement of Crimea" (*Russkoiazychnoe dvizhenie Kryma* – RiaDK) and later the Crimean People's Party *(Narodnaia Partiia Kryma)*, before entering Blok Rossiia for the 1994 elections and then splitting again after the elections.[59]

---

[58] Boris Zazhigaev, *Evoliutsiia politicheskogo ustroistva v Respublike Krym v period 1989-1998* (PhD Diss., MGIMO Moscow, 2003), 84. See also: Taras Kuzio, *Russia, Crimea, Ukraine. Triangle of Conflict* (London Research Institute for the Study of Conflict and Terrorism, 1994), 23. An even more difficult question are the activists' potential links to Soviet or Russian intelligence services, which cannot be traced with the historian's methods. There are claims in some studies that Yurii Meshkov worked for the KGB, but further substantiation is vague, and this information perhaps refers to his military service in the border guards subordinated to the KGB; Victor Tkachuk, *The Crimea. Chronicle of Separatism 1992-1995* (Kiev Ukrainian Center for Independent Political Research, 1996); and "Iu. A. Meshkov: 'Nasha tsel'—soiuz s Rossiei," *Krymskaia Pravda*, 25 December 1993, 2. In how far such a connection may have guided his political activities cannot be established by now.

[59] I have reconstructed the political socialization of the RDK/RPK and Blok Rossiia leaderships through interviews with 20 leading activists in Simferopol and Sevastopol in June/July 2008. The interviews focused on the experiences

Another group of protagonists in the Crimean movement overlapped with the Afghan war veterans: the small businessmen. A few exceptions notwithstanding, entrepreneurs in the pro-Russian movement did not stem from Soviet industrial structures. They were not the former directors of heavy industry combines, but owners or managers of newly founded, mostly small enterprises, rather in trade and services than in manufacturing. In some cases, the business model was based on economic exchanges with Russia, and thus was directly linked with the political activism of its owners. The most distinguished representative of this group among the Crimean activists was the Afghan war veteran Valerii Averkin. He was co-founder of the RDK and chairman of the import-export association "Impeks-55,"[60] which received credits and financial support from Russian banks and other institutions and financed the RDK. When the Union of Afghanistan-Veterans split from the RDK in 1992 and founded the RiaDK, the rest of the Republican Movement got into financial troubles. Both the RDK and the RiaDK now competed in Moscow for financial support from parliament committees.[61] Averkin's RiaDK, behind a thin facade of cultural politics, carried out trade operations, financial transfers, and other businesses with enterprises and state institutions in the Russian Federation.[62]

Like the Transnistrian movement, then, the Crimean movement also served not least the interests of economic elites. However, rather than being dominated by former nomenklatura

---

and the recruitment story of the interviewees. For details, see: Jan Zofka, *Postsowjetischer Separatismus*, 52–54.

[60] For details on Impeks-55 Krym: E. Korovko, "Chto zhe takoe 'Impeks-55 Krym'"? *Krymskaia pravda*, 19 March 1992, 3; and V. Medvedev, "Krymskii Beriia chistit per'ia?" *Krymskaia pravda*, 21 March 1992, 1–2.

[61] "Letter RDK to E. K. Pudovkin, Russian Supreme Soviet," 15 May 1993, GA RF, f. 10026, op. 4, d. 3514, l. 53; and "Table of expenditures for a referendum for re-elections of the Crimean Soviet," 7 June 1993, GA RF, f. 10026, op. 4, d. 3514, l. 47.

[62] "RDK—eto russkoiazychnoe obshchestvo Kryma," Interview with Valerii Averkin, *Krymskaia pravda*, 21 October 1992, 3; "RDK: Pust' naverkhu deliat kresla. My budem rabotat'!" Interview with Valerii Averkin, *Krymskaia pravda*, 24 November 1992, 3; "Chto takoe RDK?" *Krymskaia pravda*, 31 July 1993, 3; and "Report of the Russian-speaking movement of Crimea about the situation in Crimea," GA RF, f. 10026, op. 4, d. 3520, ll. 8–10.

officials, it was academics and new businessmen, keen on flanking their business model politically, who played a key role here. In contrast, regional and local elites from the Soviet power apparatuses in many places opposed Crimean separatism and aligned themselves with the Ukrainian government—as for example the elites at the center of the chemical industry in Krasnoperekopsk and the political leadership of Sevastopol.

Elites against Crimean Separatism: Krasnoperekopsk and Sevastopol

Krasnoperekopsk is the northernmost district of Crimea, which covers the isthmus between the peninsula and the mainland. Soviet planners chose the area to become a chemical industry center in the 1930s because of its natural endowments. The district town of the same name was a typical Soviet industrial town with a close entanglement of elites in party, municipality, and factory structures. The local chemical industry was hit hard by the economic crisis of the transformation and the dissolution of the Soviet Union, which cut it off from its sales market as well as from its suppliers. Conditions appear to have been favorable for a Soviet-conservative, pro-Russian mobilization. Nevertheless, pro-Russian mobilization in the town and district remained weak and local elites positioned themselves in strong opposition to the pro-Russian mobilizations in Simferopol and other places in Crimea and coalesced with the central government in Kyiv.

When in autumn 1991 the Republican Movement in Simferopol began to collect signatures for a referendum for autonomy and independence of Crimea, leading local politicians and economic officials in Krasnoperekopsk published a resolution under the slogan "Autonomy for Perekop."[63] They threatened to secede from Crimea were the peninsula to split from Ukraine. The most powerful politician of Krasnoperekopsk, Serhiy Kunitsyn, did not sign the resolution but was nevertheless a strict opponent of

---

[63] Resolution of the initiative for the launching of a movement for a federative Crimea – Movement for an autonomous district (raion); "Perekopu—Avtonomiiu!" *Frunzevets*, 19 October 1991, 1–2.

pro-Russian separatism in Crimea. Kunitsyn was anything but a Ukrainian nationalist—born in 1960 in Turkmenistan, he was an Afghan war veteran, Russian by nationality and an opponent of the dissolution of the Soviet Union, as he claimed publicly.[64] This did not hinder him in maintaining good relations with the new government in Kyiv. Through negotiations with the concurrent president Leonid Kuchma Kunitsyn achieved the declaration of the district of Krasnoperekopsk as a special economic zone named "Sivash." This bargain served his own interests, as he became Chairman of the free trade zone's administration, the local chemical industry's interests, which was freed from export limitations and import customs duties for supply, and also the Ukrainian government's interests, which won leverage in its struggle against the secessionist tendencies in the rest of Crimea.[65] For Kunitsyn this bargain was the start of a political career that would give him several Kyiv-backed power positions in the Autonomous republic: he became premier of Crimea, from 1998 to 2005 (with an interruption in 2002), and in the following years functioned as head of the city administration in Sevastopol, assigned by the president in Kyiv. On 27 February 2014, with the Crimean crisis already at its height, the temporary Ukrainian president Oleksandr Turchynov made him "Permanent Representative of the (Ukrainian) President in Crimea," a post from which he resigned a month later, reproaching Kyiv for its failure to act against the Russian take-over.[66]

To sum up, in the district of Kransoperekopsk the protagonists who stood up against pro-Russian separatism were, by

---

[64] Interview with Kunitsyn, *Frunzevets*, 11 August 1992, 1. For Kunitsyn's early biography, see: *Kto est' kto v Krymu 2001-2002: Al'manakh*, 111–12; *Kto est' kto v Krymu* (Kiew 2002), 28–29; and Kunitsyn, Sergei Vladimirovich. Biographie, unter: http://www.sevastopol.su/person.php?id=9 (originally accessed 20 June 2013; site inaccessible as at 9 February 2022).

[65] Directive of the Ukrainian President on the foundation of the experimental economic zone in Northern Crimea "Sivash"; *Frunzevets*, 4 July 1995, 1. The pro-Russian organizations criticized the Special Economic Zone and the benefits Kunitsyn was able to draw from it: "Ne dat' sebia obmanut'," *Svobodnyi Krym*, 17 June 1995, 3.

[66] *Kto est kto v Krymu* (Kiev 2002), 28–29; and Zofka, *Postsowjetischer Separatismus*, 358.

social background, similar to the protagonists of Dniester separatism. The positioning of these political and economic elites was not determined by the attitudes or even the nationality of the region's inhabitants—the 1994 election results did not differ much from the rest of Crimea.[67] Rather, an arrangement of local elites with the Ukrainian government was behind this position. This can be seen as a typical example for the matrioshka separatism during the Soviet decay, where declarations of sovereignty of administrative entities led to declarations of subordinated entities.

Sevastopol was the other peculiar case in Crimea where local elites remained loyal to Kyiv in the early 1990s mobilizations. Here too it was neither attitudes, nor ideology, nor nationality that can be seen as channeling the process of the protagonists' taking sides, but concrete institutional arrangements. In Sevastopol, as in Krasnoperekopsk, apparently favorable conditions for a Soviet-conservative, pro-Russian separatism had an unexpected impact.

Sevastopol was Crimea's most Soviet city. The structures of union-wide apparatuses, mostly linked to the military and the military-industrial complex and its conservative ideologies, were ubiquitous in this city. It hosted the Black Sea Fleet and was a cult place for Russian nationalists who viewed it as an outpost of the Muscovite state in the Black Sea. It was dominated by a heavy industry entangled with the fleet, which employed a considerable part of the population. Until 1993 it was one of the Soviet "closed cities," where movement was strictly regulated because of the presence of economic and military sensitive infrastructures. Thus, the preconditions for a Soviet-conservative pro-Russian mobilization were very favorable.[68]

---

[67] Wilson, "Presidential and Parliamentary Elections," 114.
[68] Kevin Covert, "Overlapping Imagined Communities: The Black Sea Fleet Negotiations between Russia and Ukraine," *Canadian Review of Studies in Nationalism* 24, nos. 1–2 (1997): 21–31; Karl D. Qualls, "Accommodation and Agitation in Sevastopol. Redefining Socialist Space in the Postwar 'City of Glory'," in *Socialist Spaces: Sites of Everyday Life in the Eastern Bloc*, eds. David Crowley and Susan Reid (Berg, 2002), 23–46; Karl D. Qualls, *From Ruins to Reconstruction: Urban Identity in Soviet Sevastopol after World War II* (Cornell University Press, 2009); and Serhii Plokhy, "The City of Glory: Sevastopol in

In the event, however, the pro-Russian mobilization in Sevastopol remained rather weak and the Soviet legacies partly helped the Ukrainian government to hold onto power in the city. For example, the subordination under republican jurisdiction in Soviet times had contradictory implications after Ukraine's independence. Eventually, it turned against the aspirations of the pro-Russian movement. During the years 1991 to 1993, Russian nationalist activists regularly went to Moscow to lobby for a Duma resolution declaring the Russian Federation's control over Sevastopol, which they achieved in summer 1993, as mentioned in the first section. The crucial argument was: Sevastopol had been detached from the Oblast' of Crimea and subordinated directly to the republican government of the RSFSR in Moscow in 1948. When the Crimean region was transferred to Ukraine in 1954, the Union-level Supreme Soviet did not make an extra decision for a transfer of Sevastopol, which proved, according to the Russian nationalists, that it belonged to the legal successor of the RSFSR—the Russian Federation.[69]

In fact, the Ukrainian government was able to use the traditional peculiar position of Sevastopol to put it under direct control of the presidential administration in Kyiv. Contrary to expectations of a Crimean government in Simferopol, Sevastopol was not incorporated into the Autonomous Crimean Republic, but taken under direct control by Kyiv. Thus, the city was governed not by the organs of municipal self-administration, but by officials assigned by Kyiv. The Ukrainian president did not select Kyiv-based bureaucrats or even Ukrainian nationalists for these posts, but representatives of the local Soviet power structures. The first chairman of the city administration, a sort of city mayor, named by Kyiv, was Ivan Ermakov, a longstanding member of the CPSU,

---

Russian Historical Mythology," *Journal of Contemporary History* 35, no 3 (2000): 369–83.

[69] Mal'gin, *Krymskii uzel*, 35; and correspondence of pro-Russian activists with the RF Supreme Soviet and its judiciary department 1992/1993, GA RF, f. 10026, op. 1, d. 2767, l. 191, 217; op. 4, d. 3514, l. 53. For the connection of the Sevastopol activists to Moscow, see also: Viacheslav Pikhovshek, "Will the Crimean Crisis Explode?" in *Crimea*, ed. Drohobycky, 39–65, see 43.

colonel of the Black Sea Fleet and director of an armory enterprise belonging to the fleet.[70] Not only Ermakov, but all higher-ranked officials of the city administration in the first half of the 1990s came from the port city's traditional elite.[71] This elite kept its pro-Soviet, great-Russian-imperial attitudes, but accepted the territorial status quo and arranged itself in line with its function as representatives of a new Ukrainian statehood. It was exactly this Soviet-conservative elite which ensured the almost entirely non-violent transition of Sevastopol from Soviet Hero-City to a city in the new Ukrainian state. To be sure, in 2014, the impact of this arrangement again turned towards the other side: with the fall of Yanukovych the head of the city administration resigned, and Kyiv lost its grasp on the city. Pro-Russian forces were able to install Aleksei Chalyi who proclaimed himself "people's mayor."[72]

The economic breakdown had contradictory consequences for separatism's mobilizational power in Sevastopol as well. On the one hand, shortages in consumer goods supply caused protest in winter 1992/93 with mass demonstrations, where representatives of the pro-Russian movement partially managed to position themselves as advocates of the people.[73] At the same time, the

---

[70] G. Staroverov, "Novyi mer Sevastopolia—polkovnik," *Krymskaia pravda*, 9 February 1991, 1; and I. Ermakov, "K rukovodstvu dolzhny priiti novye liudi," *Krymskaia pravda*, 4 January 1994, 2.

[71] For a list of the heads of department and secretaries of the city administration, see *Slava Sevastopolia*, 19 November 1992, 2.

[72] "Mer Sevastopolia poddal v otstavku," *Kommersant" Online-News*, 24 February 2014, https://www.kommersant.ru/doc/2415533?isSearch=True (accessed 27 May 2020); and "Aleksei Chalyi vozglavil upravlenie po obespecheniiu zhiznedeiatel'nost'iu Sevastopolia," *Kommersant" Online-News*, 24 February 2014, http://www.kommersant.ru/doc/2415882?isSearch=True (accessed 27 May 2020).

[73] "Rasporiazhenie predstavitelia Prezidenta Ukrainy. O merakh po sotsial'noi zashchite naseleniia g. Sevastopolia v sviazi s dal'neishei liberalizatsiei tsen," *Slava Sevastopolia*, 13 January 1993, 1; Iu. Sirotinskaia, "O natsional'noi gordosti v voprose o tsenakh," *Slava Sevastopolia*, 13 January 1993, 2; A. Skripnichenko, "Rozhdestvenskie mitingi otshumeli...prodolzhenie sleduet?" *Slava Sevastopolia*, 13 January 1993, 1; A. Samsonov, "Smutnye vremena v Sevastopole: snova prizrak iz Evropy?" *Slava Sevastopolia*, 19 January 1993, 1; and M. Babushkin, "Soglashenie podpisano. Liudi zhdut rezul'tatov," *Slava Sevastopolia*, 10 February 1993, 2.

economic crisis caused the city's dependency on the central government's social programs and special funds. Local taxes financed only a small part of the budget. Quickly rising prices, hidden unemployment with factories and enterprises hesitating to lay off their employees without having money to pay wages, the non-payment of wages and pensions made itself felt in the city treasury. The city administration reacted with ad-hoc social programs and subsidies, which were financed by the Ukrainian government.[74] Thus Kyiv had leverage for influencing the political situation in Sevastopol. The pro-Russian forces were far from being able to conquer power positions in the city's political apparatus in the early 1990s.

Conclusion

The Crimean and the Transnistrian pro-Russian separatist movements resembled each other strongly in their ideology and their goals, but they were very different in their social background, their recruitment patterns, and their modes of functioning. Dniester separatism was based in a sort of "factory corporatism." Enterprise directors and engineers mobilized "their" workers and built up a state apparatus in cooperation with academics, local politicians, and representatives of the Soviet security organs. The pro-Russian movement in Crimea, in contrast, resembled rather what sociology has described as a "social movement." It was based in personal networks that were created in previous political engagements outside the state apparatuses. The existing social power relations, for example in the workplace, could not be transformed into mobilization resources as in Transnistria. There was no group of actors in the Crimean movement comparable to the factory directors in the Dniester valley's separatist movement. Accordingly,

---

[74] Combined decision of the City Soviet Standing Commission's chairmen and the council of the presidential representative, 11 January 1993; "O skladyvaiushcheisia v gorode politicheskoi i ekonomicheskoi obstanovke na tekushchii moment i merakh po ee stabilizatsii," *Slava Sevastopolia*, 15 January 1993, 1; and V. Semenov, "Stabil'nost' gosudarstva – v stabil'nosti regiona," *Slava Sevastopolia*, 22 September 1992, 2.

it was not able to create long-standing organizations and state institutions which could have functioned beyond the personal networks. Rather, it consisted of small, fragile groupings which split at every occasion along personal cleavages. This background of the movement is at the heart of why, after a sweeping landslide victory in the 1994 elections, the pro-Russian forces collapsed in a few weeks, and were not able to build structures that would have opened up the possibility of entering a confrontation with the central government.

Which local actors participated and which resources they could mobilize was an important factor for what the movements were capable of. The question why certain actors took part and others did not cannot be answered theoretically, but has to be analyzed case by case. Conflict lines were fragmented and subject to a steady negotiation process. They were not predetermined by nationality or borders of historical regions. The process of taking sides was channelled by small-scale institutional arrangements. Actors of internal territorial conflicts are not ethnic groups, but complex coalitions, whose development has to be analyzed historically and cannot adequately be depicted using either the terms of ethnic conflict or comprehensive theoretical models suggesting clear causal relations. To get closer to an understanding of the internal wars and territorial conflicts after 1989 we need a mosaic of micro-studies of the actors, shedding light on the processes of coalition-building, social contexts, day-to-day practices, ambitions, and experiences of the actors and the social power relations reflected by them.

A DEBATE ON PROSPECT THEORY AND EXPLAINING RUSSIA'S ANNEXATION OF CRIMEA

Loss Aversion, Neo-imperial Frames and Territorial Expansion: Using Prospect Theory to Examine the Annexation of Crimea*

Ion Marandici

Abstract: Why did Russia's authoritarian leader decide to annex Crimea? Why was Ukraine unable to resist the Russian aggression? This study relies on prospect theory to illuminate the decision-making in Moscow and Kyiv that led to the takeover of Crimea. First, I identify the turning points of the Euromaidan crisis preceding the annexation and trace how Putin's assessment of the status quo shifted repeatedly between the domains of losses and gains. In the domain of losses, the Russian leader, influenced by a neo-imperial faction within the Presidential Administration, became more risk acceptant, annexed the peninsula, and escalated the hybrid warfare. Putin framed the intervention using nationalist themes, drawing on salient historical analogies from the past. Second, new documentary evidence such as the minutes of Ukraine's National Defence and Security Council (NDSC) and participant testimonies reveals that the decision-makers in Kyiv could not mount an effective defence due to squabbles among coalition partners, the breakdown of the military chain of command in Crimea, the looming threat of a full-scale invasion from the East, and the inflated expectations regarding the West's capacity to deter Russia's aggression. Third, the article relies on prospect theory to explain why after Crimea's annexation, Putin refrained from continuing the territorial expansion deeper into Ukraine, opting instead to back secessionism in Donbas. This account highlights the explanatory power of prospect theory compared to alternative frameworks, pointing out, at the same time, the need to incorporate

---

* I would like to thank the editors and three anonymous reviewers for their useful suggestions.

causal mechanisms from competing theoretical traditions in studies of foreign policy decision-making.

Introduction

Despite its destabilizing effect on regional security, the annexation of Crimea—the most significant territorial conquest in post-Cold War Europe—remains an understudied event. Some scholars have employed decision-making approaches to elucidate the circumstances of Russia's decision to take over Crimea and wage war against Ukraine (Bartles and McDermott 2014; Bukkvoll 2016; Lampert 2016; Forsberg and Pursiainen 2017; Fortescue 2018). Still, several interrelated questions remain unanswered. What factors influenced the decision-making processes leading to the annexation? What explains the timing and the hybrid nature of the intervention? What role did Ukraine's weakness, Putin's personality, and advisory structures play in the annexation?

The paper contributes to the foreign policy scholarship by answering these questions and conceiving of Crimea's annexation as a theory-informed case study. To use George and Bennett's (2005: 75) terminology, this study is simultaneously a disciplined configurative and a theory-testing case. Although the annexation could be used to test various international relations theories, the article focuses solely on foreign policy decision-making rather than traditional theories in international relations. Hence, the objective of the paper is twofold. First, it elucidates important aspects of the decision-making process of this significant historical case. Second, the case study assesses the external validity and drawbacks of prospect theory applied to international crises. In doing so, I argue that prospect theory provides a compelling account as to why the Russian leader took a calculated risk and engaged in territorial conquest amidst the power transfer in Kyiv, when the Ukrainian state lacked the capacity to defend itself.

Before moving on to the theory-testing part, the paper provides an overview of the annexation with the relevant facts of the case included. The sequencing of the crisis allows us to trace the changing perceptions of the status quo and reconstruct the decision-making environment in Kyiv and Moscow. Even though the collective nature of decision-making at state level presents a major difficulty for the application of prospect theory, which is an individual-level theory (Levy 1997), existing evidence suggests that the decision to annex Crimea was made by the Russian president assisted by a small group of close advisors and high-ranking officials.

The paper is structured as follows. I start off by providing an overview of the prospect theory and its foreign policy applications. Then, I distinguish three turning points in the crisis in Ukraine matching Putin's changing definitions of the status quo. The next section details Putin's shifts between the domain of losses and gains, and examines his reference points, risk propensity, and the types of frames used to describe the annexation. A separate section explains how Kyiv's weakness played into Moscow's annexation calculus, whereas the last part examines briefly how alternative explanatory frameworks might explain the foreign policy choice.

Prospect Theory and Foreign Policy Decision-Making

Developed as an alternative to the expected utility model, prospect theory is one of the main psychological approaches to the study of foreign policy decision-making (Mintz and Sofrin 2017). As such, it theorizes individual decision-making under risk (Kahneman and Tversky 1979; Tversky and Kahneman 1981; Kahneman and Tversky 1986; Kahneman, Knetsch, and Thaler 1991; Kahneman 2003).

Prospect theory postulates that decision makers perceiving the status quo in the domain of losses defined in relation to a reference point, accept more risk, whereas, in the domain of gains, they express risk aversion (Kahneman and Tversky 1979). As such, loss aversion and reference dependence feature as the core elements of prospect theory. Besides these two findings, prospect theorists identified several secondary effects pertaining to deviations from the standard rational choice decision-making. First, the endowment effect was observed, whereby goods in someone's possession are overvalued compared to objects one does not own (Kahneman, Knetsch and Thaler 1991). Then, framing effects were documented. While the expected utility model assumes that individual preferences are invariant, Kahneman and Tversky (1986) demonstrate that it matters whether choices are framed as losses or gains. Depending on wording and the order of presentation, changing the frames causes preference reversals. Next, experimental evidence confirms the declining sensitivity to gains and losses as individuals move away from the reference point as well as the tendency of decision makers to overweight low probabilities and underestimate moderate-high probabilities (Kahneman and Tversky 1979). In short, prospect theory evolved into a veritable research program with applications across social sciences.

Even though Stein (2017: 251) observed that moving prospect theory out of the lab into the field of foreign policy is a difficult process, researchers have applied the framework to study foreign policy. For instance, Farnham (1992) demonstrated that Roosevelt's preference reversal regarding the necessity to intervene in Europe during World War II was the result of a frame change induced by emotions linked to the breakdown of peace in Europe at the Munich conference. McDermott (1992) explained how the Iranian hostage crisis pushed Carter into the domain of losses, prompting the US president to pick the riskiest policy, ending with a failed rescue mission. Likewise, Haas (2001) spelled out how during the Cuban Missile Crisis, Kennedy and Khrushchev, both operating in the domain of losses, took excessive risks contrary to the expected utility model predictions. Taliaferro (2004) integrated prospect theory into his balance-of-risk theory and traced how American and Soviet officials, averse to perceived losses in terms of power, and international status, initiated risky interventions in Vietnam and Afghanistan. Such case studies demonstrate the value of prospect theory in analyzing decision-making during foreign policy crises.

A handful of scholars have employed prospect theory to study Russia's 2014 territorial expansion. Thus, Bukkvoll (2016) briefly mentions the theory to explain Putin's risk-taking in reaction to the perceived success of the Euromaidan protest, focusing mostly on beliefs, emotions, personality, and organizational politics as shaping decision-making. Similarly, Forsberg and Pursiainen (2017) invoke prospect theory as a potential framework, but then add groupthink, operational codes, belief systems, personality, and emotions as explanatory factors. Lampert (2016) compares Putin's decisions to intervene militarily in Georgia, Ukraine, and Syria, concluding that the Russian president acted in all three cases from the domain of losses. A study of the Russian foreign policy behavior by Gorenburg (2019) provides insights derived from simulations of prospect theory-based scenarios, while Lenton (2021) applies prospect theory to clarify why Ukraine's leadership did not defend Crimea but fought in Donbas. In the context of Russia's great power ambitions (Kolstø 2016), research clarifying the cognitive dimension of decision-making preceding the annexation is essential.

Despite its eclecticism, the existing scholarship has added value to this emerging field of study. Some researchers cover broadly several cases at once (Lampert 2016), while others draw on competing theoretical approaches, providing comprehensive causal stories (Bukkvoll 2016; Forsberg and Pursiainen 2017). Still, most of the annexation research employs a reduced version of prospect theory, focusing on loss aversion and glossing over elements such as the menu of policy options available to decision-makers, evolving reference points across several dimensions, alternative methods of identifying the domains of losses and gains, and the interactive nature of the crisis. That is why the relationship between prospect theory and other theories of conflict needs to be better articulated. It is often not clear what contradicts, competes, or complements prospect theory. At the same time, any theoretical explanation of the decision-making preceding the annexation cannot be complete as it is impossible to identify all influences on a particular policy outcome in highly opaque political regimes.

In line with Hudson and Vore (1995), this paper does not focus on neorealism or liberalism as major international relations theories but rather seeks to clarify foreign policy decision-making via a single case study grounded in prospect theory. There is much debate concerning the merits of single cases in theory-testing studies, hence researchers should follow Gerring (2004: 342) and carefully establish the class of phenomena to which their case belongs. The annexation of Crimea can be viewed as an instance of multiple phenomena of interest to political scientists. It can be treated as an example of hybrid warfare, a case of bloodless territorial conquest similar to the Nazi annexation of the Sudetenland or the Soviet occupation of Bessarabia, an instance of irredentist secession, or a manifestation of great power aspirations. Here, I conceptualize the annexation as a case of foreign policy decision-making in which the aggressor state faced a choice among four courses of action, opting for territorial conquest. Besides annexation, Moscow could have backed the transformation of Crimea into an unrecognized republic, abstained from intervening in Ukraine, or supported enhanced autonomy for Crimea as part of a federalized Ukraine. In this sense, the decision to occupy and annex should be regarded as one of several potential outcomes.

Studying the annexation as a case of territorial conquest carries certain theoretical and policy benefits. The case study could boost the external validity of prospect theory. By tracing how Russia's leadership reached the decision to wage a war of aggression against Ukraine and by examining the reasons guiding Kyiv's reaction to the attack, the case clarifies the distinct phases of the foreign policy choice, while providing new insights into an adjacent area of scholarship concerning the changing nature of conflict in Europe. In this sense, the present case study can be regarded as a disciplined-configurative one (George and Bennett 2005).

The case study is implemented using public sources. Archival records will remain inaccessible for decades, preventing scholars from consulting confidential materials, but new evidence, declassified documents, accounts by powerholders in Moscow, Kyiv, Crimea, and the West allow us to piece together the central elements of the decision-making process leading up to the annexation. Existing sources need to be assessed critically as some of them may be part of the information war accompanying the hostilities. For instance, it is worrying that scholarly articles about the annexation rely excessively on Kondrashov's (2015) propagandistic film *Crimea—The Path to the Motherland*, Zygar's (2016) journalistic volume, and Putin's public statements. Such evidence is problematic as Russian official sources often incorporate intentional distortions of the events. In line with previous scholarship, they have been critically examined here in conjunction with new evidence such as the declassified transcripts of the deliberations in Kyiv (NSDC 2014), post-factum statements of Ukrainian officials and accounts from participants such as Igor Girkin, one of the coordinators of the hybrid warfare attack against Ukraine.

Sequencing the Crisis in Ukraine

The sequencing of the crisis into distinct stages allows us to reconstruct the decision-making environment prior to the annexation, tracing Putin's changing perceptions of the status quo. The collective nature of decision-making at state level presents a major difficulty for the application of prospect theory, which is an individual-level theory (Levy 1997). Still, the existing evidence suggests that the decision to annex Crimea was made by the Russian president assisted by several high-ranking officials (Zygar 2016; Fortescue 2017; Rhodes 2018; McFaul 2018). Hence, the historical sketch of the annexation also provides readers with the relevant facts of the case before moving on to the prospect theoretical part.

Russia's decision to annex the peninsula was situated at the intersection of multiple processes, each guided by specific logics of action and involving complex relations among actors, operating at multiple levels. Some of the processes preceding the annexation include the cycles of protest across Ukraine, the reset of Russia's relations with the West, the rise of secessionism at Ukraine's periphery, the growing influence of conservative-neo-imperial ideas in Russia, and the negotiations concerning Russia's naval base in Crimea. For analytical purposes, the Crimean crisis is defined here as spanning from the mass mobilization on the Maidan beginning on 21 November 2013 until Russia's formal annexation of Crimea on 18 March 2014. Engaged in competition with the West, over this period, Moscow worried about the success of the Euromaidan movement, perceiving the situation as a zero-sum game. To elucidate the decision-making leading up to Russia's use of force against Ukraine, one must distinguish between three turning points of the crisis, each corresponding to Putin's transition between alternative perceptions of the status quo as either a loss or a gain.

During the initial phase, Ukraine was building closer ties to the EU and completing the negotiation of the EU–Ukraine Association Agreement (AA). The first turning point occurred before the Vilnius summit when Yanukovych decided to postpone the signing of the AA. The deferment was the consequence of Putin's pressure on Yanukovych and the promise of a $15 billion credit (Zygar 2015: 177). It was Yanukovych's turnaround that triggered the Euromaidan protests as the opposition and civil society sought to pressure the president into signing the AA (Onuch and Sasse 2016: 558). Yanukovych, closely associated with the Crimean, Southern and Eastern Ukrainian voters and known for advancing Moscow's interests, adopted a set of dictatorial laws and tried to suppress the rallies using violence, steps which further mobilized the activists (Onuch and Sasse 2016: 573–75). The Euromaidan triggered both demonstrations of solidarity as well as secessionist counter-rallies across the Russian-speaking areas of Ukraine, partially directed by Russian officials (Umland 2016).

However, the second critical juncture—Yanukovych's departure from Kyiv—is essential to understanding Putin's decision to initiate the hybrid war against Ukraine. Between 18 and 20 February 2014, unknown snipers shot tens of protesters on the Maidan. It is still unclear who the shooters were and whose orders they were following. Amid the chaos, Yanukovych and the opposition hastily negotiated a compromise to end the violence with Germany, Poland, France, and Russia serving as mediators. However, the agreement failed as the fragmented opposition could not prevent militant protesters from occupying state institutions. Fearing for his life and acting against Putin's advice, Yanukovych abandoned Kyiv, requesting Moscow's assistance (Putin 2014e). Next, the Russian president, who regarded the ongoing protests as a US-orchestrated coup, personally guided a Russian commando tasked with the extraction of Yanukovych from Ukraine (Putin 2015).

The decision to annex Crimea, the third turning point, is linked to Yanukovych's failure to remain in power. From the soft attempts to back Yanukovych and weaken the Euromaidan, Moscow switched to military intervention. Contesting the legitimacy of the new government in Kyiv, Russian officials intensified their support for the pro-Russian separatists in Crimea and the rest of Ukraine (Umland 2016). The subsequent annexation consisted of multiple events, some of which were guided by Moscow and implemented locally by various activist organizations, Russian special troops, members of the regular Russian Armed Forces, paramilitary units, rebel militias, Ukrainian defectors, and a constellation of non-state actors.

The annexation exploited long-standing separatist tendencies in Crimea.[1] Back in 1991, only 54% of Crimea's population supported Ukraine's independence (Wydra 2004: 115). A few weeks after Ukraine's independence was proclaimed, Crimea's Supreme Soviet publicized its own declaration of sovereignty. In 1992, a symbolic declaration of independence was followed by the promise to organize a referendum (Solchanyk 1994). Kyiv kept secessionism in check by offering more autonomy to the region. But tensions between Simferopol and Kyiv flared again in 1994, when Yuriy Meshkov, running on an openly secessionist platform, gained 73% of the vote in Crimea's presidential elections (NYT 1994). Sevastopol, a city enjoying a special status in Soviet times and serving as the base of the Russian Black Sea Fleet, was the epicenter of separatism. In 1994, Sevastopol's authorities requested that the city be placed under Moscow's jurisdiction (Wydra 2004: 119). To deal with secessionism, Kyiv invalidated Crimea's 1992 constitution and deported Meshkov, a Russian citizen, to Russia. Boris Yeltsin, Russia's president, refused to meet Meshkov and discuss the scenario of a merger between Crimea and Russia (Wydra 2004: 118).

Two decades later, the Ukrainian state was caught unprepared to deal with the new bout of separatism in Crimea. On 23 February 2014, while the Crimean Parliament issued a statement opposing the Euromaidan movement, participants at a small rally in

---

[1] The peninsula was annexed by the tsarist empire in 1783. The site of the Crimean War (1853–56) and the stronghold of the Whites during the Russian Civil War, the region was incorporated by Nikita Khrushchev into the Ukrainian Soviet Socialist Republic in 1954. Populated largely by ethnic Russians and Crimean Tatars, the latter deported by Stalin to Siberia in 1944, Crimea enjoyed significant autonomy as part of Ukraine.

Sevastopol, elected in an improvised manner as the city's new mayor Aleksey Chalyi, who replaced the legitimate authorities. The same tactics would be subsequently observed across Donbas. Despite accounts emphasizing the economic reasons behind the insurgence in Ukraine such as Zhukov's (2016), the Crimean secessionists focused on nationalist-irredentist themes rather than economic grievances. Chalyi (Snegirev 2014), for instance, talked about opposing the teaching of Ukrainian in schools and banning Ukraine's flag at secessionist demonstrations, and incited resistance against what he called Kyiv's assimilationist policies.

The annexation operation unfolded over three weeks, meeting no resistance. The Crimean Tatars, Kyiv's local allies, clashed with pro-Russian groups in Simferopol on 26 February. But the spontaneous Tatar resistance was quickly defused on 27 February when Moscow deployed special forces without identifying insignia, which secured control over key institutions and infrastructure hubs. On the same day, former Berkut members and Cossacks from the Cuban region of Russia set up border checkpoints (Prentice 2014), while rebel militias occupied the Simferopol airport to facilitate the landing of regular Russian troops. On 1 March, Sergei Aksenov, the new Prime Minister of Crimea, asked Putin to intervene. On the same day, Russia's Federation Council authorized the use of force against Ukraine (Federation Council 2014). Next, the Crimean Supreme Council adopted a declaration of independence (6 March) followed by a hastily organized referendum, deemed as illegitimate by the United Nations (2014), in which most participants opted for independence and the subsequent union with Russia. Despite Kyiv's references to international agreements such as the 1994 Budapest Memorandum, the 1997 Russian-Ukrainian Friendship Treaty, and the Helsinki Final Act of the Conference on Security and Cooperation in Europe, all supporting its territorial integrity, Moscow concluded the formal annexation process.

A Calculated Risk

Prospect theory refers to decisions taken under risk, hence it is essential to establish whether the annexation was a choice and whether it was the riskiest strategy.

Although the Russian leader has claimed multiple times that the annexation was a constrained action, there is sufficient evidence suggesting that the annexation was a choice among four policy options rather than a *zugzwang*. Before the annexation, Putin's advisors repeatedly stated that the federalization of Ukraine would avert the crisis (Glaz'ev 2014). A second scenario included the creation of an unrecognized republic akin to Transnistria that would have been controlled by Moscow. According to Girkin (2020), a key coordinator of the annexation and a former intelligence officer, he expected to oversee the security apparatus of an independent Crimean state and was surprised that Putin crossed the Rubicon, opting for outright annexation. Besides federalization, de facto statehood, and annexation, Moscow could have chosen to preserve the status quo, much like Yeltsin did in the 1990s. Without much warning, Putin picked the annexation option from the menu of choices.

Was the annexation a risky decision? The decision to occupy Crimea was a calculated risk rather than an expression of recklessness. In the context of prospect theory, risk refers to decisions reached without knowing their consequences as they depend on uncertain events (Kahneman and Tversky 1984). Given the high stakes and the high level of uncertainty, I concur with Forsberg and Pursiainen (2017: 5), who view the takeover of Crimea as a risky choice. Indeed, Putin and his associates were determined to invade the peninsula even though they did not estimate with accuracy the degree of Ukrainian resistance. The Russian president did, however, instruct top Russian generals to prepare for military contingencies and even conducted a closed opinion poll to gauge the support for what Russia called the "reunification" with Crimea (Putin 2015). The operation was timed to exploit the absence of a functioning government in Kyiv, a moment of maximum vulnerability for Ukraine. In doing so, Moscow reduced the risk of a full-blown confrontation and incurred minimum losses, two additional details indicating that the decision was a calculated risk.

Two equally plausible versions of events link the timing of the decision to the power struggle in Kyiv. According to Moscow's official version presented in *Crimea —The Path to the Motherland*, Putin spent the night of 22–23 February getting Yanukovych out of Ukraine (Putin 2015). Toward the morning, Putin tasked four individuals—Sergei Ivanov, the Head of the Presidential Administration, Nikolai Patrushev, the Secretary of the Security Council, Aleksandr Bortnikov, the FSB director, and Sergei Shoigu, the Minister of Defence—to prepare "the return of Crimea" (Bukkvoll 2016: 273). By and large, these officials and Putin share the same beliefs, viewing the Euromaidan protests as a US-orchestrated coup against a pro-Russian incumbent. These circumstances suggest that, despite some advance planning, the decision was made by Putin in an informal setting rather than collectively at a Security Council meeting (Fortescue 2017).

While the official version may be part of Kremlin's effort to construct a legitimizing post-annexation narrative, a second account places the beginning of the operation prior to Yanukovych's ouster. Evidence in support of the second version can be found on a state medal awarded to the participants of the Crimea campaign, specifying 20 February–18 March as the dates of the operation (Gromenko 2019). Once the detail became publicized, images of the medal were removed from official websites. Even though one can draw only weak inferences based on such a minor element, the medal would suggest that the start of the annexation was related to the bout of violence in Kyiv on 20 February rather than Yanukovych's ousting on 23 February. It is quite plausible that Putin decided to seize Crimea once he realized that the tragic events on the Maidan accelerated the transfer of power to the pro-Western opposition. If the second version is accurate, then even with a weaker Yanukovych in power, the Kremlin might have proceeded with the annexation plan. The annexation, thus, has been implemented in retaliation to the success of the Euromaidan protests, perceived as a major loss by the Kremlin.

Another aspect important for assessing the riskiness of the annexation operation concerns the level of advance planning. The Russian narrative emphasizes the adoption of a flexible approach to the unfolding events, rejecting any claims about advanced planning. Six weeks before the annexation operation, Putin (2013) stated during his annual press conference that the idea of Russia sending troops to Crimea belonged to the realm of fantasy. Three months later, the invasion was presented as a natural choice in light of the historical, religious, and strategic importance of the peninsula for Russia (Putin 2014b). Furthermore, a year after the event, Putin (2015) claimed that he came up with the initiative spontaneously and directly supervised the annexation, an assertion which aligns with the scholarly view of Putin as a gambling opportunist rather than a grand strategist (Marten 2015; Treisman 2018; Rhodes 2018; Dyson and Parent 2018: 94). Similarly, the move of the referendum date from May to March may suggest, as Treisman (2018) noted, that Putin lacked a well-thought-out plan regarding the final status of Crimea. Yet, the date change could also point to the fact that the occupation, meeting no resistance, proceeded faster than expected. Girkin (2020), a former insider, claimed that the FSB could not have come up with an elaborate plan much in advance, because the agency was going with the flow, reacting to events much like the old KGB did.

Still, Ukrainian decision-makers, pro-Russian activists in Crimea, and Ukrainian scholars contradict accounts about the lack of planning. Kuzio (2010), for instance, anticipated a decade before the events that Russia and Ukraine would clash over Crimea. Turchynov (2015), the interim Ukrainian president during the crisis, received intelligence briefings about an annexation plan from 2005 in retaliation to the Orange Revolution. Likewise, Chalyi (Snegirev 2014), the secessionist mayor of Sevastopol, spoke of two failed attempts to separate Crimea from Ukraine that took place after the Orange Revolution and the Russian–Georgian War respectively. Indeed, new parties promoting separatism in Crimea and Donbas were founded in 2006 and 2010 (Vagner 2014). Then, there were other signs of advance planning. The operation took place in the timespan between two major sporting events hosted by Russia: the

Sochi Winter Olympics (7–23 February) and the Paralympics (7–16 March). According to the Russian official version, the annexation began on the last day of the Winter Olympics, an occasion marked by enhanced national pride, which as McFaul notes (2018: 400) may have emboldened Putin to advance into Ukraine. Furthermore, two weeks ahead of the referendum, the Russian government approved the construction of the bridge over the Kerch strait, connecting Crimea to mainland Russia, a move signaling that the Russian leadership harbored no doubts about the outcome of the vote.

To minimize the costs of the annexation and confuse Western powers, Putin utilized plausible deniability. Before and immediately after the annexation, Moscow would claim that its special forces were not present on the peninsula. By denying any involvement, Putin not only misrepresented his intentions, but also sought to confer legitimacy and legality to the annexation, arguing that the independence referendum reflected the free will of the local population, engaging in a self-determination exercise. Putin's detailed admission of military involvement surfaced a year later in the celebratory film *Crimea—The Path to the Motherland* (2015), a sanitized version of events in which facts were mixed with propaganda.

Putin was aware that the West, specifically the US and Germany, could impose significant costs on Russia. A cursory analysis of the log on Kremlin's website reveals that, during the crisis, Angela Merkel called Putin at least nine times, Barack Obama—four, and David Cameron—three. Recep Tayyip Erdoğan, François Hollande, and Xi Jinping discussed Crimea too. Germany and the US were the major powers most interested in managing the crisis (Rhodes 2018: 264). In his conversations with Western leaders, Putin tried to convince them that the new powerholders in Kyiv were neo-Nazis threatening Russian speakers (Kerry 2018: 484). Germany and the US worried about a full-blown war between Russia and Ukraine, advising Kyiv to act cautiously, while hoping to deter Russian aggression through economic sanctions (Obama 2014; Merkel 2014).

Merkel and Obama could not have been sure of Putin's real intentions (Rhodes 2018: 264). Given the earlier deployment of special forces, the authorization from the Federation Council to use force was perceived by Western leaders as a step toward war. Simultaneously, the Russian armed forces were placed on high alert, conducting snap exercises in the Western and Central Military Districts (26 February–3 March) involving 150,000 army, navy, and air force personnel. Explicitly comparing the situation in Crimea to the Cuban Missile Crisis, Putin (2015) claimed that he went against the suggestions of his advisers and refused to deploy the strategic nuclear arsenal. Still, to signal posturing, Russia conducted strategic nuclear drills in late March 2014, simulating a defense against a massive nuclear attack (Vladykin 2014). In that context, German and American leaders, much like their Ukrainian counterparts, were trying to assess whether the massive troop movements were in fact preparations for a large-scale invasion or mere posturing.

Despite calls from Republicans and foreign policy hawks, the Obama administration avoided any retaliatory steps that would have escalated the crisis (Rhodes 2018: 264–67). Even though the US was quick to introduce symbolic sanctions, Putin knew that Obama reset America's relations with Russia less than a year after the war against Georgia. Moreover, the US was winding down its involvement in Afghanistan and Iraq and was unwilling to get entangled in new conflicts in Syria and even less so in Ukraine. Still, the risk of unintended escalation remained high. Apparently, without Putin's knowledge, the captain of a Russian ship threatened USS Donald Cook, an American destroyer sent to the Black Sea after the annexation (Mulrine 2014). Furthermore, in a show of resolve, Bastion, a high-precision coastal missile defense system, was swiftly brought from the mainland and deployed on the peninsula so that, easily detected by Western satellites, it would discourage NATO from intervening (Putin 2015).

The economic costs surprised Putin. Remembering the lack of a strong American response to the 2008 Russian–Georgian War, the Russians miscalculated the Western reaction. Bukkvoll (2016: 277) notes that Putin did not believe in the likelihood of sanctions, whereas other Russian officials thought of the annexation as risky. Once the sanctions were in place, Putin (2015) downplayed the costs of the annexation, arguing that defending the interests of ethnic

Russians and correcting what he regarded as a historical injustice could not be measured in material terms. Moscow, however, worried about costs. When Glaz'ev (2014), a presidential adviser, claimed with much bravado that Russia could sell its US treasuries and cause the collapse of the American financial system, the Kremlin quickly issued a rebuttal.

Decision-makers in Moscow and Kyiv were correct in assessing that the US and EU could not defend Ukraine's borders. Ukraine, unlike the Baltic States, was not offered NATO membership and thus had to rely on its own armed forces. The crisis proved right those scholars arguing in favor of Ukraine retaining its nuclear deterrent in the 1990s (Mearsheimer 1993). Even though two decades earlier the US rejected Iraq's annexation of Kuwait, the Obama administration adopted an overly cautious approach with regards to Ukraine, refusing to sell Kyiv lethal weapons to avoid further escalation (Obama 2014; Entous 2014). As Kerry (2018: 484) noted in his memoirs, the US was more interested in helping Ukrainians help themselves and keeping Europe united behind economic sanctions rather than fueling a conflict among major powers.

The riskiness of the choice may also be tied to the personality and beliefs of the chief decision-maker. Whereas prospect theory assumes that individuals have the same sensitivity to risk, it could be argued that some political leaders prefer more risk compared to others. Scholars have generally highlighted Putin's predictability. Dyson (2001: 344) observed that "Putin is unlikely to make rash, impulsive or emotional gestures that interfere with the rationality of political exchange." Gessen (2012: 58) concurred that Putin is not emotionally open. Furthermore, the absence of any information leaks during the annexation and Putin's (2014a) misrepresentation of facts during his media appearances point to the effective management of information and the ability to deny facts for the sake of operational success. Gaddy and Hill (2015: 388) note as well that Putin is a strategic planner, who can learn from his policy mistakes, rather than an improviser. The only indication of risk-acceptant behavior is contained in Putin's first official biography. Its authors claim that Putin's KGB superiors believed that their apprentice had a diminished sense of danger, while, at the same time, describing him as a predictable and boring presidential candidate (see Gaddy and Hill 2015: 12).

Despite some evidence of advance planning, efforts to minimize the costs, and concerns about a Western response, the decision to annex Crimea was a calculated risk driven by the emotions associated with Yanukovych's ousting from power and Putin's perception that the US was behind the protests in Kyiv.

Reference Points and Loss Aversion

Prospect theory explains choice under risk in relation to changes from a reference point framed as a gain or a loss. The reference point, a subjective assessment, can be the status quo, an expectation, or an aspiration influenced by social norms and interpersonal comparisons (Levy 1997; Mercer 2005). Putin's decision-making unfolded in an environment that was both fluid and strategic, suggesting that his intertemporal calculus of gains and losses evolved in relation to multiple reference points as well as his estimation of Kyiv's capacity to resist. While prospect theory explains such shifts in preferences in a dynamic setting (McDermott 2004: 292), it lacks a well-defined theory of the reference point. Scholars mention five complementary benchmarks to identify the domain of the decision-maker: status quo, aspirations, heuristics, analogies, and emotions (Mercer 2005: 4; Jervis 2017: 100).

Putin's perception of the status quo changed throughout the three critical junctures of the crisis. With Yanukovych in charge, Putin perceived control over the whole of Ukraine as the status quo (Zygar 2015: 63). Yanukovych's refusal to sign the AA was interpreted as a policy gain, while the success of the Euromaidan protests was viewed as a loss (Bukkvoll 2016: 278). As the protests continued, Yanukovych reached an agreement with the political opposition to stay in power, a compromise reluctantly supported by Moscow. Hence, Putin's second reference point must have been an adjusted definition of the status quo in which Yanukovych remained in power despite the concessions made to the opposition. Yanukovych's departure from Kyiv, contrary to Kremlin's advice, must have been interpreted by Putin as a major loss (Putin 2014e). To recoup the loss, Putin annexed Crimea. In April 2014, he took more risk by supporting the *Novorossiia* project, an expansion plan aiming to establish Russia's direct control over large swaths of Ukraine (Putin 2014d). The success of the Crimean annexation put Putin in the domain of gains. As Kyiv's resistance intensified and Moscow's efforts to kindle insurrections across Ukrainian cities failed, Putin became more risk-averse and more hesitant to support the *Novorossiia* project, preferring instead to back militarily the two Donbas republics.

Besides the changing status quo in a conflict setting, identifying the reference point when a leader faces outcomes across multiple dimensions poses a major challenge (Vis and Kuijpers 2018). Putin cared both about Russia's influence over Ukraine's security policy and his domestic approval ratings (Treisman 2018). The success of the Euromaidan was perceived as a loss across both the foreign policy and domestic dimensions, generating a perception of weakness among Putin's nationalist supporters at home. By contrast, the annexation produced a rally around the flag effect. However, once Putin accepted a partial defeat in Donbas, refusing to escalate the conflict, he lost the nationalist vote (Kolstø 2016). This aligns with prospect theory's prediction that political leaders will incur higher risks to avoid short-run losses rather than face high risks to secure moderate gains (Jervis 2017: 88).

Besides the status quo, aspiration levels and social comparisons may define the reference point (Tversky and Kahneman 1992: 1046–1047; Mercer 2005). It could be argued that Putin, who worked as a civil servant and KGB officer, having been for two decades in power, developed certain state-related goals and aspirations. For instance, he regularly promised to transform Russia into a top economy and restore its international standing. At the same time, Putin's worldview is shaped by what he perceives to be a growing competition with the US for influence in Eastern Europe. From Putin's perspective, the loss of Ukraine did not square well with his aspiration to restore Russia's great power status. In this case, it is difficult to disentangle the effects on the definition of the status quo of great power aspirations and peer comparisons with the

West. This may be an instance of multiple conjunctural causation, an aspect unaddressed by prospect theory, whereby status quo preferences, aspiration levels, and interstate comparisons, have a cumulative causal effect on the decision maker's perception of gains and losses.

Cognitive heuristics and analogical reasoning influence the way leaders define a reference point (McDermott 1992; Taliaferro 1994). Kahneman (2011: 117–55) describes three common cognitive heuristics concerning probability estimations: representativeness (i.e., substituting judgements of probability with stereotypical descriptions); anchoring (i.e., influence of a particular value on estimations of an unknown quantity); and availability (i.e., the process of judging frequency by the ease with which certain instances come to mind). While I found no evidence of anchoring and availability, evidence of representativeness can be traced to Putin's reliance on three overarching analogies. Putin viewed the Euromaidan as another Orange Revolution, an episode from which he learned that the pro-Western elites in Ukraine, once in power, would steer the country toward the EU and NATO. Ukraine's accession to NATO has always triggered Russia's opposition. In his 2007 speech at the Munich conference Putin criticized the US hegemony and NATO's enlargement, vowing to reverse the trend. Russia's opposition was one of the reasons Ukraine was not invited to join NATO at the Bucharest Summit (Gaddy and Hill 2015: 360). Moreover, Putin told the US President that Ukraine might lose Crimea and Eastern Ukraine if it were to join the alliance (Socor 2008), another detail which lends credence to the advance planning hypothesis discussed earlier.

Two additional analogies were commonly used by Putin during the crisis. The historical comparison with World War II dominated the official narrative on Ukraine. The Revolution of Dignity was characterized intentionally as the victory of ultranationalist forces (Fedor 2015). Putin, aware of the significance of World War II in Russia's collective memory, sought to elicit an emotional response from the Russian society and mobilize the Russian-speakers of Ukraine. It allowed him to reduce reality to an imaginary binary conflict between "us"—the noble, good, peace-loving, Orthodox Russians, and "them"—the stubborn Ukrainians, siding with the West, and revering controversial figures. The political exploitation of the past to fabricate the image of an aggressive Kyiv served to justify the self-determination referendum in Crimea, which would be equated to the Kosovo precedent, another equivalence invoked in Putin's (2014) Crimea speech but rejected by Western leaders (Merkel 2014).

Emotions influence the definition of the reference points too (Farnham 1992). During the crisis, Putin displayed a range of negative emotions. Kerry (2018: 487) observes that Lavrov could not negotiate successfully, because the Ukrainian issue was personal to Putin. McFaul (2018: 405) writes that Putin's stance toward Ukraine was driven by the desire for revenge as well as his ambition to restore Russia's imperial borders rather than rational cost-benefit calculations. He showed contempt for Yanukovych, whom he regarded as a weak leader. By contrast, Putin always expressed anger toward the Euromaidan activists and the US. He portrayed the West as untrustworthy, accusing it of deceit, a claim fitting the broader resentful narrative about the West taking advantage of Russia (Hill and Gaddy 2015: 42; Bukkvoll 2016: 279). A related problem concerns Putin's references to national pride combined with his refusal to acknowledge Ukrainians' right to self-identification, and his misleading portrayal of the Russian-speaking Ukrainians as threatened by cultural assimilation.

Individuals quickly renormalize their reference points after making gains, something prospect theorists identify as the instant endowment effect (Kahneman, Knetsch, and Thaler 1991). In line with the endowment effect, it seems that Putin rapidly adjusted his definition of the status quo to include Crimea, so that by 2015 Moscow rejected any negotiations about Crimea's status. Furthermore, the Russian authorities impose penalties on citizens questioning the "reunification" narrative. In contrast to Russia's quick adjustment to the new status quo, another prediction in line with the prospect theory is that in the long run, the Ukrainian leadership will refuse to accept Crimea as part of Russia.

Neo-imperial Framing

Choices made under risk are often shaped by the way the problem is framed. During the initial phase of decision-making when a range of options are available, "framing is controlled by the manner in which the choice problem is presented as well as by norms, habits, and expectancies of the decision maker" (Kahneman and Tversky 1986: 257). Kahneman and Tversky (1986) further establish that changes in the way outcomes are framed lead to violations of the expected utility model assumptions. Even though prospect theory as a reference-dependent explanatory framework lacks a clear account of how frames emerge (Levy 1997: 100), the origins of the frames used to explain the situation in Ukraine can be linked to ideological currents of neo-imperial origin.

Two types of framing processes were identified. First, the crisis was presented strategically to elicit support among the domestic audience and mobilization among the Russian speakers in Ukraine. In Putin's discourse, four types of frames were present: neo-imperial ("a lost historical Russian land"); common identity ("saving ethnic Russians from assimilation"); religious ("the Christianization of Rus' began in Crimea"); and security ("NATO ships cannot dock in Sevastopol"). The major frame in the annexation narrative was of nationalist-imperial origin, emphasizing historical claims and an endangered common identity. The annexation was, in Putin's words, a compelled, but just choice, because "we could not abandon this historical Russian land and our people to the nationalists in Kyiv" (Putin 2014b). In presenting the status quo as a major loss, Putin engaged in what Mintz and Redd (2003) called purposeful framing. The nationalist-imperial frame was built around obvious distortions regarding the nature of the Euromaidan protests. Aware of the salience of World War II in Russia's collective memory, Putin (2014b) described the social movement and the new powerholders in Kyiv in a dehumanizing manner as aggressive nationalists, whereas the state-owned media went further, using offensive terms to stir Ukrainophobia and negative emotions toward Ukraine among voters.

Second, prospect theory is silent about the origins of frames. But the nationalist-neo-imperial frame did not emerge out of nowhere. It represents a collective construct, involving Putin's entourage and the state-owned media, as well as multiple actors linked to a strain of messianic, Orthodox conservatism. Scholars studying the Russian war against Ukraine are reticent to use the term *neo-imperial* as too old-fashioned to describe the annexation, associating it with the discredited slogans of the defunct Communist regimes. However, *neo-imperial* in the context of the Ukraine-Russia relations refers to both territorial conquest as a foreign policy tool from a bygone era as well as the fact that the imperial history of Russia served as a source of inspiration for the *Novorossiia* plan. The nationalist element of the frame is noticeable in the statements of the Russian leader and his inner circle, whereby the notion of Russia as a kin-state for the ethnic Russians in Ukraine purports to protect them from assimilation. In doing so, the rights of Ukrainians to self-identify as a nation distinct from Russians and have their own state with inviolable borders are rejected. Kuzio (2020) provides multiple examples illustrating this anti-Ukrainian bias. Putin's (2021) historical essay about the unity of Russians and Ukrainians points to the continuing relevance of the nationalist-neo-imperial frame. By contrast, given Russia's ethnolinguistic and religious diversity, Putin generally refrains from articulating domestic appeals in narrow ethnic terms, preferring to speak instead of a multiethnic Eurasian civilizational identity. As such this nationalist-neo-imperial frame reflects prejudiced beliefs about Ukraine and Ukrainians held by Russian state officials.

The imperial past rarely served as a source for Russian foreign policy frames. To understand the long-term goals of the imperial faction in the Kremlin as opposed to the liberal group, one needs to clarify the goals of the failed *Novorossiia* adventure. The idea of recreating *Novorossiia*, a region of the tsarist empire stretching from Donbas to Odessa, originated in Russia's nationalist circles in the early 1990s (Solchanyk 1994). It was resuscitated by the monarchist intelligentsia with close ties to the Orthodox Church, members of the intelligence apparatus, Christian entrepreneurs, and the Presidential Administration (Coalson 2015). Putin first mentioned

Novorossiia in April 2014, when he was still in the domain of losses and willing to advance further in Ukraine. While Putin himself lacks a coherent ideology, the Security Council members and his key advisors on Ukraine—Vladislav Surkov, Sergei Glaz'ev, and Aleksandr Dugin—displayed nationalist-neo-imperial worldviews. Consequently, Putin's framing of the annexation can also be traced to the advisory structure in the Kremlin at that time.

The *Novorossiia* plan most likely originated from Putin's most hawkish advisor—Surkov, regarded as the architect of the hybrid war in Donbas. Known for formulating the doctrine of sovereign democracy, and an apologist of Putinism as a governing model, Surkov expressed the belief that Putin was sent by destiny and God to rule Russia. Surkov's views of Ukrainians are heavily prejudiced. His Ukrainophobia became apparent when he declared that individuals self-identifying as Ukrainian suffered from "mental health issues," that the Ukrainian nation did not exist, and that the Donbas war was necessary to impose brotherly relations on Ukraine (Surkov 2020). Tasked with negotiating a conflict settlement, Surkov (2020) viewed the federalization of Ukraine as a humiliation for Russia and a victory for Ukraine. Once Putin adopted a more conciliatory stance toward Ukraine, Surkov left the Kremlin, but his inflammatory statements prompted the Presidential Administration to distance itself from the former advisor.

Another key advisor on Ukraine was Sergei Glaz'ev. A critic of the Washington Consensus, Milton Friedman, and Russia's Central Bank, Glaz'ev was not part of Putin's inner circle, joining the Kremlin as a representative of the ultranationalist forces associated with the Rodina Party. As Ukraine was concluding its negotiations with the EU, Glaz'ev, a native of Southern Ukraine, started spending more time in Kyiv, persuading officials there that the AA would damage economic ties with Russia. Glaz'ev (2014) called on Yanukovych to suppress the protests and federalize Ukraine, which, in his view, would have allowed the establishment of simultaneous free trade regimes with the EU and Russia. Leaks of intercepted conversations also pointed to Glaz'ev's role in funding and guiding the anti-Euromaidan protests, which were supposed to provoke the secession of the so-called *Novorossiia* (Umland 2016).

Both Surkov and Glaz'ev overestimated the strength of the pro-Russian secessionist sentiment in Ukraine. Convinced that ethnic Russians and Russian speakers would mobilize in support of *Novorossiia*, they were surprised by the lack of popular enthusiasm for the separatist cause. Their initial overconfidence illustrates groupthink—"a tendency toward premature and extreme concurrence-seeking within a cohesive policy-making group under stress" (t'Hart *et al.* 1997: 10). The flawed deliberation style generated unrealistic expectations regarding the capacity of the Kremlin to undermine nation-building in Ukraine via exacerbations of its ethnolinguistic and regional divisions.

Besides Putin's top associates, a network of organizations and individuals pushed for an expansionist foreign policy. An unofficial advisor promoting the *Novorossiia* project, Aleksandr Dugin, the organizer of the Neo-Eurasianist movement long active in Ukraine, backed the annexation as the initial step toward the revival of a modern version of the tsarist empire (Zygar 2016: 194). The Russian Orthodox Church and the largest Christian charity sponsored by Konstantin Malofeev, a radical Orthodox monarchist millionaire, were involved too. Malofeev funded some of the annexation activities and visited Ukraine during the Euromaidan, bringing the Gifts of the Magi, a collection of ancient Christian relics, to Kyiv and Sevastopol (Weaver 2014; Girkin 2020). The Institute for Strategic Studies, a governmental think-tank led by Leonid Reshetnikov, known for his messianic beliefs about Putin as the new Tsar, produced a strategy memo, which shaped Kremlin's Ukraine policy (Coalson 2015; Sytin 2015). In addition to these figures and organizations, a fringe orthodox TV station, *Tsargrad TV*, and the Russian Imperial Movement, now banned in the West as a terrorist organization, propagated the *Novorossiia* idea. Kremlin's policy toward Ukraine was thus articulated by veteran advisers holding pro-imperial, conservative, and radical religious ideas, coupled with Ukrainophobia. Troop movements at Ukraine's borders in 2021-2022, tensions in the Kerch strait and the Azov Sea, and Putin's post-2014 statements indicate that he shares these views. However, as he adopted a more practical approach toward Ukraine, the pro-imperial faction seems to have lost its influence over foreign policymaking. It continued to hold sway in other areas of political life as demonstrated by the introduction of a series of constitutional amendments referring to religion, traditional family values, and Russian as the language of the state-forming people.

The ascendance of the nationalist-neo-imperial frame among the Kremlin elites can be tied to the broader ideological adjustment of the ruling party's conservative ideology through the appropriation of themes propagated by far-right and monarchist groups. Public figures such as Egor Kholmogorov, Nataliia Narochnitskaia, Konstantin Zatulin, Aleksandr Prokhanov, the media outlet *Zavtra* and *Tsargrad TV*, the Izborsky Club, the Double-Headed Eagle Society, radical Christian organizations, Orthodox Third Romist groups voiced enthusiasm for the war against Ukraine. In this respect, scholars citing high levels of public support for the annexation inside Russia should also consider the effect of the state propaganda and of the numerous organizations agitating in favor of war on the views of the electorate.

The origins of the Crimea annexation frames can thus be linked to the rising influence in the public sphere and state bureaucracy of groups nostalgic for the imperial era and shaping the discourse about Ukraine. The Kremlin's strategic framing of the annexation and the broader policy toward Ukraine reflect, among other things, the dominance of a neo-imperial, monarchist, conservative ideology legitimizing domestic illiberalism and militarism abroad.

Explaining the Failure to Defend Crimea

Prospect theory is largely silent on how a decision-maker's choice may be affected by interactions with other actors. But Russia's annexation calculus must have included an assessment of Ukraine's capacity to react against aggression. That is why Kyiv's inaction must be factored in when focusing on decision-making in Moscow. The decision not to escalate in Crimea was itself the outcome of collective deliberation that needs to be properly analyzed. The declassified minutes of the 28 February meeting of Ukraine's National Defence and Security Council (NSDC) and recent statements by the Ukrainian decision makers allow us to clarify the causes behind Ukraine's failure to resist in Crimea. Ukraine's vulnerability increased after its leadership defected, providing Putin with a brief window of opportunity to deploy special forces across the peninsula and take control. From a military standpoint, the Russian use of force in Ukraine was qualitatively superior compared to the military campaign against Georgia. In this sense, the annexation, largely a special troops operation, benefited from Russia's post-2008 reforms of the military sector and the creation of rapid reaction units based on military professionals rather than conscripts (Bartles and McDermott 2014).

Kyiv's inability to repel the aggression in Crimea can be traced to four factors. First, Yanukovych's exit amidst a revolutionary situation created a power vacuum, paralyzing the capacity of the Ukrainian state to react to foreign attacks. In essence, Ukraine's commander-in-chief and top state officials sided with the adversary. Russia's representative at the UN presented a letter from Yanukovych in which the deposed president requested Moscow's military assistance. Besides the defection of the commander-in-chief, Kyiv's position was further aggravated by the prolonged negotiations and intense bickering over the distribution of ministerial portfolios among coalition partners. Thus, while foreign troops were occupying Crimea, the Ukrainian state lacked a functional government and military leadership.

A second key aspect preventing an effective response relates to the weak loyalty to the Ukrainian state in Crimea. While the reluctance of the average citizen in Crimea to display allegiance to Kyiv is traceable to the 1990s, the defections of state officials deserve more attention. Russia skillfully relied on a mix of positive and negative incentives to persuade Ukrainian officers to desert. Agents of the Russian state promised material benefits, jobs, and similar career paths in the Russian military. An illustrative example is the case of Denis Berezovskii, the commander of the Ukrainian navy, who switched sides a day after his selection by the new government in Kyiv. After annexation, Berezovskii was appointed deputy commander of the Russian Black Sea Fleet. Kuzio and D'Anieri (2018: 100) mention multiple similar instances. Ihor Teniukh, a defence minister in the so-called kamikaze government, estimated that out of Ukraine's 15,000 troops stationed in Crimea, merely two thousand were willing to fight as most of the troops were local career soldiers (NSDC 2014). After being criticized for the slow withdrawal of the loyal military personnel from Crimea, Teniukh resigned (Reuters 2014). Natal'ia Poklonskaia, a former Ukrainian prosecutor became a United Russia MP out of "patriotic duty" (Gordon 2020a). Likewise, media reports alleged that the two defence ministers preceding the annexation held Russian citizenship (Gordon 2020b). Such loyalty reversals reflect a broader challenge faced by the Ukrainian state in instilling a strong allegiance among its officials.

Moscow also enjoyed a decisive informational advantage over Kyiv. Not only was Russia able to shape the narrative about the annexation via disinformation campaigns, but it always seemed a step ahead of Kyiv in Crimea. Several examples illustrate this point. In *Crimea—The Path to the Motherland*, Putin revealed that the military intelligence cut off the special communication channels of the Ukrainian army, forcing Kyiv to send orders to the units in Crimea through open channels, enabling Moscow to intercept the messages. Unsurprisingly, Putin was informed of the actions prepared by the Ukrainian military. Moscow also blocked Ukraine's military communications using the Night Wolves, an association of bikers often acting in Kremlin's interest. The Ukrainian general Koval, carrying a shooting order to the military unit in Feodosia, was captured and then released by the Night Wolves.

The key factor inhibiting a quick response pertained to the substantial disagreements among the Ukrainian decision makers on the best military strategy to counter foreign aggression. The declassified NSDC minutes from 28 February revealed that the Ukrainian leadership was split between those recommending a full military mobilization and those fearing that such an action would provoke a massive Russian invasion. Oleksandr Turchynov, the interim President, proposed the introduction of the martial law and an immediate call to arms. His initiative was not backed by other NSDC members. For instance, Yuliia Tymoshenko opposed the plan, suggesting that Ukrainians should act like "peace doves" (NSDC 2014). The NSDC members, aware of Ukraine's unprepared army, worried that decisive action would be perceived by Moscow as a declaration of war and would invite direct aggression from the East, where Russian troops on high alert were conducting tactical exercises.

It is also striking that Putin tried to directly influence the decision-making in Kyiv. During the key NSDC meeting on 28 February, Sergei Naryshkin, the Speaker of the Russian Duma, called Turchynov to convey Putin's threat that Kyiv's resistance would offer Russia a pretext to launch an invasion (NSDC 2014). Turchynov bluffed, telling the Russians that he had ordered the units in Crimea to shoot in case of an attack, a move that probably delayed the capturing of the loyal bases on the peninsula (Turchynov 2020). A misconception entertained by most NSDC members centered on the idea that the international community could deter Russia's aggression. Once they realized that NATO and the US would not intervene, decision makers in Kyiv invoked legal instruments and international organizations as ways to rally support against the invasion. The declassified documents reveal that on 28 February, the NSDC members were aware of Putin's intention to carry out annexation, the prevailing mood in Crimea, the widespread defections, the occupation of strategic infrastructure nodes, and the ongoing troop transfers from continental Russia.

In all, Moscow must have factored in Ukraine's military weakness and the lack of a functional government, expecting to meet weak resistance. The annexation operation was conducted under the most favorable conditions—a power vacuum in Kyiv, widespread disloyalty toward the state in Crimea, Moscow's interception of strategic communications, and disagreements among the Ukrainian political elite on how to respond to the Russian aggression.

Conclusion

This article contributed to the literature on foreign policy decision-making by adopting prospect theory as an explanatory framework. It demonstrated how loss aversion, reference dependence, strategic framing, emotions, aspirations, and cognitive heuristics shaped the decision-making process leading to the annexation of Crimea. Even though information regarding the deliberations in Moscow and Kyiv remains limited and potentially biased, the reconstruction of the decision-making throughout the crisis revealed evidence of advanced planning as well as the significant influence of a pro-imperial, ultranationalist faction in the Kremlin. In line with prospect theory, throughout the turning points of the Ukrainian crisis, the risk orientation of the Russian president varied, depending on whether he was situated in the domain of losses or gains. In implementing the plan, Russia did not meet significant opposition, mostly due to pre-existing secessionism, disloyalty among the Ukrainian state officials, the breakdown of order, and the Western preference for de-escalation. However, despite its military superiority and non-utilitarian rhetoric, Russia cared about costs. That is why it relied on misleading tactics, blended different modes of warfare, chose the optimal timing for the invasion, concealed its intervention plans, engaged in deceptive posturing, and even directly interfered with the decision-making in Kyiv.

While the study has privileged prospect theory over other approaches in explaining the foreign policy decision, it does not pretend to offer a comprehensive account of the annexation. The relationship of prospect theory to other theories as well as the multitude of potential explanatory factors point to the need to develop a more nuanced explanation of the decision-making process. Insights derived from alternative theoretical traditions could illuminate additional causal mechanisms. For instance, the prospect theoretical explanation could be extended to incorporate the diversionary theory of war, which assumes that leaders initiate armed conflicts to remain in power (Levy and Vakili 1992). Adopting the diversionary logic, a quick victorious campaign against Ukraine may have been planned to divert the public attention from corruption and economic stagnation, boosting Putin's domestic approval ratings via a rally around the flag effect. Putin relied on sociological surveys to gauge support for annexation, which indicates that the domain of gains extended to domestic politics as he probably would have not annexed Crimea had Russian public opinion opposed such a policy. Still, the validity of the diversionary thesis is questionable. Having suppressed the Bolotnaia protests, Putin did not face any major challenges to his rule. High oil prices ensured the viability of the regime and provided sufficient resources for the subsequent interventions in Ukraine and Syria. While the annexation boosted the popular support for the authoritarian regime, a diversionary conflict would have had to be launched at the end of the presidential term to generate more electoral gains.

Likewise, it is useful to compare prospect theory to its main rival—the standard expected utility theory of war. Following Mesquita (1980) and Fearon (1995), one could regard Putin as a rational utility maximizer, weighting gains and losses equally. Indeed, prospect theory and rational choice theory share the idea of bounded rationality. Prior to invading Ukraine, Putin (2014c) was calculating the costs of an eventual loss of the naval base in Sevastopol, the economic damage of the AA, the mobilizational potential among the Russians living in Ukraine as well as the likelihood of a Western military involvement. Still, Fearon's (1995) standard model of war is unfit to explain how changes in Putin's perception of losses during the crisis led to his choosing the riskiest option.

As new sources emerge, prospect theory explanations of the Crimean annexation should also consider organizational dynamics and bureaucratic politics. The classic analysis of the Cuban Missile Crisis by Allison and Zelikow (1999) explained how bureaucracy may constrain policymakers, demonstrating that planning in large organizations often relies on standard operational procedures, complicated by conflicting agendas, budgeting needs, inter-bureaucratic competition, and miscommunications. Along similar lines, due to the lack of information, it is unclear whether Putin tried to reach a consensus within the decision-making group, accepting input from his associates, or whether the members of his inner circle uncritically approved the choice. As prospect theory focuses narrowly on individual decision-making such group and bureaucratic processes need to be integrated as part of the explanation.

Finally, theoretical explanations of the annexation cannot gloss over the neo-imperial mindset that drove the calculus of the

Russian leadership. After all, Russia is alarmed about power transfers in the post-Soviet states precisely because it regards them as remnants of the former empire. Critics of the term neo-imperial applied in relation to Russia misleadingly assume that it refers to a grand strategy aimed at restoring the Soviet state or the Tsarist Empire through military conquest. They argue that Russia's leadership could easily occupy the neighboring republics but shows restraint. Although the Russian leader did claim that the demise of the Soviet Union was the greatest geopolitical tragedy of the twentieth century, the term neo-imperial in this paper refers to a different phenomenon—the reluctance of the Russian ruling elites to accept the outcome of the Cold War, that is, the Soviet disintegration and Russia's new post-imperial condition. The Russian leadership's portrayal of Ukraine as an artificial state populated by a fraternal population led astray by nationalist politicians and the West illustrates well the worldview behind the 2014–2015 intervention in Ukraine. The prospect theoretic calculus incorporated, among other things, frames derived from the imperial past (i.e., *Novorossiia*) and the logic whereby the former metropole refuses to accept Ukrainians as a distinct nation, having the right to a sovereign state.

REFERENCES

Allison, G. T. and Zelikow, P. (1999) *Essence of Decision: Explaining the Cuban Missile Crisis*. Reading, MA: Longman.
Bartles, C. and McDermott, R. (2014) "Russia's Military Operation in Crimea," *Problems of Post-Communism* 61(6): 46–63. doi:10.2753/PPC 1075-8216610604.
Bukkvoll, T. (2016) "Why Putin Went to War: Ideology, Interests and Decision-Making in the Russian Use of Force in Crimea and Donbas," *Contemporary Politics* 22(3): 267–82. doi:10.1080/13569775.2016.1201310.
Coalson, R. (2015) "The Plot to Seize Crimea," *Radio Free Europe*, 11 March. https://www.rferl.org/a/ukraine-russia-putin-plot-seize-crimea/2689 4212.html.
De Mesquita, B. B. (1980) "An Expected Utility Theory of International Conflict," *The American Political Science Review* 74(4): 917–31.

Dyson, S. B. (2001) "Drawing Policy Implications from the 'Operational Code' of a 'New' Political Actor: Russian President Vladimir Putin," *Policy Sciences* 34(3–4): 329–46.

Dyson, S. B. and Parent, M. (2018) "The Operational Code Approach to Profiling Political Leaders: Understanding Vladimir Putin," *Intelligence and National Security* 33(1): 84–100. doi:10.1080/02684527.2017.1313523.

Entous, A. (2014) "US Balks at Ukraine Military Aid Request," *Wall Street Journal*, 13 March.

Farnham, B. (1992) "Roosevelt and the Munich Crisis: Insights from Prospect Theory," *Political Psychology* 13(2): 205–35. doi:10.2307/379 1679.

Fearon, J. D. (1995) "Rationalist Explanations for War," *International Organization* 49(3): 379–414.

Federation Council of Russia (2014) "Federation Council Approved the Use of Russia's Armed Forces in Ukraine." 1 March. http://council.gov.ru/events/news/39851/.

Fedor, J. (2015) "Introduction: Russia Media and the War in Ukraine," *Journal of Soviet and Post-Soviet Politics and Society* 1(1): 1–12.

Forsberg, T. and Pursiainen, C. (2017) "The Psychological Dimension of Russian Foreign Policy: Putin and the Annexation of Crimea." *Global Society* 31(2): 220–44. doi:10.1080/13600826.2016.1274963.

Fortescue, S. (2017) "Russia's Security-Related Decision-Making: The Case of Crimea," in S. Fish, G. Gill, and M. Petrovic (eds.) *A Quarter Century of Post-Communism Assessed*. London: Palgrave, 295–318.

George, A. L. and Bennett, A. (2005) *Case Studies and Theory Development in the Social Sciences*. Cambridge, MA: MIT Press.

Gerring, J. (2004) "What is a Case Study and What Is It Good For?" *The American Political Science Review* 98(2): 341–54.

Girkin, I. (2020) Interview by D. Gordon, 18 May. https://www.youtube.com/watch?v=hf6K6pjK_Yw.

Glaz'ev, S. (2014) "Sergei Glaz'ev: federalizatsiia—uzhe ne ideia, a ochevidnaia neobkhodimost'," *Kommersant" Daily*, 6 February. https://www.kommersant.ru/doc/2400532.

Glaz'ev, S. (2014) "Sovetnik Putina: RF v sluchae sanktsii protiv nee otkazhetsia ot dollara," *RIA-Novosti*, 4 March. https://ria.ru/20140304/998048715.html.

Gordon, D. (2020a) Interview with N. Poklonskaia, 11 May. https://www.youtube.com/watch?v=Tj7zEHRXoI8.

Gordon, D. (2020b) "Kto i kak pomog Putinu ukrast' Krym. Dokumental'noe rassledovanie," *Dmitrii Gordon YouTube channel*, 18 March. https://www.youtube.com/watch?v=TbgMK7nJ2LE.

Gorenburg, D. (2019) "Russian Strategic Culture in a Baltic Crisis," *Security Insights* 25, George C. Marshall European Center for Security Studies.

Gromenko, S. (2019) "'Nebesnaia sotnia' i tainyi prikaz Putina", *Radio Free Europe*, 20 February, https://ru.krymr.com/a/dnevnik-okkupacii-krыma-20-fevralya-nebesnaya-sotnya-i-tayniy-prikaz-putina/29776190.html.
Haas, M. (2001) "Prospect Theory and the Cuban Missile Crisis," *International Studies Quarterly* 45: 241–70. doi:10.1111/0020-8833.00190.
Hill, F. and Gaddy, C. (2015) *Mr. Putin: Operative in the Kremlin*. Washington D.C.: Brookings University Press.
Hudson, V. M., and Vore, Ch. (1995) "Foreign Policy Analysis Yesterday, Today, and Tomorrow," *Mershon International Studies Review* 39(2): 209–38.
Jervis, R. (2017) *How Statesmen Think: The Psychology of International Politics*. Princeton: Princeton University Press.
Kahneman, D. and Tversky, A. (1974) "A Judgement under Uncertainty: Heuristics and Biases," *Science* 185(4157): 1124–1131.
Kahneman, D. and Tversky, A. (1979) "Prospect Theory: An Analysis of Decision Under Risk," *Econometrica* 47(2): 263–92.
Kahneman, D. and Tversky, A. (1984) "Choices, Values, and Frames," *American Psychologist* 39: 341–50. doi:10.1037/0003-066X.39.4.341.
Kahneman, D. and Tversky, A. (1986) "Rational Choice and the Framing of Decisions," *Journal of Business* 59(4): 251–78.
Kahneman, D., Knetsch, J., and Thaler, R. (1991) "Anomalies: The Endowment Effect, Loss Aversion, and Status Quo Bias," *Journal of Economic Perspectives* 5: 193–206. doi:10.1257/jep.5.1.193.
Kahneman, D. (2003) "Maps of Bounded Rationality: Psychology for Behavioral Economics," *The American Economic Review* 93(5): 1449–1475.
Kahneman, D. (2011) *Thinking Fast and Slow*. New York: Farrar, Straus and Giroux.
Kerry, J. (2018) *Every Day is Extra*. NY: Simon and Shuster.
Kolstø, P. (2016) "Crimea vs. Donbas: How Putin Won Russian Nationalist Support and Lost It Again," *Slavic Review* 75(3): 702–25. doi:10.5612/slavicreview.75.3.0702.
Kuzio, T. (2010) *The Crimea: Europe's Next Flashpoint*. Washington DC: The Jamestown Foundation.
Kuzio, T. and D'Anieri, P. (2018) *The Sources of Russia's Great Power Politics*. Bristol: E-International Relations.
Kuzio, T. (2020) *Crisis in Russian Studies? Nationalism (Imperialism), Racism and War*. Bristol: E-International Relations.
Lampert, B. (2016) "Putin's Prospects: Vladimir Putin's Decision-Making through the Lens of Prospect Theory," *Small Wars Journal*, 15 February.
Lenton, A. (2021) "Why Didn't Ukraine Fight for Crimea? Evidence from Declassified National Security and Defense Council Proceedings,"

Problems of Post-Communism, 15 April. https://doi.org/10.1080/1075 8216.2021.1901595.

Levy, J. and Vakili, L. (1992) "Diversionary Action by Authoritarian Regimes: Argentina in the Falkland/Malvinas Case," in M. Midlarsky (ed.), *The Internationalization of Communal Strife*. London: Routledge, 118–46.

Levy, J. (1997) "Prospect Theory, Rational Choice, and International Relations," *International Studies Quarterly* 41(1): 87–112.

Marten, K. (2015) "Putin's Choices: Explaining Russian Foreign Policy and Intervention in Ukraine," *The Washington Quarterly* 38(2): 189–204.

McDermott, R. (1992) "Prospect Theory in International Relations: The Iranian Hostage Rescue Mission," *Political Psychology* 13(2): 237–63. doi:10.2307/3791680.

McDermott, R. (2004) "Prospect Theory in Political Science: Gains and Losses from the First Decade," *Political Psychology* 25: 289–312. doi:10.1111/j.1467-9221.2004.00372.x.

McFaul, M. (2018) *From Cold War to Hot Peace: An American Ambassador in Putin's Russia*. Boston, MA: Houghton Mifflin Harcourt.

Mearsheimer, J. (1993) "The Case for a Ukrainian Nuclear Deterrent," *Foreign Affairs* 72(3): 50–66.

Mercer, J. (2005) "Prospect Theory and Political Science," *Annual Review of Political Science* 8(1): 1–21.

Merkel, A. (2014) "Policy Statement on the Situation in Ukraine," *German Parliament official website*, 13 March. https://www.bundesregierung.de/breg-en/chancellor/policy-statement-by-federal-chancellor-angela-merkel-on-the-situation-in-ukraine-443796.

Mintz, A. and Sofrin, A. (2017) "Decision-Making Theories in Foreign Policy Analysis," in C. Thies (ed.) *The Oxford Research Encyclopedia of Politics*, Oxford: Oxford University Press. doi: 10.1093/acrefore/97801 90228637.013.405.

Mintz, A. and Redd, S. (2003) "Framing Effects in International Relations," *Synthese* 135(2): 193–213.

Mulrine, A. (2014) "Russian Aircrafts Buzz US Navy Destroyer: How Big a Deal?" *The Christian Science Monitor*, 15 April.

National Security and Defense Council of Ukraine (NSDC) (2014) Declassified Minutes, 28 February. https://www.NSDC.gov.ua/files/2016/stenogr.pdf.

New York Times (NYT) (1994) "Separatist Winning Crimea Presidency," 31 January. https://www.nytimes.com/1994/01/31/world/separatist-winni ng-crimea-presidency.html.

Obama, B. (2014) Transcript of Obama's Remarks on Ukraine, *New York Times*, 28 February.

Onuch, O. and Sasse, G. (2016) "The Maidan in Movement: Diversity and the Cycles of Protest," *Europe-Asia Studies* 68(4): 556–87.
Prentice, A. (2014) "Cossacks, Berkut and Other Armed Men Dig in for Crimea Stay," *Reuters*, 2 March.
Putin, V. (2013) Annual Press Conference. 19 December. http://kremlin.ru/events/president/news/19859
Putin, V. (2014a) Press Conference, *President of Russia official website*, 4 March. http://kremlin.ru/events/president/news/20366.
Putin, V. (2014b) The Crimea Speech, *President of Russia official website*, 18 March. http://kremlin.ru/events/president/news/20603.
Putin, V. (2014c) "Porucheniia v sviazi s situatsiei na Ukraine," *President of Russia official website*, 27 February. http://kremlin.ru/events/preside nt/news/20347.
Putin, V. (2014d) "Priamaia liniia s Vladimirom Putinym," *President of Russia official website*, 17 April. http://kremlin.ru/events/president/news/20796.
Putin, V. (2014e) "Meeting of the Valdai International Discussion Club," *President of Russia official website*, 24 October. http://en.kremlin.ru/events/president/news/46860.
Putin, V. (2015). "*Krym—Put' na Rodinu,*" Production by A. Kondrashov, 15 March. https://www.youtube.com/watch?v=nbGhKfWrfOQ.
Putin, V. (2021) "Ob istoricheskom edinstve russkikh i ukraintsev," *President of Russia official website*, 12 July. http://kremlin.ru/events/president/news/66181.
Reuters (2014) "Ukraine Dismisses Defense Minister over Crimea," 25 March. https://www.reuters.com/article/us-ukraine-crisis-minister-idUSBREA2O0TO20140325.
Rhodes, B. (2018) *The World as It Is: A Memoir of the Obama White House*. NY: Random House.
Snegirev, Iu. (2014) "Aleksei Chalyi: My 20 let byli na puti privedeniia Kryma v Rossiiu," *Rossiiskaia gazeta* 174 (6446), 5 August. https://rg.ru/2014/08/05/chaliy.html.
Socor, V. (2008) "Moscow Makes Furious but Empty Threats to Georgia and Ukraine," *Eurasia Daily Monitor* 5(70), 14 April. https://jamestown.org/program/moscow-makes-furious-but-empty-threats-to-georgia-and-ukraine/.
Solchanyk, R. (1994) "The Politics of State Building: Centre–Periphery Relations in Post-Soviet Ukraine," *Europe-Asia Studies* 46(1): 47–69.
Sytin, A. (2015) "Anatomia provala", *Aleksandr Sytin personal blog*, 5 January. http://www.bramaby.com/ls/blog/rus/1841.html.
Stein, J. (2017) "The Micro-Foundations of International Relations Theory: Psychology and Behavioral Economics," *International Organization* 71(1): 249–63. doi:10.1017/S0020818316000436.

Surkov, V. (2020) Interview by A. Chesnakov, *Aktual'nye kommentarii*, 26 February. http://actualcomment.ru/surkov-mne-interesno-deystvov at-protiv-realnosti-2002260855.html.

Taliaferro, J. (2004) "Power Politics and the Balance of Risk: Hypotheses on Great Power Intervention in the Periphery," *Political Psychology* 25 (2): 177–211.

t'Hart, P., Stern, E. K., and Sundelius, B. (1997) "Foreign Policy Making at the Top: Political Group Dynamics," in P. t'Hart, E. K. Stern, and B. Sundelius (eds.) *Beyond Group Think: Political Group Dynamics and Foreign Policy Making*. Michigan: University of Michigan Press, 3–34.

Treisman, D. (2017) "Crimea: Anatomy of a Decision," in D. Treisman (ed.), *The New Autocracy: Information, Politics, and Policy in Putin's Russia*. Washington D.C.: Brookings Institution Press, 271–90.

Tversky, A. and Kahneman, D. (1981) "The Framing of Decision and the Psychology of Choice," *Science* 211(4481): 453–58. doi:10.1126/science.7455683.

Tversky, A. and Kahneman, D. (1992) "Advances in Prospect Theory: Cumulative Representation of Uncertainty," *Journal of Risk and Uncertainty* 5(4): 297–323.

Turchynov, O. (2015) "Aneksiia Krymu i viina na Donbasi hotuvalys' Rosieiu shche 10 rokiv tomu," *National Security and Defence Council of Ukraine official website*, 28 May. https://www.NSDC.gov.ua/ua/Diialnist/2161.html.

Turchynov, O. (2020) Interview by D. Gordon, *Dmitrii Gordon YouTube channel*, 18 March. https://www.youtube.com/watch?v=TbgMK7nJ2LE.

Umland, A. (2016) "What is the Nature of the Ukraine Crisis?" *OpenDemocracy*, 16 November. https://www.opendemocracy.net/en/odr/glazyevs-tapes/.

United Nations (2014) *Backing Ukraine's Territorial Integrity, UN Assembly declares Crimea Referendum Invalid*. UN News Service, 27 March.

Vagner, A. (2014) "Separatizm na Ukraine: Istoriia bolezni," *Radio Free Europe*, 16 June.

Vis, B., and Kuijpers, D. (2018) "Prospect Theory and Foreign Policy Decision-Making: Underexposed Issues, Advancements, and Ways Forward," *Contemporary Security Policy* 39(4): 575–89. doi:10.1080/13523260.2018.1499695.

Vladykin, O. (2014) "Gotovnost' k massirovanomu iadernomu udaru", *Nezavisimaia gazeta*, 29 March. https://www.ng.ru/armies/2014-03-26/6_strike.html.

Weaver, C. (2014) "Malofeev: the Russian Billionaire Linking Moscow to the Rebels," *Financial Times*, 24 July. https://www.ft.com/content/84481538-1103-11e4-94f3-00144feabdco.

Wydra, D. (2004) "The Crimea Conundrum: The Tug of War Between Russia and Ukraine on the Questions of Autonomy and Self-Determination," *International Journal on Minority and Group Rights* 10: 111–30.

Zhukov, Y. (2016) "Trading Hats for Combat helmets: The economics of Rebellion in eastern Ukraine," *Journal of Comparative Economics* 44(1): 1–15.

Zygar, M. (2016) *All the Kremlin's Men: A Short History of Contemporary Russia*. Moscow: Alpina Digital.

DISCUSSION

DISCUSSION

Competing Theoretical Frameworks for Clarifying Russia's Annexation of Crimea

Peter Rutland

Ion Marandici demonstrates that the Russian decision making around Ukraine can be translated into the framework of prospect theory. I was vaguely familiar with prospect theory, but reading this article was the first time I was forced to think about it in a systematic way, and I am grateful to the author for this exposure. Nevertheless, I remain unconvinced that this exercise, while interesting and well done, brings any particular new insights into explaining what happened. It would also be possible to translate an analytical narrative of the 2014 war into Swahili. That would be impressive: but would generate any new understanding?

Prospect theory frames decisions in terms of losses and gains, with probabilities assigned to different outcomes. There is supposedly an asymmetry between losses and gains in terms of the associated willingness to bear risk, and between high and low probability outcomes. But as Marandici concedes, it is not easy to categorize a particular strategic outcome as a loss or a gain—and he does not even try to estimate the probabilities of different scenarios.

Prospect theory came out of futures markets in economics and psychology experiments, where you see what happens when a group of students are offered the chance to win $5 or lose $5. But foreign policy decisions in the real world are much more complex than classroom psychology experiments, and harder to quantify than futures markets. The problem is: how do we define the asset position of the foreign policy decision-maker at the starting point, and hence how can we tell what is a win, and what is a loss?

For prospect theory to work it is important to define what is owned and not owned at the start of the exercise. But this is very difficult to do in the case of Crimea and the Sevastopol base. Russia had lost political control over Crimea in 1991—but it kept the right to operate the Sevastopol naval base, its most important asset there, under treaties signed in 1997 and 2010 (Treisman 2017). However, there was ambiguity over the status of those treaties: Putin feared that a new government in Kyiv could tear them up.

In 2014 Putin was afraid of the future loss of Sevastopol—so he was operating under a fear of loss framework. However, by annexing Crimea Russia was also "gaining" (or "re-gaining") a territory which it had previously lost. At the same time, while "gaining" Crimea and "not-losing" Sevastopol, Russia "lost" the chance of a closer relationship with Ukraine as a whole. So what weighed most on Putin's mind: the loss of a pro-Russian government in Kyiv (which actually happened), or the potential loss of Sevastopol, or the potential gain of Crimea?

There is also the argument that Putin's main potential loss was the fear that the Euromaidan revolution could spread and bring about regime change in Russia (Stoner 2021: 257). The Arab Spring greatly alarmed Putin (the killing of Muammar Gaddafi in particular), and this was arguably decisive in driving his decision to return to the presidency in 2012 and embrace more authoritarian methods. Marandici does not mention the fear of regime change in Moscow—but it actually fits his theory, in the sense that collapse of the Russian state is Putin's biggest nightmare.

Arguably, Realist and Constructivist frameworks are perfectly adequate for understanding Putin's actions in Crimea, and prospect theory does not materially add to our understanding. There is a risk that it adds a layer of complexity that may distract us from paying attention to the range of relevant contextual factors.

Adam Lenton (2021) also applied prospect theory to Crimea. He argues that Putin was operating with a deep historical frame of reference, and saw Crimea as a loss which could be reversed. Lenton uses prospect theory to help understand the relative inaction of the Ukrainian leadership—he argues that they were fearful of the Russian occupation of Kyiv—an even greater potential loss than Crimea, or Donbas. That fear of loss was founded on rational, Realist, calculations of the balance of power on the part of Ukraine's leadership, drawing on what happened in Georgia in 2008. Lenton suggests identity politics might also have played a role—maybe the Ukrainian leaders didn't see the Crimean population as "real" Ukrainians.

Dmitry Gorenburg (2019) uses prospect theory to analyze Russian options in the Baltics. He argues that Russia has already accepted its loss of the Baltics, which are NATO members, and are unlikely to take the risk of escalating to war—provided NATO signals its willingness to defend the Baltic states.

Paul D'Anieri (2021), writing from a neorealist perspective, explains the Russia–Ukraine conflict as the result of a structural vacuum in European security and Russia's identity narrative as a great power. So from the accounts of D'Anieri and Lenton I would conclude that the explicatory power of prospect theory stands on the back of Realist balance of power calculations and Constructivist identity narratives.

Rather than analyzing decisions in terms of probable gains and losses, Realists frame the situation in the following terms: was Putin being offensive or defensive in annexing Crimea? Was he changing the status quo, or preserving the status quo? This question is also not easy to answer. Russia already had the naval base at Sevastopol—but could it rely on Kyiv to respect the treaty in the future? If you want to argue that Russia was an aggressive, revisionist power, presumably 1991 was the point where the situation changed. But Russians could still argue that 1991 broke the status quo and they want to restore the pre-1991 strategic balance, the defensive buffer zone that Russia enjoyed (since 1783, in the case of Crimea.)

After 1991 a new status quo emerged. Kyiv maintained equidistance between Russia and the West, sometimes leaning towards the West, sometimes towards Russia. Recall that after the Orange Revolution 2004 Ukraine did not fall into the Western camp: Viktor Yanukovych became PM in 2006 then president in 2010. Russia was granted a 20-year lease to the Sevastopol base in 1997, extended for another 25 years in 2010. Moscow argues that the EU and NATO were trying to change that status quo—a neutral Ukraine—in 2014 by pushing a free trade agreement with Ukraine and then supporting the ouster of Yanukovych. Marandici does not put much emphasis on the way Ukraine was balancing between east and west under Yanukovych, nor does he mention the Sevastopol lease. This suggests that focusing on the psychology of crisis decision-making may lead the analyst to overlook or downplay crucial structural factors that are actually driving the behavior of the key actors.

In sum: the most important question that arises is how do we identify what decision-makers regard as a "gain" and a "loss," and how do we understand under what circumstances they may re-evaluate the status of a particular gain/loss? Russia seems to have accepted some past losses (such as the Baltic states entering NATO in 2004), and they seemed to have accepted the loss of Crimea in 1954/1991—until they changed their mind, in February 2014.

One striking feature of Putin's strategy towards Ukraine is that he was hedging his bets by hiding Russia's true role. Rather than deploy regular troops, he used the famous "little green men" to occupy Crimea, and mercenaries and "volunteers" to stoke the revolt in Donbas. This strategy gave Putin a degree of plausible deniability before the international community. He was able to double down on Crimea when he saw that things were going well—to proceed with incorporation of Crimea into Russia, and even admit that Russian troops had been involved from the outset. At the same time, he throttled back in Donetsk and Luhansk, refusing to recognize their independence, and declining to officially commit Russian troops to the defense of the territory. I imagine that this hedging strategy can be incorporated into a prospect theory account of the Russo–Ukrainian crisis.

Finally, a concern that I have with the prospect theory approach is that it may reinforce the already prevailing tendency to treat foreign policy as the result of rational utility-maximizing decisions by singular actors. This trend is particularly dominant in the study of Russian foreign policy, given the strong centralization of power under Vladimir Putin. However, the reality is that decision-making inside the upper echelons of the Kremlin is very opaque, and is pulled in different directions by feuding factions. Marandici to his credit does try to unpack the Kremlin decision-making during the Crimean crisis, based on the available information. We urgently need more studies of Russian decision making that go beyond unitary actor explanations to explore governmental politics and bureaucratic processes.

REFERENCES

D'Anieri, P. (2019) *Ukraine and Russia: From Civilized Divorce to Uncivil War*. New York: Cambridge University Press.
Gorenburg, D. (2019) "Russian Strategic Culture in a Baltic Crisis," Marshall Center *Security Insights* 37 (July).
Lenton, A.(2021) "Why Didn't Ukraine Fight for Crimea? Evidence from Declassified National Security and Defense Council Proceedings," *Problems of Post-Communism*, 15 April.
Stoner, K. E. (2020) *Russia Resurrected. Power and Purpose in a New Global Order*. Oxford: Oxford University Press.
Treisman, D. (2017) "Crimea: Anatomy of a Decision," in D. Treisman (ed.), *The New Autocracy*, Washington D.C.: Brookings Institution Press, 271–90.

On Reading Yanukovych and the Rhetoric of *Novorossiia* Right

Tor Bukkvoll

Dr Ion Marandici has, through the systematic use of prospect theory, given us a better understanding of the Russian decision to annex Crimea. Other authors, myself included, have used ad-hoc elements of this theory to explain Putin's behavior. None, however, until Marandici, have used the theory in both the theory-informed and theory-testing manner that he does.

I agree with the majority of empirical and theoretical claims in his study. Still, I take the opportunity to comment on three empirical issues and question one of Marandici's statements on sources. In terms of the empirical issues, I offer two alternative interpretations of reality and one small point of criticism.

First, Marandici may have a slightly misguided understanding of what kind of loss it was that prompted Putin to annex Crimea. He seems to operate under the assumption, often repeated in the press, that Putin's loss consisted in the departure of a long-time geopolitical ally. For example, Marandici portrays Yanukovych as a defender of Russian interests in Ukraine. He argues that with Yanukovych in power, Putin felt Ukraine was under relative control. I think that is inaccurate.

Why, if Yanukovych was a promoter of Russian interests, would he have started negotiations with the European Union on an Association Agreement in the first place? It would probably be more accurate to say that Yanukovych was a president who teetered between east and west and then gradually leaned more and more towards the latter. Inna Bohoslovska, who was a member of Yanukovych's Party of Regions faction in parliament, remembers a faction meeting in October 2013 where Yanukovych was present. The party was split roughly fifty-fifty between proponents of Eurointegration and membership in the Russia-controlled Customs Union. At this meeting, Yanukovych made clear to his deputies that "going to Europe" was now the party line. For example, he scolded the pro-Russian deputy Nestor Shufrich—"Have you understood nothing? Grow up, we are going to Europe!" (Vlashchenko 2017: 33). The main reason for this "going to Europe" was probably fear. Unless he did so, Moscow would always attempt to dominate Ukrainian politics and business.

Later, as the signing of the Association Agreement came closer, Yanukovych was put under tremendous political and economic pressure by Putin to change course. This pressure included threats as well as carrots (D'Anieri 2019: 200–07). In the end, Yanukovych relented and decided not to sign the Association Agreement. What is lacking in this connection in Marandici's account, however, is that this turn-around may have been about much more than alternative trade arrangements. According to firsthand interviews conducted by Ukrainian journalist Sonia Koshkina, immediately after Vilnius Yanukovych told a gathering of the most important Ukrainian oligarchs that all of Ukrainian foreign policy would now change. He had promised Putin a 180-degree turnaround of Ukrainian foreign policy orientation. Yanukovych frankly told the oligarchs in the room "we are no longer going to Europe" (Koshkina 2015: 51–52).

If these accounts by both Bohoslovska and Koshkina are true, Marandici misrepresents Putin's reference point. In prospect theory, the reference point is the state against which both loss and gain are measured. Marandici sees Putin's reference point as the loss of an enduring geopolitical ally. Instead, it may have been the unexpected derailment of his major geopolitical triumph. Putin had finally succeeded in coercing his unreliable neighbor into promising fidelity, only to lose it all again because of a popular uprising. This alternative understanding of Putin's reference point does not diminish Marandici's analytical claim. Putin decided to annex Crimea because a sense of loss with regard to a subjective reference point made him more willing to take risk. However, it questions the empirical content of that reference point.

Second, Marandici may be wrong about the role of presidential advisor Vladislav Surkov in the conflict in Donbas and about Kremlin motivations. Surkov was Moscow's main political envoy to the conflict from the summer of 2014 until early 2020. In Marandici's interpretation, he was the initiator of the *Novorossiia* plan. When the Kremlin was no longer interested in pursuing this plan, Surkov left in protest. This understanding does not seem to square well with the fact that Surkov left only in February 2020. That was long after Russian politicians stopped talking about *Novorossiia*. According to the usually well-informed head of the radio station *Ekho Moskvy*, Aleksei Venediktov, the real reason for Surkov's departure in February 2020 was that Putin made him share responsibility for the Donbas with Vladimir Kozak (Venediktov 2020). Surkov has himself partly acknowledged the veracity of this version of events (Chesnakov 2020).

Furthermore, newly available sources from the separatist camp also question Surkov's enthusiasm for the idea of *Novorossiia*. The former separatist fighter and Russian volunteer Aleksandr Zhuchkovskii recently published a biography of the separatist commander Aleksei Mozgovoi. This book is based on numerous interviews with firsthand sources both in the Donbas and in Moscow. Zhuchkovskii argues that Surkov used the *Novorossiia* rhetoric only instrumentally, in order to make the Donbas population take up arms. According to Zhuchkovskii, "Surkov was able to charm many of the commanders into thinking that he supported the idea of *Novorossiia*. Some, however, saw through this manipulation from the start" (Zhuchkovskii 2020: 229).

Thus, an alternative interpretation to Marandici's would be that neither the Kremlin nor Surkov were ever serious about *Novorossiia*. They only used this rhetoric to radicalize anti-Kiev sentiments. Nothing but an armed uprising in Donbas would in their view be sufficient to force Kyiv to political concessions. To achieve such a revolt, the Kremlin needed to deploy a sufficiently radical idea. A simple call for autonomy within Ukraine would not be enough to make people take up arms and risk their lives in battle. Zhuchkovskii confirms that when parts of the population in the Donbas initially protested in the streets of against what had happened in Kyiv, none of them "even thought about the possibilities of independent republics and armed resistance" (Zhuchkovskii 2021: 15). Girkin's armed takeover of the city of Slaviansk and introduction of the idea of *Novorossiia*, however, changed the equation, at least for some. These now started to organize armed resistance against Kyiv.

If this alternative interpretation of Surkov's dismissal and the Kremlin's motives is right, then Marandici's understanding of a shift in Kremlin policy from *Novorossiia* to Ukrainian federalization may also be wrong. Federalization of Ukraine may have been the goal more or less from the beginning. Zhuchkovskii mentions that already in spring 2014, when the separatist commander Aleksandr Mozgovoi travelled to Moscow to meet Russian political and military leaders, he was told to forget about a *Novorossiia* independent from Ukraine. Instead, he should prepare his men to fight for a "united but anti-fascist Ukraine" (Zhuchkovskii 2020: 201).

Third, Marandici spends considerable time discussing to what extent the annexation was pre-planned. The Russian narrative is that it was more or less a spur of the moment operation. Putin claims it was undertaken out of a concern for the majority Russian speaking population on the peninsula. Many Ukrainians, on the other hand, think the operation had been planned for years. Marandici argues that there is some evidence of advance planning, but that the operation still was mainly a response to events in Kyiv rather than something that the Kremlin had planned for a long time. This is a conclusion also supported by other accounts (Treisman 2018: 277–97 and Zygar' 2016: 338–42), but Marandici's discussion could have benefitted from a distinction between military and political planning. The size, speed and coordination of the military operation suggests that it could not have taken place without significant preplanning. That, however, is entirely natural and says little about the political decision making. Military organizations continuously plan for operations that may never happen. If they did not, they would be under unbearable time pressure every time politicians suddenly made the decision on the use of force.

Finally, I question one of Marandici's comments on sources. It is not clear to me why Mikhail Zygar"s journalistic account of events, based on seven years of interviews with decision makers in the Kremlin, should be less reliable as a source than Igor Girkin's accounts of his own exploits in Crimea and Donbas. Marandici is of course correct to say that journalistic accounts may contain involuntary biases or intentional misrepresentations. However, is not that danger even greater with statements from actors who took directly part in the events under discussion? The latter must have an obvious self-interest in justifying their previous actions. My position would be that if handled with skepticism, both interviews made by journalists and first-hand accounts from participants in the events themselves are legitimate sources.

Despite these points of criticism, I think Marandici has given us a good exploration of the mechanisms that led to Putin's decision to annex Crimea. Furthermore, he has provided empirical evidence in support of a theory that is currently becoming increasingly popular, also in foreign policy analysis. His account is an argument in favor of more analysts looking to prospect theory when they want to explain the international behavior of states.

REFERENCES

Chesnakov, A. (2020) Interview with Vladislav Surkov, *Aktual'nye kommentarii*, 26 February. http://actualcomment.ru/surkov-mne-intereso-deystvovat-protiv-realnosti-2002260855.html.

D'Anieri, P. (2019) *Ukraine and Russia: From Civilized Divorce to Uncivil War*. Cambridge: Cambridge University Press.

Koshkina, S. (2015) *Maidan – Nerasskazannaia istoriia*. Kyiv: Brait Books.

Treisman, D. (2018) "Crimea: Anatomy of a Decision" in D. Treisman (ed.) *The New Autocracy – Information, Politics, and Policy in Putin's Russia*. Washington DC: Brookings Institution Press, 277–97.

Venediktov, A. (2020) Interview at Echo Moskvy, 25 January. https://echo.msk.ru/programs/observation/2576395-echo/

Vlashchenko, N. (2017) *Krazha, ili beloe solntse Kryma*. Kyiv: Folio.

Zhuchkovskii, A. (2021) *Mozgovoi*. Nizhnii Novgorod: Chernaia Sotnia.

Zygar', M. (2016) *Vsia kremlevskaia rat' – Spetsial'noe izdanie dlia Ukrainy*. Kharkiv: Folio.

How Rational Was Putin's Strategy of Crimea Annexation? Prospect Theory and Security Dilemma Perspectives

Mykola Kapitonenko

Introduction

Just like World War I, the collapse of the Soviet Union, and a number of other crucial events in the history of international politics, Russia's move to annex Crimea from Ukraine in 2014 caught IR scholars by surprise. Vladimir Putin's decision seemed to be absolutely "out of touch with reality," as Angela Merkel put it in March 2014. It was too risky, too costly, and totally against the rules. Nevertheless, Moscow made this choice; and its further actions proved that it was not an accidental or just emotional one. Debates may continue about whether the intermediate cost-benefit analysis is in Russia's favor, but the decision made has already contributed to a transformation of the international order into one which arguably suits Russia's interests better.

For IR scholars this is also a theoretical puzzle. Possible explanations can certainly be put forward post-factum at different levels of analysis and within frameworks of different paradigms. Security considerations in Russia, lack of trust between Russia and the West, and the weakness of international and regional security institutions may all have contributed to President Putin's decision to annex Crimea.

But this decision can also be examined at the individual level through the lens of prospect theory. In Russia, decision-making in foreign policy, especially in crises, is limited to a very narrow circle, which makes it reasonable to address the approaches of participants personally. Rational choice theory and prospect theory provide basic frameworks for doing so.

Ion Marandici's essay provides a deep insight into how the decision to annex Crimea was taken. Its emphasis on how perception of the dynamics of events shifts strategy from risk-aversion to risk taking is especially relevant—not only for explaining the events in 2014 but also for addressing the even more dramatic decision by Moscow to start a full-scale invasion of Ukraine in 2022.

This essay opens with an analysis of how and why prospect theory is suitable for tackling issues of foreign policy crisis decision-making. It then proceeds to provide a sequence of key points in decision-making over Ukraine for the Russian leadership during the crisis of 2013–2014. After that, President Putin's possible perception of risk under conditions of security dilemma is assessed.

Prospect Theory as a Tool for Studying Foreign Policy Decision-Making

Graham Allison once outlined the way states should rationally approach their foreign policies. Within what he called the *rational actor model*, states are unitary profit maximizers, capable of prioritizing their interests and finding the best strategy out of all possible alternatives (Allison 1971).

In the real world, foreign policies of states do not usually follow Allison's rational actor model. People who take decisions deviate from optimal behavior at different levels and for different reasons. At the individual level, they tend to lack a strict hierarchy of interests and break the rule of transitivity. At the group level, they are impacted by a groupthink syndrome. At all levels, they lack capacity for exhaustive examination of all available strategies and often fall into incrementalism by opting for minor changes in current policies instead of complete revision of the strategy under new circumstances. It turns out that foreign policies of states often result not from rational decision-making, but from bureaucratic policies or organizational prescriptions.

But foreign policy often looks irrational not only due to bureaucratic routine or organizational procedures. There is a more fundamental question about the rationality of those humans who actually take decisions. Even if foreign policies of states follow the logic of the rational actor model, they can still be quite irrational.

This is because people are not very good at making rational choice. The fundamental problems are the lack of an ability to prioritize different values and the non-transitivity of their preferences. Human needs are too diversified. It's possible for someone to want a cup of coffee, a good job, and a win for a favorite football team—all at once. Moreover, these preferences, even if one could arrange them in some preferred order, can rapidly gain or lose value. Being rational under such circumstances is a challenge.

Sometimes humans know what they want—but their preferences are not transitive—i.e., preferring A over B, and B over C does not necessarily mean preferring A over C. Lack of transitivity in one's desires may lead to losses and irrational behavior (Harrington 2009). A person with one hundred dollars and an apple, with preferences of an orange to an apple, an apple to a banana, but a banana to an orange, may end up being left with no money through a series of exchanges—because of non-transitivity.

People, after all, tend to take seemingly irrational decisions quite often. They play lotteries, go to casinos, collect fines, or, say, go to polling stations. The last case, called the voter's dilemma, is telling: People invest time and effort even when there is almost no chance for their vote to be decisive. Lots of explanations have been put forward, including altruism, self-expression, and care for democracy; however, none of them fits strictly within rational choice theory predictions (Blais and Young 1999).

Apart from voting, people make a lot of irrational decisions. In some cases, they are just unaware of behaving irrationally. Very often, however, they do know that playing Caribbean poker against a casino is a decision with a negative expected value—but they still play.

There are two basic ways of addressing foreign policy decision-making at the individual level: rational choice theory and prospect theory. The former treats a choice between possible options as the way to maximize expected utility. By multiplying probabilities of gains and losses, and taking into account costs, it is possible to calculate the expected value of any decision—and that's what a rational leader should have done in Putin's place in 2013–2014. Rational choice theory assumes that decision-makers are neutral when comparing the expected values of different strategies. Only if the expected value of annexation of Crimea exceeded that of all other options, should Putin have taken a decision to annex—from a rational choice perspective.

However, this may not necessarily be the case. Putin, just like a gambler at a casino, might have been aware that the expected value of Crimea's annexation was not high enough or even lower than that of alternative options—but he still took that decision. That doesn't mean he acted irrationally. The point is that he may not have been neutral to possible gains and losses—and if that's the case, then prospect theory would be better suited to explain his decision.

Prospect theory places an emphasis on how decision-makers perceive possible gains and losses. They opt for more or less risky strategies depending on whether they face the prospect of winning or losing. It is a normative theory in the sense that it provides guiding lines for making decisions and explains how things should go (or have gone). But it can also provide a plausible explanation about why some decisions which do not fit into a rational choice approach, were nevertheless taken.

Key Points in Putin's Decision-Making over Ukraine

In 2013–2014 the Russian leadership and, in particular, President Putin faced a number of interconnected problems in dealing with Ukraine. Negotiations between Kyiv and Brussels over the Association Agreement (AA) were drawing to a close. The price of Ukraine and the EU signing an AA was perceived as quite high in Moscow: it would have put an end to Russia's attempts to engage Ukraine into Eurasian integration projects and, in the long run, limit Russia's influence in the country. Aspirations to restore most of its influence in the neighborhood and establish regional dominance would have been thwarted. On the other hand, Russia had to take into consideration the need to reinforce its lobbying power and influence inside Ukraine by promoting pro-Russian political parties and the ideology of what is now known as the Russian World. The regional dimension was also important: in dealing with Ukraine Russia also needed to keep in mind other countries in its neighborhood, which had similar concerns and kept an eye on the twists and turns of the crisis in Ukrainian-Russian relations.

At the beginning of the crisis, prior to the mass protests in Kyiv, the most fundamental issue for President Putin might have been the seeming resolve on the part of Ukraine's President Yanukovych and his government to sign an AA with the EU, a resolve that was displayed almost throughout the whole year of 2013. Putin may well have been asking himself: was Yanukovych bluffing or not?

A trade war, unleashed in August 2013, was the Kremlin's primary response to Ukraine's declared intention to sign the AA. Inspections and discriminatory treatment by the Russian customs service as well as the blocking of Ukrainian imports inflicted significant losses on Ukrainian companies. The escalation of tensions between the two countries indicated that either the Russian president had opted to call Yanukovych's bluff or that he took Ukraine's intentions seriously. Moscow's response was large-scale and expensive in terms of the damage done to future relations with Ukraine, even if Yanukovych had stayed in power. But in Putin's eyes, it may not have appeared so risky.

How risk-averse or risk-taking were Putin's responses to developments in Ukraine in the summer of 2013?

Prospect theory points out that decision-makers from the domain of losses are ready to accept more risks (Kahneman and Tversky 1979). Russia's heavy-handed response to Ukraine's preparations to sign the AA was, probably, the riskiest of all available alternatives short of application of force; but it was not excessively risky in the Kremlin's view. Rather it was in line with the usual practice of creating and managing all sorts of crises in relations with Ukraine, in which Russia enjoyed the upper hand as the stronger partner. A trade war with Ukraine in the summer of 2013 was no more risky than the series of gas wars in the 2000s.

That could mean that the Russian leader thought these measures would be enough to reverse the Ukrainian government's intentions—and he was right about that. Whether because of

Moscow's pressure or because Yanukovych had been bluffing all along in his pro-European rhetoric, the government of Ukraine changed its position and cancelled preparations for the signing of the AA. Putin must have felt himself to be distant enough from the domain of losses.

Following the decision of the Ukrainian government, mass protests erupted in Kyiv. The level of uncertainty escalated, and the Kremlin's control over what was happening in Ukraine dramatically weakened. That was the moment when decision-makers in the Kremlin must have felt that Russia's positions in Ukraine were under threat.

The alternative options available to Russia were all problematic and involved considerable risks. Moscow could have opted for non-interference; for limited assistance aimed at keeping Yanukovych in power; or for full-scale interference. In the first case the major risk was in letting the government, which seemed more pro-Russian than any possible alternative, fail. In the second case, Moscow would be betting some of its reputation and providing the Ukrainian opposition with an opportunity to link Yanukovych's corrupt regime with Russia. This could have meant spoiling future relations with the new government, should one appear as a result of the mass protests. In the third case, the same risks would have been multiplied.

But there was also another option: contributing to further destabilization of Ukraine and actually weakening Yanukovych's regime instead of helping it survive. This option is often neglected due to Yanukovych's assumed dependence on Russia and his pro-Russian foreign policy.

However, Yanukovych, especially in the late years of his presidency, was less pro-Russian than is often assumed. He had consolidated power within the country and was attempting to diversify risks internationally by promoting relations with both Russia and the EU. In 2013 his push for Ukraine's European future might well have become annoying for Moscow. In an attempt to make Yanukovych more accommodating, Putin could have actually contributed to an ongoing crisis in Ukraine instead of helping Yanukovych calm things down—but that might have been a risky decision, because any other politician in Ukraine could have been more pro-Western than Yanukovych. Were Moscow to apply this strategy, the goal would have been to weaken Yanukovych, but without driving him out of office.

In its deliberations, the Russian leadership must have been often referring to past experience—in particular, that of the Orange Revolution in 2004. At that time Moscow's restrained reaction helped it sustain influence on Ukrainian politics and public opinion; but this did not prevent the new Ukrainian leadership from choosing a pro-Western foreign policy strategy. One of the most important choices for Putin at the beginning of the crisis and right up to the annexation of the Crimea was about either saving Russia's soft power and lobbying power in Ukraine or destabilizing Ukraine as much as possible to prevent it from joining NATO and/or the EU in the foreseeable future. Geopolitical considerations and strategic uncertainty regarding Ukraine's future intentions must have played a decisive role in this choice and in the end outweighed the soft power logic.

Prospect theory states that the endowment effect makes people overvalue their possessions and undervalue what they do not have (Levy 1992). Putin's steps in the initial phase of the crisis were cautious, possibly because he believed that risky moves might have led to a loss of what he had—firm positions and influence in Ukraine. However, as tensions escalated and control vanished, the Russian president had to revise his strategy to make it more risk-taking and more driven by geopolitical considerations and negative expectations. The decision to annex Crimea was the culmination point of this approach.

Putin's Risk Perception in a Security Dilemma

Dealing with the Crimea option must have been tough for Putin and his closest advisers. Probably, in their view doing nothing was even more risky than sending "green men" to seize control over the peninsula. Why? Because of the security dilemma.

The escalating crisis in Ukraine had created profound uncertainty about the country's future policies, including those in foreign policy and national security. The Russian leadership had been quite sensitive to these issues because of energy resources supplies, the Black Sea stationing, and the overall regional security architecture. Ukraine had been an important element in Russia's grand strategy in the neighborhood and globally.

While the level of uncertainty continued to rise, a window of opportunity provided by Ukraine's weakness was opening. There was no way for the Kremlin to secure any deals with Ukraine on strategic issues—first of all because of internal instability in the country, and secondly due to previous experience of Ukraine's shifting its foreign policy priorities. The situation may have been seen from Moscow as quite difficult: with no realistic chance to get any assurances, Russia faced an inevitable loss of control and dependency on the decisions of others.

This may have been the moment when Putin found himself in the realm of losses. Letting things develop as they were would have surely led to losing Ukraine from Russia's sphere of influence, with all problems with the Russian Black Sea Fleet, natural gas supplies, and regional conflicts attached. On the other hand, more risky steps could have helped Russia minimize losses and, with some luck, to convert Ukrainian revolution into a partial geopolitical success.

These considerations would have been further enhanced by a more general framework of perception. From Moscow's perspective, there was a strategic competition, if not rivalry, between Russia and the West, in particular in Europe (National Security Strategy of Russia 2009). Ukraine, within such a framework, had become an element in a zero-sum game; and a foreign policy choice made by a new government in Kyiv could have significantly changed the balance against Russia's favor. Uncertainty and lack of control shifted Moscow's preferences and resulted in what seems to many as a more risky strategy; but for the Russian decision-makers it could in fact have been the least risky one.

A problem for President Putin was that actually all available courses of action were risky. Any possible gains were limited and hard to sustain, while the expected price was high. Immediate costs included a loss of Ukraine from Russia's perceived sphere of influence; and Western sanctions.

Losing Ukraine is often referred to as Russia's biggest possible geopolitical disaster (Brzezinski 2013). The two states have a long common history, close ties in many areas, and traditionally high levels of interdependence. Ukraine also hosts some sites which are important for Russia's statehood ideology, most importantly Kyiv as the capital of the medieval state of Kyivan Rus', from which a tradition of state of both Ukraine and Russia is often traced. Ukraine is also believed to be central to the ideology of the Russian world, which is the tool for a global projection of Russia's soft power (Putin 2021).

The symbolic significance of Ukraine to current Russia's foreign policy may be exaggerated. But control or at least significant influence over Ukraine has still been important for Russia's grand strategy in the past two decades as a precondition of regional dominance and an element of the Kremlin's plan to establish its Eurasian integration project.

Western sanctions must have been another point for decision-makers in Moscow to keep in mind. On the one hand, they must have assessed the probability of anything stronger that sanctions as close to zero. No military response from the West to Russia's actions against Ukraine was likely—because it would have been too expensive for the West. This round of poker was easy for Moscow.

On the other hand, a response "between wars and words," i.e., sanctions, was very likely, precisely because a war was impossible, while words were not enough. Annexation of a territory of a neighboring state was incompatible with the existing world order—and Putin and his advisors knew that well enough even before it was stated by Henry Kissinger (Kissinger 2014).

After all, events could have gone in a bad direction for Russia. Hybrid warfare, like all warfare, is difficult to control; and there is no way to secure victory beforehand. Thus, complications were easily foreseeable, although their scope and duration were unknown.

Regional and strategic implications must also have been seen as dangerous by the Russian leadership. A move like annexation of a neighboring state's territory sends a clear signal to other neighbors, and that is not a positive signal. Perception of Russia by its neighbors was also at stake. Strategically this has also been connected to serious risks. Russia's projects to integrate large parts of post-Soviet space into different Eurasian structures had been a priority of its foreign policy for several years before 2014. Moscow had invested significant efforts into them. Annexation of Crimea may have discounted most of those efforts and thus added to the costs of this option.

From a rational choice theory perspective, while comparing alternative decisions—non-interference, supporting Crimea's independence without annexing it, and annexation—Vladimir Putin should have calculated expected values and picked a strategy with the highest one. This would imply an assessment of the probabilities of success and failure, defining what was at stake, and measuring the costs of every option. It is likely that from this perspective, the option of annexation was not the best one—because of its extremely high costs. Sanctions had been announced by President Obama before the so-called "referendum" in Crimea in 2014. They raised the costs for proceeding further with the annexation plan and provided a withdrawal option for Putin. But even these measures did not change Moscow's intentions. It seems that the Russian president was taking decisions within a different paradigm to that of rational choice.

The realm of losses and the trap of the security dilemma might have shifted perceptions of the Russian leadership and made them more risk-accepting. This is why prospect theory is helpful in examining how the decision to annex Crimea was taken.

Conclusion

It is impossible to know exactly under which circumstances and why the decision to annex Crimea from Ukraine was taken by the Russian leadership. But that was an important decision, not only for Ukraine and Russia, but also for the general framework of international security. Understanding why it was taken in 2014 may help in assessing possible similar decisions in the future, by Russia or any other international actor.

Although it is impossible to know exactly why the decision on Crimea was taken, in order to judge whether it was a mistake, miscalculation, or a crucial element of a well-thought-out strategy, prospect theory may be helpful. Vladimir Putin must have been well aware of the high costs and uncertainty of the annexation option, but still pursued it. That may have been because of his readiness to take additional risks from the domain of losses.

It may also be possible that the Russian leadership concluded at some point that annexing Crimea might in fact be less risky than not doing so. Such an approach may be possible if decisions were taken within the logic of the security dilemma.

When applying prospect theory to foreign policy decision-making analysis, it is important to keep in mind that it is a normative individual-level theory. It may be helpful in uncovering some nuances of decision-making process, especially those dealing with risk-taking; however, the general picture will remain more complicated.

REFERENCES

Allison, G. (1971) *Essence of Decision: Explaining the Cuban Missile Crisis*. Little, Brown and Company.
Blais, A. and Young, R. (1999) "Why Do People Vote? An Experiment in Rationality," *Public Choice* 99: 39–55.
Brzezinski, Z. (2013) *Strategic Vision: America and the Crisis of Global Power*. Basic Books.
Harrington, J. (2009) *Games, Strategies, and Decision Making*. Worth Publishers.
Kahneman, D. and Tversky, A. (1979) "Prospect Theory: An Analysis of Decision under Risk," *Econometrica* 47(2): 263–92.
Kissinger, H. (2014) "Henry Kissinger: To Settle Ukrainian Crisis, Start at the End," *Washington Post*, 5 March.
Levy, J. (1992). "An Introduction to Prospect Theory," *Political Psychology* 13(2): 171–86.
National Security Strategy of Russia till 2020 (2009) *President of Russia official website*, 13 May. http://kremlin.ru/supplement/424.
Putin, V. (2021) "Ob istoricheskom edinstve russkikh i ukraintsev," *President of Russia official website*, 12 July. http://kremlin.ru/events/president/news/66181.

A Constructivist International Relations Contribution to Understanding the Annexation of Crimea

Rumena Filipova

Ion Marandici tackles one of the most consequential questions of recent international politics, namely, why Russia's President Vladimir Putin took the decision to annex Crimea. The author locates the answer to this question in prospect theory, whose main assumption is that when evaluating the status quo, decision-makers are more risk-acceptant in the domain of perceived losses and more risk-averse in the domain of expected gains. To empirically substantiate the plausibility of prospect theory, Marandici brings to bear wide-ranging evidence on how the Crimean crisis unfolded through declassified documents of the deliberations that took place in Ukraine's National Defence and Security Council and personal accounts by decision-makers. The author complements prospect theory's risk calculation model by drawing on a variety of factors that define in a more comprehensive manner the reference point against which evaluations of the magnitude and value of gains and losses are made, including status quo, aspirations, heuristics, analogies, and emotions. Special attention is paid to "neo-imperial framing" as formative of Putin's worldview and decision-making choices.

    The account thus provided constitutes a contribution to ongoing discussions as to the nature of the Russian President's psychology and behavior—whether he represents a chancy opportunist or a careful strategist. Ion Marandici shows that Putin's assessments evolved in response to the development of the crisis in relations with Ukraine leading to a calculated risk of annexing Crimea, which nevertheless aimed at reducing escalation with the West (especially through posturing on the basis of denying

Moscow's direct involvement in Crimeans' decision to become part of Russia). Evidence of pre-existing advance planning for the scenario of a potential standoff between Russia and Ukraine over Crimea is also cited as pointing towards the strategic underpinnings of Putin's actions.

The rendering of the Crimea-related events through the prism of prospect theory is, however, subject to some theoretical and empirical drawbacks. In setting out to defend the plausibility of prospect theory, the author emphasizes his focus "solely on foreign policy decision-making rather than traditional theories in international relations" (p. 112). He further states that his paper "does not focus on neorealism or liberalism as major international relations theories but rather seeks to clarify foreign policy decision-making via a single case study grounded in prospect theory." Yet, International Relations (IR) theories cannot be dismissed, even if such a dismissal stems from the premise that the analysis centers on the field of foreign policy decision-making rather than the discipline of IR, whose "proper" remit incorporates such theories as Realism and Liberalism.

As I argue in my book *Constructing the Limits of Europe*,[1] the exaggerated academic boundaries between International Relations and Foreign Policy Analysis (FPA) can obscure the avenues for cross-learning, given that both disciplines are ultimately committed to studying the international dimension of politics. The FPA approach has indeed been oriented towards the exploration of the processes, effects, causes, and outcomes of foreign policy decision-making in a comparative or case-specific manner (Foreign Policy Analysis Journal). It is generally distinguished by being agent-oriented and actor-specific in examining the policy process, whereby those with decision-making authority frame problems, assess policy options, prioritize objectives, formally settle on and implement a course of action taken with reference to a particular situation. This distinctive agentic focus, however, has been taken as

---

[1] Rumena Filipova, *Constructing the Limits of Europe: Identity and Foreign Policy in Poland, Bulgaria, and Russia since 1989* (ibidem Verlag/Columbia University Press, 2022), 119–22.

reason for the establishment of a firmly sealed disciplinary division between predominantly "systemically" concerned International Relations and "sub-systemically" focused FPA. Straddling the overblown disciplinary distinctions between IR and FPA can thus illuminate the close affinity between international relations and foreign policy, otherwise obscured by stringent academic boundaries—since the general interactions and dynamics between states in the international system have implications for foreign policy decisions, which in turn affect international trends and structures. Hence, the inseparable association between international relations and foreign policy means that they are not the exclusive research preserve of IR and FPA, respectively (especially when examinations are attuned to multiple levels of analysis). They can be studied by both IR and FPA, which can borrow from each other's theoretical and conceptual assumptions.

The potential for such cross-fertilization is also implicitly revealed in Marandici's analysis through the emphasis on neo-imperial framing. The argument that such "framing is controlled by the manner in which the choice problem is presented as well as by norms, habits, and expectancies of the decision maker" (p. 131) and that the "major frame in the annexation narrative was of nationalist-imperial origin, emphasizing historical claims and an endangered common identity" (p. 131) resonates with Constructivist theorizing in IR. Constructivism provides the analytical guidelines for exploring how socially constructed rules, norms, identities, and ideas shape decision-making environments and international politics. Therefore, Marandici's paper can benefit from exploring how Constructivism and prospect theory relate to each other.

A more sustained dialogue with the structurally-oriented insights of IR could also remedy a problem of levels of analysis in prospect theory that the author himself identifies: that the "collective nature of decision-making at state level presents a major difficulty for the application of prospect theory, which is an individual-level theory" (p. 113). Although this problem is said to be resolved in the paper by the fact that the decision to annex Crimea was made by the Russian President, subsequent elements in the analysis point to the significance of intersubjective rather than strictly individual views. This is reflected in the discussion of the nationalist-neo-imperial frame as representing a collective construct that involves Putin's close circle, state-owned media, and a variety of other actors, who share the conservative ideational positions. Hence, prospect theory's individualist focus cannot be left unexplored and applied to empirical cases that could fit its premises but requires an incorporation of an investigation of how tensions between subjectivity and intersubjectivity can be dealt with.

Furthermore, the focus of the paper on Russia–Ukraine interactions and assessment of Kyiv's capacity to resist, not least determined by domestic power struggles, as factoring in Putin's decision-making sheds important light on how the cycle of bilateral perceptions unfolded. Yet, the fact that Ukraine is altogether weaker than Russia in relative power terms—and could not have mounted an effective challenge even in the presence of greater internal cohesion and resilience—suggests the importance of rebalancing attention to Russia's calculations vis-à-vis Western countries, which were the ones that could impose significant costs on the Kremlin for its annexation of Crimea.

Indeed, the annexation of the Black Sea peninsula is part of a repetitive pattern, whereby the Kremlin acts in a forceful—and what might be deemed irrational, manner, leading to reputation costs and negative political-economic consequences (such as sanctions). For example, Russia has continued to conduct clandestine operations as in the poisoning of former Russian military intelligence officer Sergey Skripal on UK soil despite widespread condemnation of an earlier poisoning of former officer of the Russian Federal Security Service Alexander Litvinenko, again in the UK. The Russian authorities also imprisoned opposition politician Alexey Navalny upon his return to Russia in early 2021 and cracked down on his political allies in the run-up to the Russian parliamentary elections in September 2021 still within the context of international normative pressure and support for Navalny.

So the key question is: why does Russia take aggressive stances without regard for the attendant consequences and responses from the West? The reasons can be found in a new degree of (oftentimes exaggerated) self-confidence on the part of authoritarian regimes such as Russia and China, which has spurred them to act assertively, going so far as to interfere in the domestic politics of Western countries via disinformation and funding far-right groups, among others. As Walker and Ludwig have argued, policymakers in democracies grossly underestimated the determination of authoritarian powers and their capacity to alter and reforge international norms and institutions.[2] At the same time, Putin's understanding of the psychology of Western leaders has predisposed him to taking gambles in the expectation that the scope of retaliation would be limited. Volker has pointed out that one of the main Western mistakes that the Russian President exploits includes a default toward de-escalation rather than confronting aggression.[3]

Overall, taking risks in international relations involves a constant calculation of gains and losses conditioned by a wider framework of international dynamics, cultural and psychological factors. Only a clearer comprehension of the motivations behind authoritarian leaders' audacious actions—as provided in Marandici's paper—can inform strategies that feature the right combination of policies of engagement and containment to defend the international liberal order and democracy against authoritarian designs.

---

[2] C. Walker and J. Ludwig, *A Full-Spectrum Response to Sharp Power. The Vulnerabilities and Strengths of Open Societies*, Sharp Power and Democratic Resilience Series (National Endowment for Democracy, 2021).

[3] K. Volker, "How Putin Keeps Winning," *Europe's Edge*, Center for European Policy Analysis, 23 July 2021.

On the Application of Prospect Theory to the Annexation of Crimea: Possibilities for Optimization

Martin Malek

It should be noted at the outset that the application of prospect theory (or: theory of choice under risk) to the events of February and March 2014 in and around the Black Sea peninsula is scientifically justified. Therefore, the comments and objections to be made here refer to details rather than the *big picture*.

The exact "circumstances of Russia's decision to take over Crimea" in February and March 2014 will probably not be revealed for many years (or perhaps never), as the Russian archives containing the relevant documents will not open up for research. The author himself admits the lack of information, but only towards the end of the paper: "public information regarding the deliberation processes in Moscow and Kyiv remains scarce." The ultimately decisive "Russian factor" can thus only be recreated to a limited extent, and for this reason alone all conclusions—based on whatever theory—are provisional.

The author outlines the course of events in and around Crimea in February and March 2014 without illusions. He correctly identifies Russia's "imperial ambitions," its "war of aggression against Ukraine" and a "neo-imperial messianic strain of conservatism on the state apparatus in Russia." He also clearly calls Russia an "aggressor state," and that is what counts—even if many political scientists in Western Europe and North America do not dare to say so openly, fearing accusations of "partisanship," "Russophobia," etc.

The author elaborates that Russian President Vladimir Putin took advantage of a power vacuum in Kyiv after the overthrow of Ukrainian President Viktor Yanukovych on 22 February 2014, who was known for "advancing Moscow's interests in Ukraine." It is also true that Putin's decision to annex Crimea was linked to Yanukovych's inability to remain in power in Kyiv. Undoubtedly, Yanukovych's flight from the capital was also crucial for the Kremlin's decision to launch a hybrid war against Ukraine. But were Russian efforts to keep Yanukovych in power and to weaken the Euromaidan really only "soft"? It can be taken for granted that Russian intelligence services made considerable efforts to prop up Yanukovych. And one cannot exactly speak of a "bloodless territorial conquest" of Crimea, as six people were killed.

Terms like "popular mayor"—pro-Russian-minded people who wanted to seize power on the ground in the Donbass in spring 2014—should definitely be put in inverted commas, which is not the case throughout the author's article (but it is when mentioning Aleksei Chalyi, "popular mayor" of Sevastopol). It is also questionable to refer to Sergei Aksenov as the "newly installed Prime Minister on Crimea" without mentioning how he was "installed": there was a "vote" in the Crimean regional parliament on 27 February 2014 where the quorum of MPs was not reached and members of the Russian armed forces were present in the meeting room with weapons at the ready.

The author mentions "scholarly accounts emphasizing the economic reasons behind the insurgence in the East" of Ukraine. — What "accounts" are these exactly, and what "economic reasons" should be involved here? Russian intelligence services instigated a war in the Donbass in the spring of 2014 in order to separate the region from Ukraine by force; there was no need for any "economic reasons."

The "referendum" in Crimea on 16 March 2014 was "deemed as illegitimate by the international community." —Does this mean that—apart from this opinion—there are other views that could claim to be serious? This "referendum" was forced by the Russian occupying power without any legal basis. To be sure of this, one does not really need the opinion of the "international community," because a look at Ukraine's constitution is sufficient.

Contrary to the position of Thomas Forsberg and Christer Pursiainen, with which the author agrees, the "takeover of Crimea" was at no time "a risky choice": the interim government in Kyiv that took office after Yanukovych's fall, was paralyzed, and military intervention by other, third actors in order to support Ukraine's territorial integrity was never even under discussion. Moreover, the author even mentions below that "Germany and the USA [...] advised Kyiv to act cautiously." This "advice"—and the fact that Kyiv "followed" it (for whatever concrete reasons)—is one of the main reasons for Ukraine's loss of Crimea and Putin's instigation of a war in the Donbas. Washington's and Berlin's actions therefore need to be reflected much more critically than it has been usually done in scientific literature.

The author correctly assesses the roles of the UN and the US: "In the absence of US leadership, the invasion of Ukraine [by Russia] proved that the UN as an organization representing the post-Cold War order failed to provide relief for countries targeted by wars of aggression [...]." It is also true that support for the *"Novorossiia"* project among ethnic Russians in Ukraine was much lower than expected in the Kremlin. It is largely because of this that things did not get even worse in 2014 or that Ukraine did not break up in the first place.

The author states that Russia's decision to invade Ukraine was partially affected by Moscow's assessments of Kyiv's capacity to resist. This, of course, is as true as it is trivial: those who start a war only do so if they believe (or are even certain) that they can actually win it. The reasons the author gives for the weakness of Ukraine as a state in February/March 2014 are basically correct, but possibly incomplete: many people inside and outside Ukraine still believe that it would have been possible to launch an attempt to counter the invading Russian troops by force. However, such an order was either not given in Kyiv or not carried out by the Ukrainian troops in Crimea (on this important point, the accounts differ).

It would be important for the topic and its theoretical coverage to examine the question of when the preparations for the Russian military intervention against Ukraine and the occupation of Crimea actually began. Almost certainly wrong is the claim made by many Western European and North American politicians and political scientists that this was a "short-term," "spontaneous" or even "defensive" decision on Putin's part. But anyone who is even somewhat familiar with military affairs knows that preparations for the deployment of tens of thousands of soldiers and several branches of the armed forces take drastically longer than just a few days. It is therefore much more plausible to assume a run-up time of months, if not years. Some argue that the preparations go back to 2005, i.e., immediately after the victory of the first Maidan in Kyiv (which was also directed against Yanukovych). The author himself mentions such a possibility, but without evaluating it.

Most of those (Aleksandr Dugin etc.) whom the author calls "public intellectuals" are public, but not remotely intellectual.

The author uses the term "West" at several points. However, this is questionable and not suitable as a scientific category of analysis—for many reasons that cannot be discussed in detail here. It must suffice to point out that there are considerably more political differences between various countries that one likes to count as "Western" than between this mythical "West" as a whole on the one hand and Russia and China on the other.

28 September 2021

Follow-up Observations on Prospect Theory, the Annexation of Crimea, and the Second Invasion of Ukraine

Ion Marandici

It was a great honor to receive so many insightful comments from such a distinguished group of scholars. Hence, I would like to thank them for taking the time to provide their thoughts on the applicability of prospect theory to the study of the annexation of Crimea. Written before Russia's 2022 war against Ukraine, my paper relied on prospect theory to clarify the decision-making processes leading up to what is termed here as the first Russian invasion, a multi-stage event including the annexation of Crimea and the war in Donbas. As Rumena Filipova and Mykola Kapitonenko observed, the paper steered away from the grand theoretical debates in international relations, adopting instead a foreign policy analysis (FPA) approach. In doing so, it contributed to the growing academic literature on prospect theory and foreign policy. Besides its theoretical and empirical focus, the article stemmed from the normative belief that Russia's 2014 war of aggression against Ukraine needs to be studied closely in order to understand what drives Kremlin's hostile policy toward its peaceful neighbor.

Consequently, it might be useful to respond to some of the questions raised in the comments, while simultaneously drawing several parallels between the decision-making processes preceding the two invasions. At first sight, both military incursions can be regarded as part of the same long-term aggressive strategy adopted by Russia toward Ukraine. Many observers would probably agree that the 2022 invasion represents a continuation of the war in Donbas, which resulted in a stalemate unresolved for eight years. Still, upon carefully considering the way in which force was used in both cases, the two interventions should be classified as distinct types of conflicts. The annexation and the war in Donbas were instances of hybrid warfare with Russia adopting plausible deniability and denying its military involvement. This caused some ambiguity with regards to the nature of the conflict, which was adeptly exploited by Moscow. One cannot but agree with Martin Malek, who has noted that some Western political scientists, observers, and politicians stubbornly refused to identify Russia as the aggressor state, preferring to describe the annexation as a "spontaneous" and "unique" event, and the war in Donbas as a typical civil war. Often the blame for the lack of progress in peace talks was placed on domestic forces within Ukraine.

By contrast, the 2022 conflict constitutes a war of aggression conducted in a conventional manner, which leaves no doubt about the identity of the invading state, revealing the actual intentions of the power incumbent in Moscow vis-à-vis Ukraine. Since Ukraine posed no threat to Russia, the 2022 war is not a preventive war as Moscow tries to frame it. Without a casus belli, Russia sent into Ukraine circa 150,000 troops, shelled cities, killed civilians, captured nuclear power plants, attacked the capital, and launched airstrikes on military and civilian infrastructure as far West as Yavoriv near the NATO border. The war caused a humanitarian and refugee crisis not seen in Europe since World War II.

Unlike the annexation of Crimea, which caught many scholars and policymakers by surprise, the 2022 war was long expected. Multiple intelligence reports were published prior to its onset with most of them correctly estimating that the likelihood of an invasion was high. Such forecasts prompted Western diplomats to leave Kyiv before the fighting even began. Unlike the 2014 war, the 2022 war did not generate mass euphoria inside Russia. Instead, harsh Western sanctions were imposed with a devastating effect on the economy. The sanctions weakened the authoritarian leader, who used the war as an excuse to crack down on independent media and anti-war protesters. Nor was the 2022 war accompanied by anti-governmental protests in Ukraine, a fact pointing to the consolidation of a civic national identity. Likewise, the goal of the 2022 war went beyond the *Novorossiia* plan, with Moscow now seeking to establish control over the whole of Ukraine by removing the legitimate authorities and installing a puppet-government in

Kyiv led by pro-Moscow loyalists, including some figures who had defected to Russia back in 2014.

Yet, the two wars feature similar characteristics in terms of decision-making dynamics. The same individuals, who annexed Crimea, started the 2022 war using similar pretexts. Much like in 2014, the Duma and the Security Council backed Putin's decision to recognize the secessionist republics of Donbas. After the two breakaway regions signed friendship treaties with Russia, the Federation Council authorized the use of military force, ostensibly to defend them.[1] In reality, this sequence of decisions served to mask the upcoming invasion. The pre-taped Security Council deliberations on the recognition of the two secessionist republics were made public in an effort to present Putin as a consensus-seeking leader, who consulted with other state officials before making a significant foreign policy move.[2] For the sake of accuracy one should note that the Security Council members did not endorse formally the invasion but only the recognition of the two secessionist republics. Similarly, in 2014 and 2022, Russian officials denied the existence of any invasion plans prior to the attack and engaged in nuclear posturing to deter Western involvement once hostilities started.

The published Security Council deliberations also revealed that Russia's leadership drew some misguided lessons from the wars against Georgia and Ukraine. Dmitry Medvedev argued that Russia would survive any type of Western sanctions, which suggests that the West's failed attempts to impose high costs on Russia for its past aggressions have emboldened Putin to initiate another war. Much like in 2014, the absence of disagreements within Putin's inner circle points to what scholars of decision-making call "groupthink," a manifestation of collective irrationality as members of the group

---

[1] Vladimir Putin, Address to the Nation, *President of Russia official website*, 24 February 2022, http://kremlin.ru/events/president/news/67843; Vladimir Putin, Federation Council Request on Authorizing the Use of Military Force beyond Russia's Borders, *President of Russia official website*, 22 February 2022, http://kremlin.ru/events/president/news/67836.

[2] Minutes of the Security Council Meeting, *President of Russia official website*, 21 February 2022, http://kremlin.ru/events/president/news/67825.

become reluctant to express any dissent. In this sense, Rumena Filipova raises an extremely relevant point in her comment, echoed as well by Peter Rutland, concerning the potential of constructivist theories in exploring the intersubjective construction of Ukraine and Ukrainians among the Russian elites. How else would one explain the fact that Putin's advisors and associates refer to Ukraine using the same boilerplate phrases?

Both Russian–Ukrainian wars illustrate why the beliefs of Russia's authoritarian leader matter more than his advisors' worldviews or even the actual developments on the ground. Consequently, debates about Putin's sanity have reappeared in the public sphere. As a side note, sometimes the madman theory serves well the "madman," who in bargaining situations can extract more concessions from the adversary. Other accounts allege that Putin's staff withholds inconvenient information from him out of fear. Still, the head of state is the key official responsible for starting the war, which means that an individual-level theory is needed to explain why Putin moved from the domain of gains to the domain of losses again. It is thus quite plausible that in 2021–2022 Putin perceived that he was in the domain of losses and launched the invasion to prevent Ukraine from acceding to NATO and the EU. After some initial gains, the strong Ukrainian resistance combined with Russia's blunders may have pushed Putin back into the domain of losses, which then resulted in a second phase of the war marked by reckless behavior such as the destruction of the port-city of Mariupol, the use of hypersonic missiles, and open nuclear threats. These are, of course, predictions derived from prospect theory. Still, I agree with Peter Rutland, Tor Bukkvoll, and Mykola Kapitonenko on the need to develop appropriate methods to identify what constitutes the status quo from the perspective of the decision-maker. Despite the extensive research on the topic, it seems that scholars largely rely on their judgement and knowledge of the case when identifying deviations from the reference point.

Distinguishing the reference point is further complicated by imperial legacies. If one thinks of post-imperial revanchism as the default mode of thinking in the Kremlin, one could argue that in a broader sense Putin will constantly perceive himself in the domain of losses, regretting the Soviet demise and formulating narratives inspired by the tsarist past to justify military campaigns against weaker states. In annexing parts of neighboring countries populated by Russian speakers, complaining about Russia being wronged at the end of the Cold War, and expressing nostalgia for an imagined glorious past, Putin bears resemblance to resentful fascist leaders, who similarly took over countries invoking nationalist themes, expressed nostalgia for defunct empires, and lamented that their countries had been abused and deceived by other major powers. Such analogies proliferate in 2022. If one adds the fact that Putin refuses to recognize and respect Ukrainians as an equal nation, rejects Ukraine's borders as artificial, constantly refers to Russian exceptionalism, and is building a regime centered on a cult of personality praising masculinity, traditional values, and religious messianism, then the affinities of his regime with the ideology of the far-right becomes evident.[3]

Another striking aspect pertains to the similarity of the frames used to present the wars to the Russian public. The repetition of the same discursive frames over time suggests that after Crimea's annexation, a symbolic victory of sorts, Putin, failing to influence Ukrainian politics via proxy parties, returned to the domain of losses. Specifically, even though Putin emphasized NATO's enlargement as a key issue in 2022, he articulated again the misleading claims about a "cultural genocide" against Russian speakers and the need "to denazify" the country, portraying it as an anti-Russian Western-backed project created by the Bolsheviks.[4] Both in 2014 and 2022, Putin referred to the Russian speakers of Ukraine as an oppressed group waiting "to be liberated." His essay published in mid-2021 illustrated his obsessive preoccupation with

---

[3] The analogy between Putin's Russia and Nazi Germany has sparked a vigorous academic debate. For diverging views on the matter see Timothy Snyder, *The Road to Unfreedom: Russia, Europe, America* (Tim Duggan Books, 2018); Marlene Laruelle, *Is Russia Fascist? Unraveling Propaganda East and West* (Cornell University Press, 2021); and Marcel van Herpen, *Putinism: The Slow Rise of a Radical Right Regime in Russia* (Palgrave Macmillan, 2013).
[4] Vladimir Putin, Address to the Nation, *President of Russia official website*, 24 February 2022, http://kremlin.ru/events/president/news/67843.

"losing Ukraine" and demonstrating "the cultural unity" of the two nations.[5] Since such expectations preceding both wars proved to be wrong and far from reality, one natural question to ask is: why do Putin's distorted beliefs about Ukrainian identity persist over time? Shouldn't such beliefs change in light of the robust resistance mounted by Ukrainians in 2014 and 2022? Besides cognitive dissonance as a potential explanation, another one may be age. An ageing Putin is unlikely to change his core beliefs about the world.

Then, there are some empirical aspects mentioned by commentators that need to be clarified. First, in the original paper, Yanukovych was presented as a politician defending Russia's interests in Ukraine. I agree with Bukkvoll, Kapitonenko, and Rutland, who note that Yanukovych did not have a consistent pro-Russian stance, maneuvering between the EU and Russia. While Yanukovych did indeed oscillate between West and East, during the crisis he sided with Russia, receiving advice from Putin on how to deal with the demonstrators. Moreover, the Kremlin extracted the former president from Ukraine via a special aerial operation, offering him and his associates a safe harbor to form a government-in-exile of sorts.[6]

Second, two remarks are in order on the issue of advance planning. I agree with Malek's and Bukkvoll's contention that the military preparations for annexation may have started months before the political decision was made. This, however, raises another problem. Prospect theory is generally applicable to explain decision-making in crisis situations marked by high uncertainty and risk. If the military component of the annexation plan was rehearsed well in advance, then the event may not have been perceived as a risky choice after all. Such a redefinition of the crisis situation would force us to come up with an alternative identification of the reference point. One might thus ask: did the military advance planning begin

---

[5] Vladimir Putin, Essay on the Unity of Russians and Ukrainians, *President of Russia official website*, 12 July 2021, http://kremlin.ru/events/president/news/66181.
[6] "Ex-PM Azarov, In Moscow, Proclaims 'Salvation Committee' For Ukraine," Radio Free Europe, 3 August 2015, https://www.rferl.org/a/ukraine-ex-pm-azarov-forms-salvation-committee/27167032.html.

in reaction to an event preceding the Euromaidan or after? My point on planning referred narrowly to the discrepancy between the official Russian timeline and the inconvenient facts casting doubt on the narrative that the plan to annex Crimea was primarily designed in response to Yanukovych's departure from Kyiv. As pointed out in the article, Ukrainian officials accessed intelligence documenting three unsuccessful attempts to separate Crimea from Ukraine after the Orange Revolution. Moreover, the protracted military exercises along Ukraine's borders prior and during the annexation were perceived by decision-makers in Kyiv as preparations for a full-scale invasion much like the lengthy build-up along Ukraine's borders in 2021–2022. This could mean that Putin might have intended to launch a full-scale invasion back in 2014 to restore Yanukovych but pulled back only to intervene massively at Ilovaisk and Debaltseve, where the Ukrainian army began gaining ground against the rebels. In the absence of credible accounts from Putin's inner circle, the scenario of a Russian occupation of the entire country in 2014 was not even contemplated in this article as it was deemed too risky and brazen. However, with the benefit of hindsight, a full-scale invasion of Ukraine back in 2014 appears as a plausible development.

A minor point of disagreement concerns Bukkvoll's suggestion that neither Putin nor Surkov were serious about *Novorossiia* and only used such rhetoric to radicalize the secessionist groups. This is a key point that requires a longer discussion. If one assumes that Putin and Surkov were true believers, ideologically committed to the *Novorossiia* plan, then prospect theory and rational utility maximizing models are inapplicable in this case as pursuing ideological goals when faced with extremely adverse conditions can be viewed as a sign of fanaticism rather than rational calculus. While Kremlin officials employ narratives in a strategic manner, the wars against Ukraine point to both Putin and Surkov displaying a neo-imperial-nationalist mindset. Driven by nationalist imaginings of the nation, Putin expected in 2014 and 2022 to garner the Russian-speakers' support for the break-up of Ukraine into separatist republics in

Kharkiv, Dnipropetrovsk, Kherson, and Odessa.⁷ Such attempts succeeded only in Crimea, Donetsk, and Lugansk and failed elsewhere.

Along similar lines, the role of local militant secessionist groups should not be downplayed. One should keep in mind that the *Novorossiia* Movement led by Pavel Gubarev transformed into a party in the so-called Donetsk People's Republic, advocating continuously for its territorial expansion. The movement included radical figures such as Andrei Purgin, who as early as 2005 was propagating the idea of secession. Bukkvoll's assessment may be accurate in the sense that Putin and Surkov were not as extreme as Gubarev, Purgin, and other local activists, who were anyway removed from their positions of power in Donetsk precisely due to their conflicts with the moderate factions backed by the Kremlin. In this sense, Surkov's involvement in the political life of Donbas is well-documented, as is his opposition to federalization, which he regarded as a shameful defeat of the secessionist cause.⁸ His accession to the party of Zakhar Prilepin, who fought alongside the Donbas insurgents, may further indicate that Surkov's views were too radical for Kremlin's changing agenda after Zelensky's victory. By contrast, Surkov's successor, Dmitrii Kozak, a long-time friend of Putin, was the author of the 2003 federalization plan for Moldova and could have added some value to the relaunched negotiations on Donbas.

---

7 In 2022, Russia attempted the creation of the Kherson People's Republic. For the failure of separatism in Kharkiv and Dnipropetrovsk in 2014–2015, see Quentin Buckholz, "The Dogs That Didn't Bark: Elite Preferences and the Failure of Separatism in Kharkiv and Dnipropetrovsk," *Problems of Post-Communism* 66:3 (2019): 151–60. On the attempt to set up a Bessarabian Republic see Thomas de Waal and Balazs Jarabik, "Bessarabia's Hopes and fear on Ukraine's Edge," *Carnegie Europe*, 24 May 2018, https://carnegieeurope.eu/2018/05/24/bessarabia-s-hopes-and-fears-on-ukraine-s-edge-pub-76445.

8 Sanshiro Hosaka, "Welcome to Surkov's Theater: Russian Political Technology in the Donbas War," *Nationalities Papers* 47(5) (2019): 750–73. doi:10.1017/nps.2019.70); and Aya Shandra and Robert Seely, "The Surkov Leaks: The Inner Workings of Russia's Hybrid War in Ukraine," *Occasional Papers Series*, Royal United Services Institute (2019), https://static.rusi.org/201907_op_surkov_leaks_web_final.pdf.

Finally, Rumena Filipova posed a crucial question worth returning to as it will remain relevant for some time: "Why does Russia take aggressive stances without regard for the attendant consequences and responses from the West?" The answers will probably differ depending on what level of analysis one focuses on. To explain Moscow's behavior, my article adopted the FPA approach and prospect theory. In doing so, the proposed account relegated systemic factors such as the global power transition and balance of power considerations in Europe to scholars working within the IR field. Yet, system-level causes matter as well. As Paul D'Anieri has pertinently observed, Russia's desire to achieve great power status seems incompatible with Ukraine's aspiration to remain democratic and sovereign and to "return to Europe."[9] This situation is eerily reminiscent of the Cold War Brezhnev Doctrine, which stipulated that the USSR's satellite-states in Eastern Europe could not enjoy full sovereignty in running their foreign and military affairs. Deviations were met with brute force. Thus, the Prague Spring ended with the Soviet occupation of the country.

As we know, neorealist scholars would also put much emphasis on the systemic level and argue that NATO's enlargement was perceived by Russia as a threat, which then attacked Ukraine to prevent it from joining the alliance. Neorealist narratives may point to other system-level processes such as the American decision to end the costly wars in the Middle East as well as the strategic repositioning of the US military forces to project power more effectively in the Indo-Pacific region.[10] Such perspectives discount Ukraine as an inevitable victim of great power politics, lacking any agency. However, the Ukrainian–Russian war of 2022 may prove neorealists wrong as the Russian army faces a highly motivated medium-sized nation acting in self-defence—a scenario unforeseen by both Kremlin and Western officials alike.

---

[9] For an eclectic perspective see Paul D'Anieri, *Ukraine and Russia: From Civilized Divorce to Uncivil War* (Cambridge University Press, 2019).

[10] See Biden Administration, Indo-Pacific Strategy of the United States, *White House official website*, February 2022, https://www.whitehouse.gov/wp-content/uploads/2022/02/U.S.-Indo-Pacific-Strategy.pdf.

ARTICLES

ARTICLES

Mikhail Putin (1894-1969) and Socialist Competition: Exploring a Neglected Branch of the Putin Family Tree*

Chris Monday

Abstract: *This article examines the biography of Mikhail Eliseevich Putin (1894-1969) and investigates the possibility that he may have been related to Russian President Vladimir Vladimirovich Putin. Mikhail Putin was a peasant turned factory worker, a champion wrestler who also played an important role in promoting "socialist competition," a key institution of Stalinist modernization. While he is largely forgotten today, in the late Soviet period he was a prominent and well-connected figure whose life was celebrated on the pages of the Brezhnev-era press. Early in Vladimir Putin's political career, some commentators claimed that the two men may have been related, but as public discussion of Vladimir Putin's biography has become more tightly controlled, references to a connection between the two men have apparently been "cleansed." While solid evidence is lacking, the existing circumstantial evidence makes the possibility of this familial connection worth considering. This article sets out the existing evidence and investigates the possibility that the trajectory of Vladimir Putin's early life and career may have been shaped by privilege arising out of a kin relationship to this former Soviet icon. An exploration of Mikhail Putin's biography also sheds light on aspects of Sovietization, urbanization, and modernization during his lifetime.*

---

*   The author wishes to thank Julie Fedor, Andreas Umland, Mykhailo Minakov, the anonymous reviewers, Jason Crouthamel, Tatiana Zhdanok, the Research Laboratory at the Russian, East European, and Eurasian Center (University of Illinois), and the National Library of Russia.

Vladimir Putin is often portrayed as a scrappy kid from an underprivileged background whose judo skills allowed him to become a lone-wolf master operative.[1] At the same time, there is much about his biography which remains obscure. In this article, I question the standard account of Putin's early life by examining the possibility that he may have benefited from a familial connection to a quite prominent member of the Soviet elite, Mikhail Eliseevich Putin (1894–1969). Today Mikhail Putin is a largely forgotten figure. In his time, he was a Soviet icon, "a name familiar to all Soviets,"[2] a man who played an important role in establishing "socialist competition," a crucial institution for Stalinist modernization whereby workers were encouraged to contend for social recognition instead of wages, and which was designed to help adapt peasants to factory life.

As Fiona Hill and Clifford Gaddy pointed out in 2015, there is a noticeable lack of reliable information on Vladimir Putin's biography, and the information that is available on his life has "declined over time. Above all, the information that does emerge has been increasingly controlled and manipulated... after 15 years, we remain ignorant of some of the most basic facts about a man who is arguably the most powerful individual in the world."[3] Western research on Vladimir Putin's biography and worldview has been hampered by reliance on "inside" sources. Often they throw out red herrings to purposely mislead, as seen in the notorious Steele dossier. These insiders, moreover, are too scared for their safety, and/or too removed from the echelons of power, to provide reliable information. Frequently, they are beholden to the traditions of the *intelligentsia* which viewed the secret police as a macabre, prime

---

[1] Fiona Hill, "The One-Man Show the West Doesn't Understand," *Bulletin*, 7 December 2020, https://thebulletin.org/premium/2020-12/putin-the-one-man-show-the-west-doesnt-understand/; and Steven Lee Myers, *The New Tsar: The Rise and Reign of Vladimir Putin* (Doubleday, 2015). All URLs cited in this article were accessible on 30 July 2021.

[2] This phrase is found in many Soviet-era texts on Mikhail Putin, for example: Piotr Pospelov, *Istoriia Kommunisticheskoi partii Sovetskogo Soiuza* (Politizdat, 1965), vol. 4, part 1, 595; and "Putin," *Pravda*, no. 64, 5 March 1969, 1–2.

[3] Fiona Hill and Clifford Gaddy, *Mr. Putin: Operative in the Kremlin* (Brookings Institution Press, 2015), 6–7.

mover.⁴ Putin is thus depicted as a sinister, deep-state mastermind. The real man, in contrast, especially in off-the-cuff performances, often comes across as unsure. Another problem with relying on Russian insiders is their ingrained penchant for following unspoken "understandings," such as never discussing elite families.⁵

Researchers, moreover, have been limited in what they can publish on Putin: Even the blandest of biographies have to be cleared by Kremlin handlers.⁶ The Putin foundation legend, *First Person* (2000), continues to serve as an analytic touchstone.⁷ In a 2020 interview, one of its authors, Andrei Kolesnikov, could not say whether Putin had re-married: "I honestly don't know, and it's better not to know."⁸ Access to archival material on Putin ancestry is restricted.⁹ Some researchers apparently fear writing even on ancient kin, and rely on material provided by the Kremlin.¹⁰ The main source on Putin's genealogy is Aleksandr Putin, a cousin.¹¹

---

4   Michael Kimmage and Matthew Rojansky, "The Problem with Putinology," *New Republic*, 24 July 2020, https://newrepublic.com/article/158616/problem-putinology.
5   Anna Nemtsova, "Putin Rumors Run Wild as He Shrouds Himself in Secrecy," *Daily Beast*, 28 December 2020, https://www.thedailybeast.com/alleged-nashville-bomber-anthony-quinn-warner-hated-cops-and-loved-weed-former-co-worker?ref=scroll.
6   Author's conversations with Russians who have published on Putin, 2007–2011. Notoriously, journalist Oleg Blotskii wrote what was meant as a hagiography of Putin in 2001. His book, *Istoriia zhizni*, has all but disappeared and the author has since faced legal problems; see "Na avtora biografii Putina zaveli ugolovnoe delo," *Vedomosti*, 13 October 2017, https://www.vedomosti.ru/politics/news/2017/10/13/737806-biografii-putina-ugolovnoe.
7   Nataliia Gevorkian, Natal'ia Timakova, and Andrei Kolesnikov, *Ot pervogo litsa* (Vagrius, 2000).
8   Yurii Dud', "Andrei Kolesnikov, letopisets Putina," *vDud'*, 18 February 2020, https://www.youtube.com/watch?v=aiOcgApMVcY.
9   Ekaterina Sazhneva, "Semeinye tainy Putina," *Moskovskii komsomolets*, 5 October 2017, https://www.mk.ru/social/2017/10/05/semeynye-tayny-putina-rodstvennik-prezidenta-raskryl-istoriyu-roda.html.
10 See for example comments by genealogical researcher Sergei Kotel'nikov; "Pervyi predok Putina," *Komsomol'skaia pravda (Kazan')*, 18 July 2002, https://www.kazan.kp.ru/daily/22592/18989/.
11 Some journalists have hinted that Aleksandr Putin has used his name to get ahead in business; Aleksandr Luchek, "Vsia pravda o rode Putinykh," *Kommersant'*, 7 October 2002, https://www.kommersant.ru/doc/344728; and Maria Podtserob, "Kak naniat' rodstvennika Putina v gendirektory," *Vedomosti*,

Thus it is not surprising that we can find little discussion in the Russian sources on the topic of Vladimir's possible relationship to Mikhail Putin. There have been occasional articles speculating on this, but some of these seem to have subsequently been taken down.[12] In his 2002 Putin genealogy, Aleksandr Putin noted that work was underway to ascertain the possibility of a kinship relation between Mikhail Putin and the "Pominovo Putins,"[13] that is, Vladimir Putin's father's branch of the family, but this phrase does not appear in the 2015 edition (which does however include several pages on Mikhail Eliseevich).[14] Latvian-Russian politician and Member of the European Parliament Tatjana Ždanoka (Tat'iana Zhdanok), who is herself related to Mikhail Putin by marriage, is one informed source who has shared with the author a detailed account of her knowledge of Mikhail Putin, including family photos, and whose account squares with the facts presented in this paper.[15]

---

28 March 2018, https://www.vedomosti.ru/management/articles/2018/03/28/755117-nanyat-rodstvennika-putina.

[12] The author has searched for online information about Mikhail Putin since 2014 and has noticed that articles on him seem to disappear. One exception, still available at time of writing, is Sergei Achil'diev's article, which argues that it seems plausible that the two men were related; Sergei Achil'diev, "Mikhail Putin. Moral'nyi stimul," *Mozgokratiia*, 18 March 2019, https://mozgokratia.ru/2019/03/mihail-putin-moralnyj-stimul/ (accessed 9 June 2022). Sometimes the topic pops up in articles on the local or regional history of Tver', such as one article that notes the fact that, "In several sources we find mention of a quite famous ancestor of the Russian president, Mikhail Eliseevich Putin"; "Kalininskii raion: istorii tverskoi Rublevki," *Krai spravedlivosti*, 10 November 2017, https://ks-region69.com/statiianalitika/46598-kalininskij-rajon-istoriya-tverskoj-rublyovki.

[13] "Mikhail Eliseevich Putin, ch'ia rodstvennaia sviaz' s pominovskimi Putinymi ustanavlivaetsia [...]"; Aleksandr Putin, *Rod Putinykh* (Syktyvkar: Sever, 2001), 174.

[14] Mikhail Putin is listed here in the section titled "Izvestnye odnofamil'tsy"; Aleksandr Putin, *Rod prezidenta V.V. Putina. Materialy issledovaniia 1986–2002* (Dashkov i Ko, 2015), 247–50. It is of course possible that the text in question was removed once the existence of a kinship relation was definitively ruled out.

[15] In a 2007 interview, Zhdanok said: "My mother's cousin was named Mariia. She was married to Mikhail Eliseevich Putin. He was from the same village, where all Putin's ancestors came from... My mother also knew well both Putin's grandfather and their son, Vladimir Putin's father... After my parents left Leningrad, my mother kept up a correspondence with her cousin. And the latter told her in one of her letters that the Putins had a new grandchild, Volodia";

The lack of substantial discussion on the topic may arguably be read as telling in itself. Sherlock Holmes concluded that the remarkable part of his investigation was what did *not* happen; the hound did not bark. It is possible that this is not a matter that will ever be satisfactorily resolved, partly because the genealogy of any peasant family will always be a murky affair.[16] Nevertheless, in this paper I set out to discover what we can learn about Mikhail Putin and his possible relationship to the current President of Russia. I utilize a broad range of sources, including pre-revolutionary, Soviet, and post-Soviet historiography, newspapers, propaganda tracts, popular accounts, reminiscences, government documents, interviews, and site visits, to reconstruct the life and times of the man behind the legend. To understand Mikhail Putin and disentangle fact from fiction, we must also examine the movement he was associated with: socialist competition. To this end, I draw upon specialized Soviet journals, Soviet and Russian dissertations, North Korean and Ukrainian propaganda as well as western intelligence reports, to analyze the scope of socialist competition. On the Putin family, many sources provide nothing more than talltales, hagiography, and out-right falsification. Nonetheless, other sources provide reliable information: telephone directories; author interviews; published archival material, including several work questionnaires completed by Mikhail Putin and internal intelligence reports produced during the Stalinist years; articles published in the factory newspaper *Krasnovyborzhets* and material from the Krasnovyborzhets Museum (which was aimed primarily at fellow workers and would therefore need to provide at the least plausible propaganda); off-the-cuff speeches by Mikhail Putin given to inspire the youth; remembrances published during the period from 1980 to 1990 when Putin and "socialist competition" meant little; archive/interview-based studies produced by professional Soviet

---

Tatiana Zhdanok, cited in Andrei Mamykin, "Teorema Zhdanok," *Rus.tvnet.lv*, 21 January 2007, https://rus.tvnet.lv/6079024/teorema-zhdanok.

[16] Russian peasants under serfdom did not use last names, for example, and village elders were addressed as "uncle" or "aunt." Disruptions brought by migration, famine, and war further complicate matters. At the same time, in this context, an extended kin-network also took on additional importance.

historians; and non-official remembrances from people disconnected from one another in space and time. Thus some details remain murky, but the broad narrative is clear.

This article will further our understanding of Putinism by going beyond propaganda to uncover underlying social structures. One key component of social governance, scrutinized by Max Weber, is family.[17] Communism, advancing the hegemony of the proletariat, brutally eradicated competing social institutions: all that was left to bind society together was family.[18] The Putin-mythos has obscured Russia's princeling system. The first section discusses how the family institution allowed peasants, such as the Putins, to work in the city while maintaining roots in the village during the period 1850 to 1914. The second section shows how Mikhail Putin, living at the margins of village and city life, marshalled peasant skills to become a professional wrestler. The next argues that the factory where Mikhail worked, Red Vyborzhets in St Petersburg, was crucial to the Bolshevik drive to power, but was torn between the peasantry and the proletariat. The following section, focusing on Stalinist industrialization (1928–34), shows how the Bolsheviks, realizing that Russia was far from Marxist ideals, depended on authoritative half-proletarians, such as the former wrestler Mikhail Putin, to lead socialist competitions, thereby appealing to semi-literate workers through sports imagery. The article contends that while Soviet chieftains, such as Sergei Kirov, crafted the socialist competition program, much was initiated from below, by Mikhail Putin and other self-interested workers. The next section shows how Mikhail Putin became a Soviet legend. The article speculates that Mikhail may have exerted a key influence on Vladimir's upbringing, and that the existence of a kin relationship between the two men would help

---

[17] Max Weber, *Economy and Society* (University of California Press, 1968), 356–68.
[18] Soviet totalitarianism threatened all institutions, including the family, as seen by the "model son," Pavlik Morozov. This changed over time. As in North Korea and China, the Soviets began to see the family as a bulwark of the regime; see Chris Monday, "Family Rule and the Post-Marxist State Family Rule and the Post-Marxist State," in *Ideology After Union: Political Doctrines, Discourses, and Debates in Post-Soviet Societies*, eds. Mykhailo Minakov and Alexander Etkind (*ibidem* Verlag, 2020), 155–234.

to explain certain puzzles linked to Putin's biography. I speculate that it may well have been Mikhail who got young Vova hooked on sports; Mikhail may even have launched his KGB career. As Vladimir himself has acknowledged, personal connections provided the standard route into the Soviet secret service.[19]

Half-Proletarians

This section describes the peculiar way Russian peasants, such as the Putins, adapted to city life during the period from 1850 to 1914. According to Aleksandr Putin, the Putins, who today number around 3000, all hail from Tver, a bucolic province that lies between Moscow and St. Petersburg.[20] During the Mongol period, Tver rivaled Moscow, but soon declined: for Soviet Russians, the city was perhaps best known as the home of crooner Mikhail Krug (1962–2002). Tver documents mention a certain Faddei Putin in 1682 living in Bordino, a patrimony-estate (*votchina*) of boyarina Domna Bogdanova.[21] Other Putins inhabited the nearby *votchinas* of Turgenovo and Pominovo, owned by Ivan Romanov, an adviser to Tsar Mikhail. Ravaged during the Time of Troubles, only a handful of households (*dvory*) ever inhabited these villages which were later owned by relatives of Count Apraksin.[22] Thus by end of the

---

[19] Putin said: "Of course, I wanted to serve in intelligence which was considered the white-collar work of the secret service. Many exploited their connections [Ochen' mnogo blatnikov bylo], of course. Unfortunately, that's how it was"; Gevorkian *et al.*, *Ot pervogo litsa*, 47. This interview comes from the year 2000 at a time when Putin lacked self-confidence and poise. At the very least, this quote highlights the rampant nepotism of those times and that this issue was on Putin's mind when first presenting himself to the public.

[20] Aleksandr Putin, *Rod prezidenta V.V. Putina*, 235–50. Vladimir Putin told the director Nikita Mikhalkov (a scion of one of Russia's most elite families), "I'm not joking. All my ancestors, from the 16th century, were peasants who lived in two or three villages in Tver: they all attended the same church"; *Vesti nedeli*, 13 June 2022, https://smotrim.ru/video/2425115.

[21] Iaroslav Leont'ev, "Vse my nemnozhko Rurikovichi," *Novaia gazeta*, 7 October 2002, https://novayagazeta.ru/articles/2002/10/07/13560-vse-my-nemnozhko-ryurikovichi.

[22] "Tverskie korni Vladimira Putina," official website of the Turginovskoe rural settlement, Kalininskii district, Tverskaia' oblast', 5 October 2012, https://turginovosp.ru/selo-turginovo.html. According to one possible interpretation, the

nineteenth century, there were 226 males and 264 females living in Turgenevo.[23] The climate in Tver was relatively harsh so that agriculture demanded intense work, 125 days out of a year. Towards the beginning of the twentieth century, inefficient peasant communes (*obshchina*) still harvested the vast majority of the land in this former citadel of serfdom.[24] During the long, non-farming seasons, the men would make their way to St. Petersburg to earn cash.[25]

In the mid-nineteenth century, French sociologist Frédéric Le Play produced a detailed study of Russian peasant life. In his examination of Russian migrants, Le Play argued that family bonds connected village to city. Village life revolved around ritualized drinking, fighting, weddings, and barn-raising. Children began productive work by age seven, gathering berries or making sandals *(lapti)*. By ten, they would take animals to pasture and soon engaged in serious farm work.[26] At eighteen, youths would have to pay the *obrok*, lordly tithe, and thus would go to the cities to earn cash. Extended family enabled them to travel long distances. During springtime, when the ice thawed, they would embark, traveling in groups of twenty. Expenses were controlled by an elder selected by

---

name "Putin" suggests that his people were administrators *(putniki)* for the Boyar's property. "An income-producing property was called put' and the officer in charge of it [...] putnik"; Richard Pipes, *Russia under the Old Regime* (Penguin Books, 1974), 45.

[23] N. A. Troinitskii, *Naselennye mesta Rossiiskoi imperii v 500 i bolee zhitelei* (Obshchestvennaia pol'za, 1905), 183. This Putin homeland, which was under Nazi occupation, today has neither factories, nor fast food, only a lone war memorial.

[24] Boris Mironov, *Upravlenie etnicheskim mnogoobraziem Rossiiskoi imperii* (Bulanin, 2017), 79.

[25] On the family structure and migrant workers, see: Boris Mironov, *Sotsial'naia istoriia Rossii perioda imperii* (Bulanin, 2000), vol. 1, 219–359; N. M. Druzhinin, *Russkaia derevnia na perelome. 1861-1880* (Nauka, 1978); J. Bradley, *Muzhik and Muscovite: Urbanization in Late Imperial Russia* (University of California Press, 1985); and T. Dennison, "Household Structure and Family Economy," *Cambridge Studies in Economic History* (Cambridge University Press), vol. 2: 50–92.

[26] Frédéric Le Play, *Les ouvriers européens*, vol. 2, Les ouvriers de l'Orient (Tours: A. Mame, 1879), 196; and Chris Monday, "Le Ple v Rossii," *Voprosy statistiki* 12 (1999): 65–82.

the family as the most trustworthy. On return, earnings were handed to this elder, who would guard the funds in his *sunduk* (trunk). The amount a villager could bring back would determine the possibility of making an advantageous marriage. After seven years of apprenticing under older siblings, the migrant workers would assume higher-paying jobs, as coachman, mason, or cook. Skilled workers typically would spend around 19months in Saint Petersburg and then, every two years, return to the village for a spell of several months. The *artel* complemented the family in the city by allocating work, organizing housing, and distributing wages. According to Le Play:

> In Russia, each member of the working class is surrounded, throughout his life, by a large family, with which he lives in a regime of absolute community, sheltered from all unfortunate eventualities. Emigrant workers find themselves for the first time deprived of this protection, so that they rush to join voluntary associations, *Artèles*.[27]

By age 36, the successful migrant-worker would return to the village to assume the role of elder. According to Le Play, the family structure enforced habits of sobriety: even far from the paternal eye, the peasant youth scrupulously saved their money. Le Play favorably compared this practice to the profligate French peasant migrants.[28]

Le Play's notion that the peasant family formed a kind of autonomous economy was shared by the Populists.[29] Migration *(otkhozhie promysly)* was also studied by Vladimir Lenin who wanted to demonstrate the disintegration of the peasantry. Lenin found that many peasants in Tver were entering the bourgeoisie. They were building hothouses, planting crops (potatoes and flax) for commercial production, and hiring workers.[30] Nonetheless, Lenin was mistaken: neither Russian capitalism, nor the Bolshevik Revolution, ultimately destroyed the family: the next section will

---

[27] Le Play, *Les ouvriers européens*, 217–18.
[28] Ibid., 195–218.
[29] Chris Monday, "An Intellectual's Revolt against the Sun: Chayanov and Bragin's Albidum," *Russian History* 42(3) (2015): 304–42.
[30] Vladimir Lenin, *The Development of Capitalism in Russia* [1899] (Foreign Languages, 1956), 118, 235, 278.

show how the history of the Putin clan vindicates Le Play's position that the family-based economic unit created a path to modernity.

Mikhail Putin's Leningrad

The Putin men, starting with Ivan Petrovich (1845–1918), the President's paternal great-grandfather, were migrant workers in the manner outlined by Le Play. Establishing connections in the city, Ivan was followed by Spiridon, the President's grandfather, and Mikhail Eliseevich, respectively. The Putin women, for the most part, stayed in Tver, serving as anchoring matriarchs, for example, Spiridon's sister Paraskeva Ivanovna (1884–1969), Zinoviia Ivanovna (1845–1940), Matrena Ivanovich (1825–1907), and Olga Ivanovna, Vladimir's grandmother (1886–1976). As with many Russian families, "home" remained the village; during times of hardships the Putins returned to Pominovo.[31] A family legend passed from generation to generation held that the smallpox outbreak of 1771 had wiped out all the Putin line except a 13-year-old, Alesha, who was quickly married off so that he could receive a land-allotment.[32]

Another Putin to migrate from Tver to the cities was Mikhail (1894–1969). His father, Eliseev, was a switchman for the Nikolaivskii Railroad at the Bezhetsk Station in Tver, about 140 km from Pominovo. The train stop, a ten-hour ride from St. Petersburg, remains a humble outpost. Between Turgenevo and Bezhetsk, there was a post office, a two-year government school, and a bazaar. Traders would bring in small-scale household items while peasant would carry oats, potatoes, flax, and firewood.[33] Young Misha would thus have come into contact with other Putins.[34] Thanks to his father's stable job, he would have been well-fed during the brutal

---

[31] Gevorkian et al., *Ot pervogo litsa*, 8.
[32] Sazhneva, "Semeinye tainy."
[33] K. I. Vorob'ev, *Statistiko-ekonomicheskoe izsledovanie gruntovykh dorog Tverskoi guberni n. Tver* (Gub. Zemstvo, 1911), 93.
[34] Viktor Senin, "Budem sorevnovat'sia!," *Neva* 1 (1983): 177; I. Kuz'min, "Pervyi dogovor," *Molodoi kommunist* 3 (1979): 50; Putin, *Rod prezidenta*, 248; Tat'iana Zhdanok, cited in Andrei Mamykin, "Teorema Zhdanok," *Rus.tvnet.lv*, 21 January 2007, https://rus.tvnet.lv/6079024/teorema-zhdanok.

famine years of the 1890s. Moreover, Misha, meeting travelers from various walk of life, became socially mature.

With nine siblings, Misha started work by age nine. He would help his father who would show him how to switch the tracks, warning that a slight mistake could spell prison.[35] Along the way, Misha received a few years of elementary education *(nizhnee obrazovanie)*.[36] At twelve, he began traveling to St. Petersburg, lodging with relations.[37] Perhaps he would have stayed with Vladimir's grandfather, Spiridon, on Gorokhovo Street.[38] Born in Pominovo, at age sixteen, Spiridon apprenticed under a relative as a cook at the swanky Astoria.[39] Thanks to Spiridon, Misha became a bus-boy at the cafe of Jean Pierre Cubat, a "cuisinier des tsars."[40] Located near today's Herzen University, the restaurant "Cubat," *(Kiube)* boasting of one of the city's first electric signs, was a see-and-be-seen restaurant.[41] Its success depended on young men like

---

[35] Senin, "Budem sorevnovat'sia!", 177; "Putin," *Tsvetnye Metally* 7 (1982): 117; and Kuz'min, "Pervyi dogovor," 50.

[36] S. I. Tiul'panov (ed.), *Industrializatsiia Severo-Zapadnogo Raiona v gody Pervoi Piatiletki* (Izdatel'stvo Leningradskogo universiteta, 1967), 386; and Kuz'min, "Pervyi dogovor."

[37] Putin loved recounting his life but was never clear on details: he claimed to have started working at age 7, 9, 14, and 17; N. S. Zelov, "Pervye kavalery ordena," *Sovetskie arkhivy* 3 (1970), 5; and *Pravda*, 1969, 1.

[38] Too young to live on his own, it seems likely that Mikhail may have bunked with Spiridon as was typical for peasant families of the time. They worked a few minutes from one another at prestigious restaurants. Spiridon and Mikhail remained close; Zhdanok, cited "Teorema Zhdanok." Nikolai Petrovich Putin, working as a tailor on Gorokhov Street 58, gave shelter to his nephew, Spiridon. Throughout the years, several Putins and other Pominovo boys would live at this appartment working at local restaurants; Aleksandr Putin, *Rod Prezidenta Putina* (Daskova, 2013),31, 33, 63, 65, 69.

[39] Later, Spiridon became a cook for Stalin; Leont'ev "Vse my nemnozhko Rurikovichi"; Gevorkian *et al.*, *Ot pervogo litsa*, 7; Ol'ga Vandysheva, "Ded Putina kormil zhenu Lenina, mat' Khrushcheva i lichno tov. Stalina," *Komsomol'skaia pravda*, 10 November 2000, https://flb.ru/info/4728.html; and Oleg Blotskii, *Vladimir Putin. Istoriia zhizni* (Mezhdunarodnye otnosheniia, 2001), 36–38.

[40] Kuz'min, "Pervyi dogovor," 50; and Aleksandr Putin, *Rod prezidenta V. V. Putina*, 248.

[41] "Dokhodnyi dom M. F. Ruadze," *City Walls: Arkhitekturnyi sait Peterburga*, 2021, https://www.citywalls.ru/house22991.html.

Mikhail Putin who guaranteed it was "the only restaurant of that type where a respectable lady could go without a chaperone."[42] Mikhail recounted how he "tended to the samovars and lanterns, and performed errands for the gentlemen."[43] There he may have witnessed famous scenes such as on 20 June 1906, when Kadet Party leader Pavel Miliukov had a quiet word with Tsarist right-hand Dmitri Trepov about forming a liberal-leaning Duma.[44]

For Europeans, the city remained "rustic, swarmed by hordes of bearded men."[45] But for teenage provincials, St. Petersburg imparted modernity. Mikhail became a "half-proletarian" (*poloproletarskii*) torn from the pages of Maxim Gorky.[46] As a teenager, the muscular Mikhail lugged 100 kg cargo for a longshoreman *artel* in the rough-and-tumble beer-manufacturing docks at the Kalashnikov Embankment.[47]

During breaks, Mikhail Putin would wrestle peasant-style *(bor'ba na opoiaskakh)*. One lad would tie a red dock sash around his shoulder. His opponent, gripping this sash, would try to topple him. This was not an MMA free-for-all, but rather a test of skill, similar to Korean *Ssireum*.[48] Local sportsmen noticed Putin and invited him to workout at Sanitas, a gym precursor. During the Belle époque fitness craze, sports became a way for workers to distinguish themselves from peasants. Echoing the dandies who found a way to express cultivation through fashion rather than aping posh

---

[42] Dmitrii Likhachev, *V blokadnom Leningrade* (Algoritm, 2017), 17.
[43] Senin, "Budem sorevnovat'sia!," 177; and Aleksandr Putin, *Rod prezidenta V. V. Putina*, 248.
[44] P. N. Miliukov, *Vospominaniia* (Politizdat, 1990), vol. 1, 378.
[45] Christopher Clark, *The Sleepwalkers* (Harper, 2012), 433–34.
[46] The Putin boys loved to take stylish photos of themselves in the city. For photos of Spiridon and Aleksandr (another Putin from Tver') from 1900–1914, see: E. Evseeva, "Kto vy, Putiny? Korni prezidenta Rossii—v tverskoi derevne," *Argumenty i fakty (Tver')*, 8 May 2018, https://tver.aif.ru/society/persona/kto_vy_putiny_korni_prezidenta_rossii_-_v_tverskoy_derevne.
[47] Kuz'min, "Pervyi dogovor," 50; and Aleksandr Putin, *Rod prezidenta V. V. Putina*, 248.
[48] Senin, "Budem sorevnovat'sia!," 177. See also: S. Frank, "'Simple Folk, Savage Customs?' Youth, Sociability, and the Dynamics of Culture in Rural Russia, 1856-1914," *Journal of Social History* 25, no. 4 (Summer 1992): 711–36.

aristocratic dress, a peasant path to status was through cultivating a refined physique.

Sanitas was founded by a Pole, Ludwig Chaplinsky. Chaplinsky's father, a successful lawyer, moved to Nevsky Prospekt and encouraged his son to combine the study of foreign languages and sports. Ludwig turned several rooms of his apartment into gyms. The atmosphere, perhaps similar to Venice Beach in the 1970s, was international. Sanitas was frequented by the Cossack Ivan Chufistov, the Estonian Oskar Kaplur, and the Ukrainian Ivan Piddubnyi: history's great wrestlers. Chaplinsky's gym, moreover, was located in the Tolstoy apartment complex, home to writers, such as Arkady Averchenko.[49] Sanitas workouts were based on the teaching of physiologist Peter Lesgaft, who wrote: "mental and physical activities should be in complete harmony, for only then is it possible to fully attain self-comprehension." According to Lesgaft, "when working with machines and equipment, it is necessary to use as many muscles as possible since the more muscles that take part in work, the slower the moment of fatigue [...] This theory of muscularity can be applied to mental activity." For Lesgaft, harmonious development of the body should constitute the goal of education. Instead of isolation exercises, he urged doing balance training, such as walking on hands. Citing Plato and Rousseau, he adumbrated a philosophy of wrestling.[50] Sanitas training involved stretching, running at a set pace, cold and hot water showers, lectures in physiology, and full-body power-lifts, such as the get-up. Many Sanitas athletes were vegetarians.[51]

---

[49] Ia. V. Grinval'd, *Russkie silachi: Ocherki o proshlom russkoi tiazheloi atletiki* (Fizkul'tura i sport, 1950), 160; and M. N. Kolotilo, *Tolstovskii dom. Sozvezdie imen* (Iskusstvo, 2011).

[50] Petr Lesgaft, *Izbrannye pedagogicheskie sochineniia* (Fizkultura, 1951), 17, 18, 37. Sports and the intelligentsia were intertwined: Lesgaft's son-in-law, Lev Kleinbort, was a radical leftist who fought for the ideal of a state run by worker-intellectuals; Chris Monday "Kopyl'skii marksist: L.N. Kleinbort," *Belorusskii sbornik* 4 (2008): 79–103.

[51] "Retrokul'turizm: kak trenirovalis' otsy russkogo bodibildinga," *Men's Health.ru*, 18 December 2019, https://mhealth.ru/form/fitness/retrokulturizm-kak-trenirovalis-otcy-russkogo-bodibildinga.

Wrestling became a popular entertainment so that successful wrestlers gained fame doing tricks in the circus for semi-literate workers. Leading wrestlers, such as Ivan Piddubny, entered high society. Others trained the police. A few studied martial arts. Mikhail Putin, a middleweight, never reached Olympian heights, but received some notoriety.[52] In 1914, he lost to "the Captain of the Wind and King of Iron" Ivan Zaikin in the New Circus during an amateur national championship.[53] Zaikin could lift a 400 kg anchor. The lads at the docks began calling Putin, "Mishka the Wrestler."

During the Civil War, as trade froze up, the dock *artel* organized show matches. In Tomsk, the workers wanted to see who could last the longest against the legendary Piddubny. Putin entered the ring, but out of fear retreated. Piddubny, smiling, pulled him aside and told him, using Ukrainian slang, "Why are you chickening out? [*Chto tikaish'?*] Scary, yes, but suck it up!" Putin took his advice to heart and lasted seven minutes in the ring against this Samson.[54] In 1923, Mikhail defeated Yan the Gypsy (Ivan Kusenko).[55]

Mikhail Putin's training was interrupted by war.[56] According to government documents from 1931, he served in the Red Army from 1917 to 1923, "fighting against Admiral Kolchak."[57] By other accounts, Putin served nine years in various armies, training troops in wrestling.[58] In none of the accounts is any actual fighting mentioned. During the First World War, many members of the Putin family returned to the village outside Tver. Perhaps Mikhail did the same.[59]

---

[52] Aleksandr Putin, *Rod prezidenta V. V. Putina*, 248.
[53] Kuz'min, "Pervyi dogovor," 50.
[54] A. Zuev, "Vyzyvaem na sotsialisticheskoe sorevnovanie," *Neva* 3 (1979): 122–29; Kuz'min, "Pervyi dogovor," 50–51; Aleksandr Putin, *Rod prezidenta V. V. Putina*, 249; Iurii Pompeev, *Khochetsia zhit' i zhit'* (Politizdat, 1987), 83–85.
[55] Aleksandr Putin, *Rod prezidenta V. V. Putina*, 249; Senin, "Budem sorevnovat'sia!," 177; and N. Aleksandrov, "Yan Tsygan" (1959), http://www.ruscircus.ru/arhiv-press/cigan596.
[56] "M. E. Putin," *Pravda*, no. 64, 5 March 1969, 1; and Kuz'min, "Pervyi dogovor," 50–51.
[57] Zelov, "Pervye kavalery" 5.
[58] Kuz'min, "Pervyi dogovor," 51.
[59] Zelov, "Pervye kavalery," 3–7. According to Vladimir Putin, during the war Spiridon would often shelter in Tver; Gevorkian *et al.*, *Ot pervogo litsa*, 7–8;

In 1923, Putin returned to his dock-worker *artel* but could not adjust to the slipshod NEP-era. The workers, he recounted later in a retrospective article in the Brezhnev-era press, were shirking and drinking. The boss would bark at them, "this is not a political meeting with your 'comrades.' Get moving!" Putin had trouble landing wrestling gigs. Eventually, his father helped Mikhail get a factory job in 1923.[60] This section has shown how Putin's upbringing, at the railroad and café, plus serious sports training, established him as a charismatic figure for the half-proletarians flooding into the factories in the 1920s.

The Red Factory

This section describes Mikhail Putin's new workplace, a factory torn between the peasantry and proletariat. The Rosenkranz factory, founded by a Baltic mechanic, Fedor Gosh, in 1857, was located at the banks of the Neva: it specialized in bronze and aluminum pipes. Typical for Russian capitalism, it possessed an "advantage of backwardness."[61] European managers, the Rosenkranz brothers were able to import foreign technology which was adapted by *artel* peasants. Serving the military and transportation needs of the state, the factory produced the pipes for a steam-driven economy. Rosenkranz went bankrupt several times, but wars and government contracts brought the factory back into prosperity. Also typical of Russian industry, the factory was involved in tariffs disputes with the United States. Rosenkranz became important enough to head a trade syndicate which included the fading Demidov factories. The factory boasted of vast machines, such as a thousand-ton hydraulic press: Peasant-workers innovated electrolysis methods.[62] Worker

---

[60] Aleksandr Putin, *Rod prezidenta V. V. Putina*, 35; Perhaps Mikhail may have also returned to the villages of Tver.
[60] Kuz'min, "Pervyi dogovor," 51.
[61] M. I. Tugan-Baranovskii, *Russkaia fabrika v proshlom i nastoiashchem* (Pantelieeva, 1898).
[62] N. B. Lebedeva and O. I. Shkaratan, *Ocherki istorii sotsialisticheskogo sorevnovaniia* (Lenizdat,1966), 59; and Leonid Beilin, *Kak rodilos' sotsialisticheskoe sorevnovanie* (Profizdat, 1960), 41–43.

pride was bolstered by stunning architecture: the unmissable director's wooden house, still visible in 2014, was built by Nicholas Benois. (The factory was torn down in 2020.)

Under the Soviets, Rosenkranz, renamed Red Vyborgskii district, Krasnyi Vyborzhets, became a factory capable of producing a multitude of products at short notice, which was crucial not only for industrialization, but also to the state's efforts at creating a communist lifestyle. Notably, vanguard-workers minted money, forged statues (including the Lenin at the Finland Station) and produced musical instruments. Today, the factory is remembered for kettles and canteens.[63] Workers garnered high wages. A roller *(val'tsovshchik)* earned up to 200 rubles a month; a roller's assistant would earn 160 rubles, while the less skilled workers in Leningrad received a meager 25 rubles.[64] Pay at the factory was chaotic: the same job could earn from 45 to 122 rubles.[65] Vyborzhets was relatively small for a significant factory. While Putilivets had 10,405 employees, in 1925, Krasnyi Vyborzhets had 4,433. A large proportion, 28%, were communists.[66]

Because of its importance for the Revolution, the factory became politicized. It was located in the blue-collar Vyborgskii region, the industrial center of Leningrad where 20% of industrial production took place. Lenin, arriving at the nearby Finland Station, made Vyborgskii a Bolshevik bastion. At Smol'nyi Monastery, Lenin, an "ideal bureaucrat" working from morning until midnight, managed adjacent factories personally, a *ruchnoi* regime. Top Bolsheviks, such as Viktor Kingissepp, agitated at Krasnyi Vyborzhets, whose workers breathed politics. Typical meetings involved sending collective get-well letters to "Dear Lenin, captain of the revolutionary ship"[67] or expressing concern over the

---

[63] Valentin Simonov, "Estafeta aktsionerov," *Neva* 11 (1995): 166–74.
[64] A. I. Kartus, "Vospominaniia," *Istoriia Peterburga* 3 (31) (2006): 36.
[65] G. N. Sevost'ianov (ed.), *"Sovershenno sekretno": Lubianka–Stalinu o polozhenii v strane* (Institut istorii, 2001), 3:2: 595.
[66] S. S. Khromov, *F. E. Dzerzhinskii vo glave metallopromyshlennosti* (Izdatel'stvo Moskovskogo universiteta, 1966), 252.
[67] Viktor Mushtukov (ed.), *Dorogoi tovarishch Lenin* (Lenizdat, 1969): 146.

"bourgeoisie raising its head."[68] In 1925 workers demanded: "Capitalists, hands off China!"[69] Even Soviet historians acknowledged that Trotsky's "dangerous rightward deviation" gained palpable factory support.[70]

In 1923, Mikhail Putin became a furnace stoker at this war-ravaged factory.[71] He looked back on this period in a memoir published in the Brezhnev era:

> It was my job to put copper rods into the kiln. Simple, yet difficult! It was so hot that at times my canvas robe nearly caught fire. We drank 40 cups of water per shift; our clothes were covered with salt from sweat. My diligence was noticed: the foreman of our workshop, Mikhailov, proposed I lead a brigade. "I have strength, but no experience in managing," I protested. "Don't worry, lad," laughed the foreman, "It's not the gods who make pots!"[72]

But it was thanks to wrestling that Putin gained real authority *(avtoritet)*[73] among his illiterate mates.[74] Putin organized a wrestling club. Impressed by this, the party supervisor asked him to form a brigade with 8 *artel* wrestling mates, in part for propaganda purposes.[75] Putin recalled:

---

[68] N. B. Lebina, *Povsednevnaia zhizn' sovetskogo goroda* (Neva, 1999), 58.
[69] I. A. Rosenko, *Internatsional'nye sviazi rabochikh Leningrada 1921–1937* (LGU, 1977), 21.
[70] V. M. Ivanov, *Iz istorii bor'by partii protiv "levogo" opportunizma: Leningradskaia partiinaia organizatsiia v bor'be protiv trotskistko-zinov'evskoi oppozitsii* (Lenizdat, 1965), 150.
[71] Aleksandr Putin, *Rod prezidenta V. V. Putina*, 178; Senin, "Budem sorevnovat'sia!," 177; *Pravda*, no. 64, 1969, 1–2; V. I. Kuzakova, *XVI Konferentsiia VKP(b)* (Politizdat, 1978), 78; A. F. Zanin (ed.), *Rabochaia entsiklopediia* (Lenizdat, 1986), 38; and Zuev, "Vyzyvaem na sotsialisticheskoe sorevnovanie," 122–29.
[72] M. E. Putin, "Dogovor Ruda," in V. F. Finogenov and V. A. Smyshliaev (eds.), *Neizvedannymi putiami* (Lenizdat, 1967), 167–79. The line "gods who make pots" was used by Lenin in "How to Organize Competition" published in 1929. Thus we are likely dealing with another embellishment.
[73] V. Gurinovich, "Kyl'ia pochina," *Sovetskie profsoiuzy*, 6 March 1979, 22–23.
[74] Zelov, "Pervye kavalery," 5.
[75] Aleksandr Putin, *Rod prezidenta V. V. Putina*, 178; and Senin, "Budem sorevnovat'sia!," 177–78.

> Seven sturdy lads were selected for our brigade. Besides myself, there were two communists, three Komsomol members, and two non-party members. From the first days, we established strong discipline. [...]
>
> The Party made me the brigade agitator. I had no experience, but with great zeal, I took up my duties. At first, I wearied my listeners.
>
> "We'll hold political studies at lunchtime," I announced resolutely, pointing to a stack of newspapers.
>
> "But we need to eat," the guys shot back.
>
> I wouldn't let up. "OK, then we will lunch and study at the same time!"[76]
>
> The brigade would sit in a circle to read newspapers. Gradually this took on a conscious character: Instead of mindlessly reading one item after another, we would focus on the political and economic issues that interested the workers. The guys asked questions, many of which, I could not immediately answer. Therefore, I wrote everything down and sought advice from the Party bureau. These conversations raised our consciousness. We became aware of important events in our country and abroad: we saw our place in the struggle for socialism.[77]

In 1924, Mikhail Putin joined the Party and started work as agitator.[78] Soviet sources allow us to reconstruct his propaganda activities during the period leading up to 1929. Putin would have been sent to one-year evening *(politekhnicheskie)* indoctrination courses, available for those with a smattering of literacy: in 1923, Krasnyi Vyborzhets sent 95 workers for such training. Putin would read to illiterates from leaflets like "Our Factory" *(Nash Zavod),* a *stennaia gazeta.* Posters on the factory floor enjoined: "Educated, teach the illiterate!"[79] "Wagon mechanic shop, be ready! Accept the challenge of the car locksmith to reduce costs by 9.5%."[80] Putin would have organized "voluntary" book clubs in factories: Red

---

[76] I. G. Lupalo (ed.), *Govoriat stroiteli sotsializma* (Gospolitizdat: 1959), 221–25.
[77] M. E. Putin, "Dogovor," 169–70.
[78] Zelov, "Pervye kavalery," 5.
[79] Zuev, "Vyzyvaem na sotsialisticheskoe sorevnovanie," 122–29; V. I. Nosach and A. A. Ushanov, *Sovetskie profsoiuzy v bor'be za sotsialisticheskuiu kul'turu* (Profizdat, 1986), 99.
[80] Kuzakova, *XVI Konferentsiia*, 79.

professors, such as literary critic Petr Kogan, gave talks at Krasnyi Vyborzhets. Much worker time was consumed by omnipresent indoctrination and agitprop activities: demonstrations, rallies, meetings, "roll calls," work teams, *subbotniks*, campaign gatherings, mass excursions.[81] During 1926–28, newspaper printing in Leningrad increased three-fold; the number of radios in the city increased at an astonishing rate, from 670 to 62,530.[82]

Putin helped organize his factory's participation in May-first processions which recalled Renaissance-era extravaganzas.[83] Initially, these were Zinoviev-era spectacles where workers carried caricatures of European "bourgeois" politicians, which dumfounded the proletariat. By 1929, the "festivals" became more down-to-earth. According to one account, "the streets overflowed with an avalanche of workers. Volleys of guns rang out. Thousands of demonstrators poured into the square: the Narvskii, Vyborgskii, Tsentral'nyi and Volodarskii districts go side by side next to 18 new tractors." Workers carried posters: "War on truancy, drunkenness, laxity." The truants, drunkards and wreckers were depicted vividly by actors in make-up. "You cannot envy the amateur worker-artists who had to play the role of these enemies of the working class. [...] One of the factories came up with a kind of competition [...] for the best drunkard." There were also caricatures of priests, rabbis, bureaucrats, and, of course, of the turn-coat Trotsky.[84]

Despite all these exertions, discontent at Krasnyi Vyborzhets was high, as noted by secret OGPU reports *(Obzory politicheskogo sostoianiia)* based on the testimony of informers who infiltrated the factory meetings. In 1924, workers complained that members of the factory administration were leading a "degraded lifestyle" *(razgul'nyi obraz zhizni)*. In 1925, factory workers sent a collective

---

[81] On the omnipresence of propaganda under the Bolsheviks, see: Peter Kenez, *The Birth of the Propaganda State: Soviet Methods of Mass Mobilization, 1917–1929* (Cambridge University Press, 1985).
[82] V. G. Zakharov (ed.), *Ocherki istorii leningradskoi organizatsii KPSS*, vol. 2 (Lenizdat, 1968), 326.
[83] Richard Stites, *Revolutionary Dreams: Utopian Vision and Experimental Life in the Russian Revolution* (Oxford University Press, 1989), 92–95.
[84] N. I. Levchenko and V. P. Tolstoi, *Agitatsionno-massovoe iskusstvo, oformlenie prazdnestv* (Iskusstvo, 1984), 135, 180–81.

letter with 30 signatures demanding production norms not be raised, threating an "Italian" strike, where workers over-rigorously follow all regulations thereby hindering production. Making matters worse, without explanation, wages would be reduced, often by 40%. Informants reported that workers purposely wrecked production. Skilled workers left, at the pace of 12 a day, for higher pay. Lack of raw materials caused breakdowns. "With the goal of economizing," the factory got rid of the hot-water banya, serving 400 workers.[85] Soon every month brought 40 strikes, with a total of 3,000 participants. In one incident, upset workers summoned the plant manager, who said: "Nothing can be done, this is economizing." The workers turned to the Party secretary, who went to the factory committee, where he angrily declared: "The earnings of workers of the fifth category dropped from 150 to 80 rubles!" Often a commission would be too intimidated to announce wage reductions. Workers were dumbfounded by NEP-era "speculation." One worker at Krasnyi Vyborzhets was overheard at a political meeting: "The speaker was carried away by talk of imperialist gouging, but we are outdoing them!"[86]

The conundrum was how to transform peasants into proletarians: the Bolsheviks had no blueprint. Disdaining the detailed plans of utopian visionary Charles Fourier, Karl Marx had only nebulously sketched what the post-market society would actually look like. In particular, it was never clear why the proletarians would work for free. On seizing power, the Bolsheviks, only about 200,000, were far too few to impose any grand schemes.[87] Rather, they relied on guiding elemental social forces, *stikhiinost'*.[88]

---

[85] Sevost'ianov, "Sovershenno sekretno," 4:1: 527, 660.
[86] Ibid., 265, 527, 556, 64. See also: B. N. Kazantsev, "Materialy gosudarstvennykh, partiinykh i profsoiuznykh organov," in I. I. Kir'ianov and W. Rosenberg (eds.), *Trudovye konflikty v Sovetskoi Rossii* (Éditorial, 1998), 38–66; Vladimir Brovkin, *Russia After Lenin: Politics, Culture and Society* (Routledge, 1998), 124–25; and M. P. Kim and L. S. Rogachevskaia, *Pervye shagi industrializatsii SSSR* (Politizdat, 1959), 404–08.
[87] Robert Service, *The Bolshevik Party in Revolution: A Study in Organization Change, 1917–1923* (Palgrave Macmillan, 1979), 89–92.
[88] On the vision of early socialists, see: Jonathan Beecher, *Charles Fourier. The Visionary and His World* (University of California Press, 1987). On the

Lenin, who had talent for quickly applying Marxist doctrine to real-world issues, was quite clear-eyed. By 1917, Lenin realized revolution in agrarian Russia was possible, but he knew perfectly well that proletarian self-governance was years away. Because Russia was an agricultural society, the Party must rely on a few "conscious" worker-intellectuals to overcome the lethargy of the peasant-proletariat. "It is necessary," argued Lenin,

> to destroy the distinction between city and country, as well as the difference between physical and mental labor. [...] To accomplish this, we must overcome the resistance (often passive, which is especially difficult to overcome) of workers attached to small-scale production: the enormous force of habit associated with these residual forces must be overcome. To assume that all "working people" are equally capable of this would be an illusion of antediluvian, pre-Marxist socialism. The ability [to move to genuine communism] is not a given, but grows only from material conditions of large-scale capitalist production. At the beginning of the path from capitalism to socialism, this ability, is possessed only by the true proletariat. [Unfortunately,] in backward capitalist countries, such as Russia, the majority belong to the semi-proletariat, that is, people who spend only part of the year as proletarians. Those who try to solve the problems of the transition from capitalism to socialism based on general phrases about freedom, equality, abstract democracy, labor democracy [...] only prove their true nature as petty bourgeois [...] The solution to the problem [of achieving communism] can only be found by a concrete study of the peculiar relations among the class that won political power, namely the proletariat, the non-proletarian, and the semi-proletarian.[89]

Lenin was correct to worry that the "semi-proletarians" would create their own sub-culture.[90] Party reports in the 1920s noted that

---

Bolsheviks and revolutionary chaos: Katerina Clark, *The Soviet Novel: History as Ritual* (University of Chicago Press, 1981; Alexander Rabinowitch, *The Bolsheviks in Power: The First Year of Soviet Rule in Petrograd* (Indiana University Press, 2007); and Iaroslav Leont'ev, *"Skify" russkoi revoliutsii: partiia levykh eserov i ee literaturnye poputchiki* (AIRO-XXI, 2007).

[89] V. I. Lenin, *Velikii pochin* (1919) at https://leninism.su/works/78-tom-39/640-veliki-pochin.html.

[90] On the ruralization of Soviet cities, see: Reinhard Bendix, *Work and Authority in Industry: Ideologies of Management in the Course of Industrialization* (Harper & Row, 1963), 351–433.

hooliganism, committed by young workers, was rampant.[91] Often these were not crimes but their way of adapting to the city. Notably, workers would engage in fist fights, that were not simply brawling, but rather the symbolic, holiday shows of strength practiced in the village. Notoriously, Krasnyi Vyborzhets workers would challenge other factories to these fist-fighting competitions.[92]

The contradictions of the New Economic Policy exacerbated these difficulties.[93] The Party elite especially worried about the growth of nationalism among the semi-proletarians. Later, the infamous Barshai case (1929), in which a young Jewish woman factory worker was assaulted in an antisemitic attack, brought conflict between Jewish and Russian workers into the open.[94] In short, the Bolshevik factory was far from a Fourier Phalanx.[95]

What was needed was a way to present factory life in a fun, theatrical light, so as to unite illiterate workers from various cultures. In Stalinist fashion, the solution would be found by supposedly turning back to Lenin. Drained from the revolution, Lenin had taken an improbable Christmas break: On 24 December 1917, he left St. Petersburg for a sanatorium in Finland. Although Stalin had requested his return a few days later, he had time to draft an essay "How to Organize Competition."[96] According to this ferocious text, workers must initiate a ruthless terror. "The rich and

---

[91] One of the main struggles of the Bolsheviks was not theoretical, but rather concerned containing a flood of violence and crime; Dmitrii Ereshchenko, *Prestupnost' v Petrograde v 1914–1917 gg.* (kandidatskaia dissertation, History) (Herzen University, 2003).

[92] Lebina, *Posvednevnaia zhizn'*, 58.

[93] Sheila Fitzpatrick, *Stalin's Peasants: Resistance and Survival in the Russian Village after Collectivization* (Oxford University Press, 1994).

[94] M. Ia. Aleksandrov, *Klassovyi vrag v maske* (Gosizdat, 1929), 15, 50, 79.

[95] Archival research has found that ethnic tension and resentment towards efforts to "internationalize" the workers by importing foreign laborers dominated the early years of Stalinist industrialization; Sarah Davies, *Popular Opinion in Stalin's Russia: Terror, Propaganda and Dissent, 1934–1941* (Cambridge University Press, 1997), 73–90; Hiroaki Kuromiya, *Stalin's Industrial Revolution: Politics and Workers* (Cambridge University Press, 1988), 87–99; and Arkadii Zel'tser, "Mezhetnicheskie politiki i sovetskaia politika," *Yad Vashem* (2010); available at: https://historicus.ru/525/.

[96] Robert Service, *Lenin: A Biography* (Harvard University Press, 2000), 333–34.

the swindlers, these are two sides of the same coin, these are the two categories of parasites [...] They must be dealt with [...] mercilessly." This text, cited by scholars today as proof of Lenin's inhumanity, was perhaps edited by Stalin.[97]

Stalin had "How to Organize Competition" published in *Pravda* in 1929 to justify forced industrialization. According to Lenin, the Bolsheviks must experiment with different methods to motivate the "half-proletarians." The revolutionaries were similar to a Japanese doctor testing remedies for syphilis.[98] Lenin suggests that socialist competition, similar to a sports competition, might be one way to get the "half-proletariat" motivated. "Socialism," thundered Lenin, "does not extinguish competition. On the contrary, socialism creates the first real opportunity to apply competition broadly, on a massive scale, by drawing the majority of laborers into the arena of real work, where they can prove themselves [...] Our task is to organize competition."[99] By March 1929, a copy of this work had been sent out to the agitator of every brigade at every major factory, including Mikhail Putin.[100]

This section has shown that Mikhail Putin's factory, central to Bolshevik plans, was plagued by discontent. Stalin hoped that Lenin's musings could be refashioned into a campaign to motivate the half-proletariat. For "socialist competition," the state needed a man like Putin.

---

[97] This text would only be published in 1929; Lenin never saw fit to publish it. The only background source for this strange "Christmastime" work is a brief reminiscence by Alexandra Kollontai written in 1946; Alexandra Kollontai, "Lenin Thought of Both Great and Small," available at: https://www.marxists.org/archive/kollonta/1946/lenin.htm.
[98] Lenin, *Velikii pochin* (1919).
[99] V. I. Lenin, "Kak organizovat' sorevnovanie" (1929) at https://www.politpros.com/library/13/264/. Lenin, in passing, mentioned the idea of "competition" several times, for example, in 1920 in discussing plans for electrification.
[100] I. P. Ostapenko, *Uchastie rabochego klassa SSSR v upravlenii proizvodstvom: proizvodstvennye soveshchaniia v promyshlennosti v 1921-1932 gg.* (Nauka, 1964), 135-36; and L. S. Gaponenko, *Vedushchaia rol' rabochego klassa v rekontruktsii promyshlennosti SSSR* (Mysl', 1973), 97; and F. N. Shcherbak, *Moral'nye stimuly v trude* (Lenizdat, 1973), 124-25.

Wrestler to Competitor

This section describes how the often clumsy Bolshevik attempts to override worker autonomy by creating top-down initiatives, such as worker "roll calls," led eventually to socialist competition. Mikhail Putin proved crucial in this effort to use sports and village values for adapting the peasant-worker to regulated Soviet factory life. The peasants had organized life in the city as they knew it in the villages with the councils *(sovety)* and *artel*. The Bolsheviks gradually overrode these with state-controlled institutions.[101] For example, in 1924 Party-led "worker production circles" were introduced to outline production goals to the *artels*.[102] In this drive, Krasnyi Vyborzhets, under Komsomol tutelage, staged showy contests, judged by "worker juries," which awarded token prizes: theatrical "production inspections" began in 1927.[103] The first "shock brigade" was established in 1926 at "Red Triangle" factory.[104] But these half-hearted efforts seemed to only annoy the workers: the Party instituted widespread purges *(chistki)*: at Krasnyi Vyborzhets, the Party bosses were sacked while new cells were created.[105] In 1927 the *Partshkoly* trained an army of 3000 agitators who would conduct "talks" *(besedy)* with disgruntled workers.[106] In 1928, the regime turned to public shaming, imposing "self-criticism" *(samokritika)*

---

[101] A Bolshevik dream was to have the peasant-workers leap past the bourgeois stage to an "advanced" stage of continuous production that would eliminate idle machinery. Under the "continuous work week" scheme, Sundays would disappear. Factory work would consist of a five-day week, with a seven-hour shift each day, followed by one day of rest. This created a "year" comprising sixty work weeks and sixty days of rest. Work schedules, moreover, would be staggered in such a way that a brigade would be stationed at a factory machine continually throughout the year. In 1929, this utopian scheme was pushed onto the Leningrad metalworkers, thereby exacerbating confusion and resentment; Namsub Kim, "The Changing Labor Conditions of the Leningrad Metalworkers between the Late 1920s and Early 1930s," 러시아연구 23, no. 1 (2013): 297–300.

[103] *Ocherki istorii leningradskoi organizatsii*, 74–78.

[104] P. V. Grechishnikov, *Ekonomicheskie problemy sotsialisticheskogo sorevnovaniia v sel'skom khoziaistve* (Ekonomika, 1968), 38; and V. N. Bernadskii and A. E. Suknovalov, *Istoricheskoe proshloe Leningrada* (Uchebno-pedagogicheskoe izdatel'stvo, 1958), 292–29.

[105] G. E. Evdokimov, "Zaiavlenie G.E. Evdokimova plenumu CK VKP(b), 31 marta 1926," *Istoricheckeskie materialy*, http://istmat.info/node/59792.

[106] *Ocherki istorii leningradskoi organizatsii*, 322–25.

and "comrade courts" on the factories. Posters were hung on building facades stigmatizing truants. The wives of Krasnyi Vyborzhets workers were encouraged to declare a public fight against drunkenness. "Enough of being passive!" They were told to keep a vigilant eye over their husbands.[107] Workers publically volunteered to stay at their factory, and not look for higher paying work.[108] On 21 November 1928, the Smolensk Katushka factory instituted short-lived "roll-call rallies" *(mitingi-pereklichki)*, where workers melodramatically "summoned" other factories to compete for the best production results. "Roll-call" became the prototype for socialist competition.[109] These precursors to socialist competition seemed to have been clumsily conducted and were quickly forgotten.

The early history of socialist competition is a jumble of names and dates: the "initiator" depended on the regional audience. In January 1929, *Komsomol'skaia pravda* issued an appeal to start an All-Union competition to reduce production costs, *"sebestoimost',"* in pseudo-Marxist terminology.[110] Ukrainian-language accounts highlighted that the Donbas coal miners published a challenge on 31 January 1929 which soon involved all Soviet mines.[111] On 20 January 1929 *Tverskaia pravda* announced a challenge by textile workers. On 26 January *Komsomol'skaia pravda* made an appeal to the Komsomol members about organizing all-union youth competitions.[112] On 10 February, the shoe factory Parizhskaia Kommuna summoned the Komsomol youth of sister factories to

---

[107] A. M. Lazareva, "Kommunisty Vyborgskoi storony Leningrada v bor'be za razvitie sotsialisticheskogo sorevnovaniia," *Trudy* [Leningradskii inzhenerno-ekonomicheskii institut] vol. 38 (1961): 83, 92.

[108] I. P. Ostapenko, *Uchastie rabochego klassa SSSR v upravlenii proizvodstvom: proizvodstvennye soveshchaniia v promyshlennosti* (Nauka, 1964), 172.

[109] D. A. Baevskii (ed.), *Politicheskii i trudovoi pod"em rabochego klassa SSSR* (Politizdat, 1956), 223–24.

[110] A. M. Valov and I. A. Garaevskaia, *Sovetskie profsoiuzy v gody industrializatsii* (Profizdat, 1987), 101.

[111] Ostapenko, *Uchastie rabochego klassa SSSR v upravlenii proizvodstvom*, 135–36; and G. P. Alekseev, *Istoriia sotsialisticheskogo sorevnovaniia v SSSR* (Profizdat, 1980), 81.

[112] N. B. Lebedeva, *Partiinoe rukovodstvo sotsialisticheskim sorevnovaniem* (Lenizdat, 1979), 65–66.

competition.¹¹³ "The whole atmosphere of those days was saturated with the idea of competition," remembered Mikhail Putin.¹¹⁴ Contemporaries at first imagined that "competition" would go the way of the short-lived "roll calls." Although Putin's effort was one out of many, Krasnyi Vyborzhets was canonized to become the template for industrialization. "Vyborzhets," recalled Putin,

> one of the only factories producing rolled non-ferrous metals, played a huge role in industrialization. But what was our plant like in those years? The equipment was outdated, heavy manual labor prevailed. [...] Most workers arrived recently [from the village]. Many were untrained and did not yet accept the rich revolutionary traditions of the "Vyborg-side [of Leningrad]."

> In 1929, the plant was really lagging. Of course, quite a few workers in the collective cared about the honor of the plant, and upbraided laggards. The management, Party, trade unions and Komsomol launched attacks on truants. But the old methods of organizing production were no longer suitable, and new ones had not yet emerged. [...] A strong impetus was needed [...] The draft of the first five-year plan was discussed at all factories.¹¹⁵

In particular, factory managers hoped "competition" could resolve problems with the supply chain. Vyborzhets was not receiving needed raw materials from sister factories. In February 1929, Vyborzhets workers "challenged" the supply-chain factories, Kamensk and Metallolampa.¹¹⁶ Their challenge, published in *Pravda* on 5 March, read: "In accordance with the directives of the government and our party to reduce costs, we, the workers of the Krasny Vyborzhets, undertake to improve production and the fight against defects, rest time and absenteeism [...] We have three tasks: an increase in labor productivity, rationalization, and a struggle to tighten the work day. If we manage to condense rest-time by 15 minutes a day, our factory would receive 500 thousand rubles in savings." On 21 March, *Pravda* published a letter from the Kamensk

---

113   Others claim that the first socialist competition was held in 1928 while building the Volkhostroi hydroelectric dam; Leonid Rakhmanov, "Za davnost'iu let," in A. M. Beilin (ed.), *Nachinaetsia den': rasskazy o leningradskikh rabochikh* (Sovetskii pisatel', 1972), 42–59.
114   V. Mikhailov, "Podniavshie znamia," *Izvestiia*, 5 March 1969, no. 52, 3.
115   M. E. Putin, "Dogovor," 167–79.
116   Lebedeva and Shkaratan, *Ocherki istorii sotsialisticheskogo sorevnovaniia*, 92.

factory describing how the workers had answered the challenge.[117] But this was only the beginning. Putin recalled:

> Our pipe shop was the largest at Vyborzhets. [...] Every day hundreds of demands came from all over the Soviet Union. Ships, tractors, and automotive construction depended on our pipe shop [...] Our factory had issued challenges, but it was not clear how we should organize socialist competition. We had no idea.[118]
>
> Semenov,[119] a Party Secretary, handed me Lenin's "How to Organize Competition." "Read it and then explain it to your comrades." That article turned our lives upside down.[120]
>
> It seemed that Ilyich appeared at our factory [...] to our brigade and uttered: "[...] For the first time after centuries of labor for strangers, forced labor for exploiters, there is an opportunity to work for oneself!"[121]
>
> I experienced an extraordinary state of mind, as if a wave had picked me up. Thoughts, thoughts, thoughts. From Lenin, I understood the deep meaning of socialist competition: no one should be defeated. On Wednesday morning, 15 March 1929, I brought the article to the shop.[122]

Another account continues the story:

> Putin began to read. Raising his head to observe how his mates reacted, Putin repeated phrases the workers especially liked. Finishing, he neatly folded the newspaper. So great was the impression of Lenin's simple words [...] that everyone was lost in thought. "Will we compete?" they asked. "We will!" [Budem!]— thundered Putin.[123]
>
> "But competition is not enough for us because the success of the plant depends on the work of each of us, each team." Everyone began speaking at once.[124]

---

[117] N.a., "O priniatii vyzova na sotsialisticheskoe sorevnovanie," *Pravda*, no. 65, 21 March 1929; *Politicheskii i trudovoi pod"em*, 199–200; and Kuzakova, *XVI Konferentsiia*, 79.
[118] M. E. Putin, "Dogovor," 167–79.
[119] Perhaps this is A. P. Semenov, a milling machine operator *(frezerovshchik)*.
[120] V. T. Senin, "Budem sorevnovat'sia!," 177–78.
[121] N.a., "Krasnyivyborzhets: Estafeta sorevnovaniia," *Agitator* 5 (1979): 7–11.
[122] N.a., "M. E. Putin," *Krasnyivyborzhets*, 11 January 1969, 2.
[123] Senin, "Budem sorevnovat'sia!," 177–78.
[124] M. E. Putin, "Dogovor,"167–79.

"This was written for us!" exclaimed young, cocky Boris Kruglov.[125]

"Lenin's program is simple," continued Kruglov, "understandable: so that everyone has bread, so that everyone walks in sturdy shoes, not trashy clothes, has warm housing, and works conscientiously!"[126]

"What do we have to do?" exclaimed the workers. "How can Leninist thoughts be realized?"

Wanting to record our conversation on paper, I suggested: "Let's write a contract."[127]

"Contract?" wondered the guys.

"A contract that we will compete with each other, and challenge our fellows."

"And win a prize?" Kruglov simplistically exclaimed.

"It's not who wins," I objected, "this is not our principle. But to finish the job faster, better." I found a student notebook and we began to draw up the first contract of socialist competition.[128]

"We must strive for something concrete, take on obligations. Let's say increase labor productivity by 10 percent."[129]

But we did not make exact calculations: it was all intuition.[130]

"If we increase productivity, wages will also increase. People will think we are after rubles?" Aleksei Goriunov doubted. "It's a sin to complain about wages."

---

[125] Senin, "Budem sorevnovat'sia!," 177.
[126] By some absurd accounts, Sergei Kirov "happened" to overhear the brigade's discussion. "Success depends on each brigade," intoned Kirov. "And your shop is the only one in the country where pipes are made for tractors"; Pompeev, *Khochetsia zhit'*, 85–86.
[127] In another variant: "For some reason, it seemed that our decision must be fixed by a contact"; P. E. Nikitin, *Muzei V. I. Lenina. Leningradskii filial* (Lenizdat, 1969), 157–58.
[128] M. E. Putin, "Dogovor," 167–79.
[129] "Krasnyivyborzhets: Estafeta sorevnovaniia," 7–11.
[130] Shcherbak, *Moral'nye stimuly*, 124–25.

"How will the other brigades react to this?" Grigor'iev asked skeptically.[131]

Our wages were already declining. "This won't do," insisted Pavel Mokin. "We don't know if we can actually increase productivity: we will hit our own pocketbooks." Mokin, conscientious, honest, didn't hide doubts from his comrades. He died defending Leningrad.[132]

But then, it seemed to him that we were wrong to call for wage cuts.[133]

There was a heated dispute. Putin remembered the advice of Piddubny: "Don't chicken out: fight!"[134]

Lunch-break ended and they came to an agreement. Kruglov exclaimed: "Wages need to be reduced: that's that!" Mokin acquiesced: "I'm with you!"[135]

We wrote the first paragraph: "We, aluminum workers, challenge to socialist competition: cleaners, red copper cutters [...] We, for our part, will voluntarily reduce the cost-price by 10% and will take all measures to increase labor productivity by 10%. We invite you to accept our challenge and conclude a contract with us. Aluminum cutters: M. Putin 2287. Mokin 2116. Ogloblin 2485. Kruglov 2292."[136]

All seven signed the declaration in the school notebook. My comrades asked me to go challenge the cleaners.[137] They immediately accepted our challenge, but one old worker, Stepanov, who before the Revolution had participated

---

[131] Pompeev, *Khochetsia zhit'*, 85–86. This version also, improbably, includes a scene featuring Kirov: "How others react depends on you," Kirov remarked and, deciding not to interfere, walked away.
[132] M. E. Putin, "Pervoe bolee reshaiushchii, chem sverzhenie burzhuazie. Vzgliad skvoz' gody," in V. A. Ezhov and N. V. Kuz'micheva, *Desiat' piatiletok leningradtsev* (Lenizdat, 1980), 17–19.
[133] Gurinovich, "Kyl'ia pochina," 22–23.
[134] Pompeev, *Khochetsia zhit'*, 86–87.
[135] In another variant: Putin: "I stayed up to 1 am, writing the contract, as if it was poetry. In the morning, everyone signed"; Z. V. Stepanov, *Rabochie Leningrada* (Nauka, 1963), 207.
[136] The numbers indicate personnel IDs; Senin, "Budem sorevnovat'sia!," 177–78. Original documents mention others on Putin's brigade: "Korobkin" and "Gorunoi": the cleaner "Stepanov" is never mentioned. "We, cleaners, accept the challenge: Tumanov 2182, A. Wels 2128, Beldovsky 2558, Yakovlev 2441, Smirnov 2087, Shelgunov 2475"; Beilin, *Kak rodilos' sotsialisticheskoe sorevnovanie*, 51–52.
[137] In another variant Putin claimed: "On 15 February 1929, together with the chairman of the factory committee, comrade Zykov, I went to challenge other brigades"; V. N. Bernadskii and A. E. Suknovalov, *Istoricheskoe proshloe Leningrada* (Uchebno-pedagogicheskoe izdatel'svo, 1958), 292–93.

in monarchist organizations, refused: "Mikhail, your contract is politically harmful."

"How would this agreement make things worse for workers?" Kruglov protested "You *[ty]*, Stepanich, became used to secretively counting your kopecks under the old regime and cannot be weaned away. The [conscious workers] will not be deceived!"

"You're painfully clever!" another old cleaner interrupted. "You *[ty]* haven't been weaned from mother's milk and complain about us counting kopeks! Ugh! You may fly in the clouds and live without a kopek, but I can't."

"Clinging desperately to the old regime, Stepanov went wild: "Maybe you *[ty]* destroyed the tsarist regime with your friends? You *[vy]*, Putin, can actually read. Interpret Lenin's article without any distortions. Read it, wrestler, out loud," challenged Stepanov, pointing to a paragraph.

"This great historical shift, the shift of from forced to free labor cannot happen without friction and conflicts," Putin read.

"Well, I'm in 'conflict!'" Stepanov sneered. "I'm off to our union to declare that Mishka is forcing us to sign some document."

Putin was summoned to factory headquarters. Chairman Yakovlev, asked sternly: "What is this collection of signatures, Putin?"

After Putin explained, Comrade Yakovlev immediately appreciated its importance. "Putin is doing the right thing: Nobody is pressuring the workers."

"Maybe I didn't completely understand," the repentant Stepanov mumbled. "And now I have decided to add the following condition to the contract: So that there will be no defects!"[138]

Our challenge was accepted by the welders. Craftsman Misha Pevzner[139] also promised to eliminate defects. Within a few days, all our factory shop signed contracts. "Work in such a way so as not to get mud on our face, Putin intoned. Or else people will cry: "They promised a lot, but failed, the con-artists! *[brekhuny]*"[140]

---

[138] Pompeev, *Khochetsia zhit'*, 88–89.
[139] In other variants, "Pezner" (the one non-Slav mentioned) is a Komsomol activist.
[140] M. E. Putin, "Dogovor Ruda," 167–79. For other accounts see: A. Balatin, "Geroi s vyborgskoi vyzov krasnogo Vyborzhtsa," *Pravda*, 64, 5 March 1969, 1; "Krasnyi

Подписание первого в стране договора о социалистическом соревновании на заводе «Красный выборжец». На переднем плане (второй справа) бригадир бригады обрубщиков коммунист ленинского призыва М. Е. Путин.

Figure 1. Mikhail Putin and his brigade signing the competition agreement. Mikhail Putin is second from the right. Source: *Leningradskaia promyshlennost' za 50 let* (Leningrad: Lenizdat, 1967), 18.

According to Putin, many "Dear guests" came to Vyborzhets. "It is impossible to convey with what great enthusiasm workers

---

Vyborzhets," *Leningradskaia Pravda*, 6 April 1929, 1; "Krasnyi Vyborzhets," *Pravda*, 11 April 1929, 1; *Politicheskii i trudovoi pod"em*, 223-24; A. V. Kol'tsov, *Kul'turnoe stroitel'stvo v RSFSR v gody pervoi piatiletki* (Akademii Nauk, 1960), 92; N. V. Tsapkin and V. I. Kazakov, *Leningradskaia promyshlennost' za 50 let* (Lenizdat, 1967), 221; A. V. Koshurin, "Dostizhenie vysokikh konechnykh rezul'tatov—glavnaia tsel' v sorevnovanii," in A. I. Miliukov, *Sorevnovanie i khoziaistvennyi mekhanizm razvitogo sotsializma* (Mysl', 1979), 119; I. P. Ostapenko, *Uchastie rabochego klassa SSSR v upravlenii proizvodstvom: proizvodstvennye soveshchaniia v promyshlennosti* (Nauka, 1964), 136; "M.E. Putin," *Krasnovyborzhets*, 10 January 1969, 2; and V. D. Soldatenkov, "Partiinoe rukovodstvo politiko-nravstvennym vospitaniem trudiashchikhsia promyshlennosti v gody pervoi piatiletki," *Vestnik Leningradskogo universiteta. Istoriia KPSS*, 3 (1988): 7-8.

joined competition"[141] which "was supported by the entire factory, then all of Leningrad, then the entire country."[142]

Бригада обрубщиков трубного цеха завода «Красный выборжец», подписавшая первый договор о социалистическом соревновании. *1930 г.*

Figure 2. Mikhail Putin's Brigade in 1930. Source: Ia. M. Dakhiia (ed.), *Leningradskie rabochie v bor'be za sotsializm 1926–1937* (1965), 197.

Today this all seems preposterous, but socialist competition, deftly exploiting a cultural code, was perfect for adapting the peasant mentality to regimented, regulated modernity. The competition *fabula* highlighted bold decisiveness, a *postupok,* that Mikhail Bakhtin found was central to identity formation.[143] Russia's grand novels all feature heroes, Onegin, Raskolnikov, whose personal decisions, hold metaphysical stakes. Furthermore, the competition involved a theatrical demonstration of manhood *(muzhestvo),* another theme pervading Russian culture from Akhmatova to Ayn Rand. Legitimacy was created by the quasi-

---

[141] Aleksei Zakhartsev, "Leningradtsy sami vyzvalis' spasti Rossiiu," *Voenno-promyshlennyi kur'er,* 1 March 2019, https://www.vpk-news.ru/articles/48893.
[142] "Putin," in A. F. Zanin (ed.), *Rabochaia entsiklopediia* (Lenizdat, 1986), 38.
[143] Mikhail Bakhtin, "K filosofii postupka," in *Filosofiia i sotsiologiia nauki i tekhniki. Ezhegodnik* (Nauka: 1986), 80–138.

religious act of reading and signing the pledge, seemingly torn from Goethe's seminal depiction of man crossing the threshold into Modernity. Thanks in part to competition, Soviet factories "once a woman's domain, became masculine and a source of national pride."[144] Contemporaries would have noted that all *personae dramatis* were of "Great-Russian" nationality. Most of all, socialist competition became a rite of initiation for the peasant into the factory-family. Workers cried genuine tears when they left for promotion.[145] Thanks in part to Mikhail Putin, the Bolsheviks thus created a ritual that legitimized industrialization.

Figure 3. Mikhail Putin in 1931. Source: V. N. Bernadskii and A. E. Suknovalov, *Istoricheskoe proshloe Leningrada* (Leningrad: Gos. uchebno-pedagog. izd-vo, 1960), Kn. 2, 293.

---

[144] Joshua Freeman, *Behemoth: A History of the Factory and the Making of the Modern World* (W. W. Norton, 2019).
[145] Kartus, "Vospominaniia," 37–38.

How "Spontaneous" Competition was Stage-managed by the Party

It's clear that "competition" with half-proletarians debating over the quasi-Marxist term *sebestoimost'* ("self-cost," basically production costs) was a fabrication.[146] Soviet scholars, complaining about the over-focus on personality, highlighted factual errors.[147] Nonetheless, *the-Man-who-shot-Liberty-Valence* myth prevailed. A comparison of available documents allows a more realistic account.

One former worker, A. I. Kartus, remembered being dragged to endless Party meetings. In March 1929, the factory director at Krasnyi Vyborzhets boasted that *sebestoimost'* had been reduced by 14%, but no one really understood if this was for the year or the quarter. After more presentations, a committee adopted a resolution to challenge "all the enterprises of the Soviet Union" to socialist competition. This resolution was adopted "unanimously" by "a meeting with 300 people: no one saw it as a significant event. Things soon got carried away, it was all forced *[prinuditel'no]*. There were idiots in the Party." Kartus recalls Mikhail Putin as "a plain *muzhik*, who had no idea he would become famous. I was proud to know him."[148]

Moscow's propagandists determined to make socialist competition different from similar failed initiatives. The Leningrad bureau of *Pravda* received an urgent call from Moscow: Mariia Il'inichna Ul'ianova (Lenin's sister) wanted reports published on how factories were competing to lower production costs. Petr Lukst, an old Bolshevik and envoy (*polpred*) of *Pravda* went to the Party

---

[146] S. R. Gershberg, "K piatiletiiu dvizheniia kollektivov i udarnikov kommunisticheskogo truda," in R. P. Dadykin (ed.), *Velikoe dvizhenie sovremennosti* (Nauka, 1964), 32–38; and L. A. Beilin, "O retsidivakh odnoi oshibki," *Istoriia SSSR* 3 (1965): 244–45.

[147] L. A. Beilin, *Ekonomicheskie osnovy sotsialisticheskogo sorevnovaniia: voprosy teorii* (Ekonomika, 1975), 34, 49–50; I. I. Kuz'minov, *Metodologicheskie problemy ekonomicheskoi nauki* (Mysl', 1967), 34; I. I. Changli, *Sotsialisticheskoe sorevnovanie i novye formy kommunisticheskogo truda* (Sotsiekgiz, 1959): 13; and N. A. Tsagolov (ed.), *Kurs politicheskoi ekonomii, t. II. Sotsializm* (Nomizdat, 1963), 199–200.

[148] Kartus, "Vospominaniia," 35.

Committee (Obkom) and was told to focus on Vyborzhets. He sent the skilled reporter Andrei Zverintsev to embellish the story. Zverintsev recalled: "I went around the workshops, meeting with workers. The factory's challenge, along with my correspondence and photographs, were sent to Moscow, and on March 5 published in *Pravda*."[149]

A special Party headquarters (*shtab*) was set up to supervise competitions at Vyborzhets. At first, 186 workers, under strict supervision, were to "compete." The Party bosses asked machine operators Murav'ev and Cherepagin to formalize their obligations in a written contract, but they refused. By April, the Party had browbeaten several brigades to sign contracts. Putin's brigade was the only one which agreed to wage reductions. They signed, not in March, but on 13 May.[150]

There does seem to have been some initial progress. Mikhail Putin bragged: "By the first month, our team had fulfilled the plan by 150 percent [...] In the first quarter, we increased labor productivity by 10.2 percent and reduced production costs by 7.1 percent." (Vyborzhets which was never able to fulfill quotas began to produce 120% of the plan.[151]) Putin proclaimed, "despite the panicked whimpers of right-wing evaders, Vyborzhets promises to

---

[149] A. B. Zverintsev, *Leningradskie rabochie i "Pravda"* (Lenizdat, 1982), 42–44.

[150] "Trubniki vypolniaiut obiazatel'stva," *Krasnovyborzhets*, 1 July 1929; Beilin, *Kak rodilos' sotsialisticheskoe sorevnovanie*, 51–52; Lebedeva and Shkaratan, *Ocherki istorii sotsialisticheskogo sorevnovaniia*, 98; L. S. Rogachevskaia, *Sotsialisticheskoe sorevnovanie v SSSR* (Nauka, 1977), 706; I. E. Vorozheikin, *Letopis' trudovogo geroizma* (Politizdat, 1984), 66; *Ocherki istorii Leningrada* (Akademiia nauk, 1955), 300–01. Other sources give 30 April as the day Putin and his brigade signed the contract; "Initsiatoram sorevnovaniia vrucheno znamia," *Pravda*, no. 120, 1 May 1941; and *Pravda Ukrainy*, no. 100, 29 April 1949. Yet other sources insist on 15 March as the day the contract was signed; M. I. Eskin, *Osnovnye puti razvitiia sotsialisticheskikh form truda* (Sotsekgiz, 1936), 6; Nikitin, *Muzei V. I. Lenina*, 157–58; D. Sherikh, *Gorodskoi mesiatseslov: 1000 dat iz proshlogo* (Peterburg-XXI vek, 1993), 23; and S. G. Strumilin, *Ekonomicheskaia zhizn' SSSR: khronika sobytii i faktov* (Sovetskaia entsiklopediia, 1961), 209.

[151] Stepanov, *Rabochie Leningrada*, 207; R. P. Dadykin, *Nachalo massovogo sotsialisticheskogo sorevnovaniia* (Politizdat, 1954), 97–99; and Dakhiia, *Leningradskie rabochie v bor'be za sotsializm* (Lenizdat, 1965), 197.

fulfill the five-year plan in four years."¹⁵² Accounting data was always spotty. Nonetheless, it appears production costs in 1929 decreased by around 6.3% while the plan called for 8.9%.¹⁵³ Absenteeism went from 41 in October to 11 workers in March.¹⁵⁴

Economically, competition was never successful.¹⁵⁵ As one report noted: "What hinders the development of socialist competition? Lack of tools, especially band saws, several of which were sent by express mail from Germany [...] we switched to circular saws but these proved useless. Skilled workers refuse to compete."¹⁵⁶ One Soviet historian noted: "Vyborzhets workers set out with even greater energy to storm [in 1930]. But unsatisfactory leadership disrupted implementation [...] Unfortunately, the factory got carried away with the pursuit of quantity at the expense of quality." Competition involved empty sloganeering and "pseudo-storming."¹⁵⁷

It was the young half-proletarians who propelled competition while professionals realized that it was preposterous. Komsomol lads would harangue senior workers about the need to arrive on time and work quickly. These initiatives were laughed at by seasoned workers. For example, the Racklasts (textile printers)

---

152 "Postanovlenie Obshchego Sobraniia rabochikh i sluzhashchikh leningradskogo zavoda 'Krasnyj Vyborzhets' o shefstve nad kolkhozami i sovkhozami," *Krasnovyborzhets* 37, 19 November 1929, 1.

153 "Informatsionnyi obzor leningradskogo oblastnogo komiteta Profsoiuza metallistov o khode sotsialisticheskogo sorevnovaniia na leningradskom zavode Krasnyi Vyborzhets," *Krasnovyborzhets*, 175, 25 October 1929, 1.

154 "Raport rabochikh leningradskogo zavoda Krasnyi Vyborzhets XVI Vsesoiuznoi partiinoi konferentsii. O proizvodstvennykh uspekhakh zavoda," *Pravda*, 92, 21 April 1929, 2; L. I. Arapova, *Marsh udarnykh brigad* (Molgvardiia, 1965), 212–14; and A. M. Lazareva, "Kommunisty Vyborgskoi storony," 92–93.

155 Even North Koreans zealots noted: "Socialist competition does not work well without effectively stimulating the material interests of members. Of course, it is of the utmost importance to educate workers with communist thoughts to increase their consciousness, but at the same time, they must be stimulated materially to increase their enthusiasm and elevate production;" Kim Il-song, *Kim Il-song seonjip* (Tongbangsa, 1965), 376.

156 *Politicheskiii i trudovoi pod"em*, 304–05; and CIA, "Of Domestic Difficulties," 1 June 1951, https://www.cia.gov/library/readingroom/docs/CIA-RDP80-00809A000700100201-5.pdf, 1–2.

157 M. E. Putin, "Dogovor Ruda," 178–79.

claimed "competing" would only lower quality.[158] Unions ignored the campaign completely. In 1929 Vyborzhets engineer bureau chairman, declared "until you stop writing about us in the newspaper and fix the relationship between the Commissars and the engineers, there can be no competition." Craftsmen tried to have over-eager youth fired.[159] In 1930, Leningrad workers yelled: "down with May Day, hurrah for Easter!" At Vyborzhets, even after threats, workers would not attend meetings. At a typical political meeting, out of 750 workers, only 98 showed up.[160]

The main "achievement" of competition was signing more agreements, a propaganda coup. As one contemporary gloated in 1930: "Future historians of the October Revolution will emphasize two events: the approval of the Five-year Plan and the powerful scope of socialist competition. This is not a dream, not a fantasy, as our enemies imply."[161] Perhaps using family connections, Mikhail Putin's call to competition was endorsed by textile workers in Tver. This became a propaganda set-piece, the "Agreement of Thousands."[162] Importantly, the competition soon moved to the villages: "At a plenum of the Morozovskii village council, the challenge of Vyborzhets was thoroughly discussed. Working peasants, unanimously resolved: 'Let the workers reduce the cost of production for factory goods by 7%. For our part, we, the peasants, undertake to expand the sown area in the upcoming spring

---

[158] M. Dosov, *Trekhgorka na sitsevom fronte* (Molgvardiia, 1929), 85. On conflict between skilled workers and newly arrived peasants, see: Lewis H. Siegelbaum, *Soviet State and Society Between Revolutions, 1918-1929* (Cambridge University Press, 1992), 105–10; and Hiroaki Kuromiya, "The Crisis of Proletarian Identity in the Soviet Factory, 1928–1929," *Slavic Review* 44, no. 2 (1985): 280–97.

[159] V. Ol'khov, *Za zhivoe rukovodstvo sotsialisticheskim sorevnovaniem* (VTsSPS, 1930), 20.

[160] "*Sovershenno sekretno,*" vol. 8, part 1 (1930), 305; and "Pervoe bolee reshaiushchii," 17–19.

[161] M. Shul'man, *Nashi dostizheniia na fronte sotsialisticheskogo sorevnovaniia* (Gosizdat, 1930), 3.

[162] *Podpisanie dogovora tysiach* (1929) available at: https://www.youtube.com/watch?v=6Y_Rkozpl5Q.

campaign.'"¹⁶³ By the end of 1929, two-thirds of the workers in large enterprises were competing.¹⁶⁴

Competition was soon simplified to a manageable point-based system: The base was 100 points. For exemplary working morale it was possible to receive as much as 110 points. For an 8-hour workday, the standard points would be given. Over-time would garner bonus points. Workers were allowed a 7 percent defect rate: anything under that earned more points. Finally, over-fulfillment of the norm would add points to the competition score.¹⁶⁵

"Competition" soon reached comical proportions. In 1935 at the prestigious Leningrad History Institute, the "USSR" department challenged Medieval Studies to competition.¹⁶⁶ Stalin apologist Fredrick Ward offered an unintentionally ghoulish description of how father was challenged by son, how African workers swore to work like simbas (lions).¹⁶⁷ Socialist competition was used with prisoners of war, and at beauty pageants.¹⁶⁸

As with other Stalinist innovations, such as the 1936 USSR "Constitution," competition served to disorient foreign enemies:¹⁶⁹ It was declared "the principal means" of making labor more

---

163 V. A. Smyshliaev, *Po leninskim zavetam* (Leningradskii universitet, 1969), 66.
164 Kuzakova, *XVI Konferentsiia*, 81; and Nikitin, *Muzei*, 157–58.
165 Jiri Cysar, "Criticism of Conduct of Socialist Competition" (1953), accessed via Freedom of Information Act Electronic Reading Room, https://www.cia.gov/readingroom/document/cia-rdp80-00809a000700100201-5.
166 P. N. Bazanov, *Zhizn' i tvorchestvo Nikolaia Ul'ianova* (Vladimir Dal', 2018), 124–25.
167 H. Ward, *In Place of Profit: Social Incentives in the Soviet Union* (C. Scribner's, 1933), 128, 149; and "'Socialist Competition' Carried Out During the Changkufeng Fighting," *New York Times*, 2 September 1938.
168 CIA, "Prisoners of War. Methods of Increasing Labor Productivity," 10 March 1952, https://www.cia.gov/library/readingroom/docs/CIA-RDP82-00039R000100230030-3.pdf; and "Beauty Pageants to be Held in Manner of Socialist Competition," *New York Times*, 22 October 1967, https://timesmachine.nytimes.com/timesmachine/1967/10/22/93874360.html?pageNumber=1.
169 A.N. Medushevskii, "Kak Stalinu udalos' obmanut' Zapad," *Obshestvennye nauki i sovremennost'* 3 (2016): 122–38, http://ecsocman.hse.ru/data/2018/11/18/1251870720/122-138_Meduchevskii_.pdf.

productive than in capitalist countries.[170] Competition was introduced into every country that came under Soviet domination.[171] Ukrainian sources first mention "Putin" in connection with his appeal to "sotsialistychne zmahannia".[172] North Korea continues to diligently organize socialist competitions (사회주의 경쟁).[173] Thus, although competition was economically inefficient, it became a widely used indoctrination tool.

사회주의경쟁열풍 더욱 세차게 각지 피해복구전투장들에서 들어온 소식 외 1건

Figure 4. Socialist Competition in North Korea: "sa-hoe-ju-ui gyeong-jaeng-yeol-pung" ("intense socialist competition"); from a news report broadcast on (North) Korean Central Television and posted by the North Korean propaganda outlet *Uriminzokkiri*, 2020, available at: https://www.youtube.com/watch?v=l9Z_2ODIVPY (screen shot taken on 26 October 2020).

---

[170] "Czechs Stressing Worker Contests," *New York Times*, 14 May 1949, https://timesmachine.nytimes.com/timesmachine/1949/05/14/96455918.pdf?pdf_redirect=true&ip=0.

[171] "Socialist Competition at Cuban Schools to Stop Cheating," *New York Times*, 19 March 1965, https://timesmachine.nytimes.com/timesmachine/1965/03/19/97187779.pdf?pdf_redirect=true&ip=0.

[172] O. S. Kudlai, *Vid komunistychnykh subotnykiv do brygad komunistychnoi pratsi* (Politvidav, 1962), 49–50, and S. M. Bilousov (ed.), *Istoriiia Ukrains'koi RSR* (Akademiia nauk Ukrains'koi RSR, 1958), v. 2, 341.

[173] Uriminzokkiri, "Sa-hoy-cwu-uy-kyeng-cayng-yel-phwung te-wuk sey-cha-key kak-ci phi-hay-pok-kwu-cen-thwu-cang-tul-ey-se tul-e-on so-sik oy 1ken," October 2020, https://www.youtube.com/watch?v=l9Z_2ODIVPY.

Competition and Totalitarianism

That worker initiative created competition is ludicrous. Instead, socialist competition gave the Bolsheviks an ideal means of horizontal monitoring by coaxing groups of workers into regulating each other. The Stakhanov movement, by rewarding a few of the most outwardly productive workers, further marginalized management and divided the labor movement.[174] Socialist competition thus hindered the formation of a true working class that could challenge the regime.[175] Notably, Hannah Arendt found socialist competition was integral to totalitarian control: "The Stakhanovite system [...] broke up all solidarity and class consciousness among the workers, first by the ferocious competition and second by the temporary solidification of a Stakhanovite aristocracy whose social distance from the ordinary worker naturally was felt more acutely than the distance from the ordinary workers and the management."[176] Indeed, for Stalin, competition was a perfect way to outwit left-wing supporters of Trotsky and Zinoviev by liquidating old cadres and promoting ambitious, uneducated peasant-workers. At the same time, competition challenged Bukharin's policies by marginalizing markets and returning to the "true" Lenin.

In the "Year of the Great Breakthrough" (on 3 November 1929) Stalin promulgated socialist competition as a harbinger of a new society. For Viacheslav Molotov, competition was creating a "fundamentally new" worker characterized by partisanship, collectivism, initiative, firmness, perseverance, heroism, "hegemonism."[177] Maxim Gorky was dispatched to describe this

---

[174] Isaac Deutscher, *Soviet Trade Unions: Their Place in Soviet Labour Policy* (Royal Institute of International Affairs, 1950), 107–14.
[175] Hiroaki Kuromiya, *Stalin's Industrial Revolution* (Cambridge University Press, 1988), 88–100.
[176] Hannah Arendt, *The Origins of Totalitarianism* (Cornell University Press, 1988), 321. See also: Michel Heller, *Cogs in the Soviet Wheel: The Formation of Soviet man* (Harvill: please add year), 147; and Robert Conquest, *Industrial Workers in the U.S.S.R* (Praeger, 1967), 73–83.
[177] V. Molotov, "Novoe sredi rabochikh," *Pravda*, 21 January 1930, available at: http://rt-online.ru/p10075591/.

"new" culture, visiting Vyborzhets on 4 July 1929.[178] Gorky wrote: "Many things at Vyborzhets surprised and delighted me, most of all aluminum production. Not only because workers extract silver and gold from garbage. It is an amazing, creative process, but there is a deeper meaning. This is how the working class must isolate the dirt and litter of the past, from the chaotic legacy of the bourgeoisie."[179] Socialist competition was promulgated by a propaganda state through novels such as Aleksandr Peregudov's *Solnechnyi klad* (Solar Treasure) (1933); movies, such as *Vstrechnyi (Counterplan)* (dir. Fridrikh Ermler and Sergei Yutkevich, 1932); songs like "Udarnyi trud vpered!" ("Shock work forward!") (1929); new holidays, such as Den' Industrializatsii (Industrialization Day) which replaced Transfiguration Day (6 August) from 1929; and first names, such as Gertruda (a portmanteau formed from the words for "hero" and "labor").

The 16th All-Union Party Conference (April 1929) approved the first five-year plan calling for competition in all areas of socialist construction. Competition, by awakening "the creative energy and initiative of the masses,"[180] was key to the Five-year plan.[181] Mikhail Putin reported: "We are pleased that, at our call, hundreds of factories have entered competition, introducing the creative initiative of the masses into the country's economic and political life."[182] Ominously, the Central Committee warned against overbureaucratizing this heroic struggle.[183] Of the elite shock-workers at this conference, only half had a school education while one-fifth had

---

[178] S. V. Zhuravlev, *Fenomen "Istorii fabrik i zavodov"* (Insitut rossiiskoi istorii RAN, 1997), 55–70; V. I. Grechnev, *Gor'kii v Peterburge-Leningrade* (Lenizdat, 1968), 213; and S. D. Balukhatyi, *Literaturnaia rabota M. Gor'kogo* (Akademii nauk, 1941), 105.
[179] Kuzakova, *XVI Konferentsiia*, 79; and L. Rakhmanov, *Nachinaetsia* (1972), 42–43.
[180] Lebedeva, *Partiinoe rukovodstvo*, 65–66.
[181] D. A. Baevskii, "V. I. Lenin i rost tvorcheskoi aktivnosti mass," *Istoricheskie zapiski* 84(1969): 81–84; and F. Mikhail and D. Reznikov (eds.), *Samoe vazhnoe, samoe glavnoe* (Profizdat, 1933), 143.
[182] Lazareva, "Kommunisty Vyborgskoi storony," 81.
[183] Kuzakova, *XVI Konferentsiia*, 81; *Ocherki istorii Leningrada* (Akademiia nauk, 1955), 300–1; and G. P. Alekseev, *Istoriia sotsialisticheskogo sorevnovaniia v SSSR* (Profizdat, 1980), 86.

no education at all. Many were peasants with landholdings who resented factory life.[184]

The conference barely hid the true Stalinist goals. Competition would sideline counterrevolutionary "independent" unions and "rightist" opposition. A key slogan was "Unions, face up to production!"[185] There were blunt calls to push aside older workers with the "young and energetic."[186] "Local party organizations took the lead in working collectives, organizing them to fulfill the tasks of the first five-year plan."[187] Mikhail Putin, often a willing stooge, uttered absurd propaganda lines, such as "the revolutionary impulse, awakened by the party's enthusiasm for building a new life, helped to overcome obstacle after obstacle, difficulty after difficulty."[188] In reality, worker autonomy was crushed.

Stalin made clear what he felt about opposition to competition: "Some 'comrades' among the bureaucrats think that competition is the next Bolshevik fad and will stall by the end of the 'season.' These 'comrade' bureaucrats, of course, are mistaken. In fact, competition is a communist method of building socialism based on the maximum activity of millions of workers."[189] Chief economic planner V.V. Kuibyshev also gave centrality to competition.[190]

---

[184] M. P. Kim and U. S. Borisov, *Rodina Sovetskaya* (Politizdat, 1987), 117–18.
[185] P. I. Kabanov (ed.), *Ocherki istorii sovetskogo rabochego klassa*, (Prosveschenie, 1966), 151; Politburo, "O chistke profapparata" (1930), at http://istmat.info/node/58756; and Lazareva "Kommunisty Vyborgskoi storony," 80.
[186] V. I. Kuz'min, *Vremia velikogo pereloma: kommunisty vo glave trudovogo pod"ema moskovskikh rabochikh v 1928-1929* (Moskovskii rabochii, 1979), 74–75; N. N. Amosov (ed.), *Pokoleniia udarnikov: Sbornik dokumentov* (Lenizdat, 1963); "Postanovlenie Soveta Narodnykh Komissarov 19 iiulia, 1929 O meropriiatiiakh po usileniiu proizvodstvennykh soveshchanii i ispol'zovanii initsiativy rabochikh," *Istoriia rabochego klassa Leningrada* (Leningradskii Universitet, 1962), 69–70.
[187] Lazareva, "Kommunisty Vyborgskoi storony," 80–81.
[188] S. S. Khromov, *Istoriia sovetskogo rabochego klassa*, vol. 2 (Nauka, 1984), 239.
[189] I. Stalin, "Sorevnovanie i trudovoi pod"em mass," 11 May 1929, at *Fond Aleksandra N. Iakovleva*, https://www.alexanderyakovlev.org/fond/issues-doc/1014536.
[190] Khromov, *Istoriia sovetskogo rabochego klassa*, 264; and V. V. Kuibyshev, "Sotsialisticheskii plan i tvorchestvo mass (1929)," in *Izbrannye proizvedeniia* (Gosizdatpolit: 1958), 134–43.

Soviet Icon

Figure 5. Mikhail Putin. Source: P. N. Pospelov (Ed.), *Istoriia Kommunisticheskoi partii Sovetskogo Soiuza* (Moscow: Politizdat, 1970),vol 4, pt. 1, 596.

Nonetheless, the notion that the initiative for competition came from below cannot be completely dismissed. Stalinism was in part propelled by ambitious men seeking upward mobility.[191] Self-interested youth willingly glorified competition.[192] As a contemporary noted: "Shock brigades were created spontaneously [*stikhiino*], at the initiative of the youth [...] At every factory, mine, and workshop, despite the lack of assistance from the trade unions

---

[191] Sheila Fitzpatrick, *Education and Social Mobility in the Soviet Union 1921–1934* (Cambridge University Press, 1979).
[192] For the related case of the Stakhanovites, see: Lewis H. Siegelbaum, *Stakhanovism and the Politics of Productivity in the USSR, 1935–1941* (Cambridge University Press, 1988), 179–209.

and party functionaries, workers arose to compete. Many in the Party saw competition as a threat."[193]

While not the "initiator" of competition, Mikhail Putin was no mere cog in the machine. Along with other Bolshevik chiefs, Kirov and Voroshilov frequented Vyborzhets.[194] Putin would have come to their attention. The athletic Putin embodied the ideal of the "new" worker and would have been sought after by Party leadership who saw wrestling as exemplifying Aleksandr Bogdanov's God-building *(bogostroitel'stvo)*. Putin served as the semi-nude model for the I.D. Shadr sculpture "Cobblestone: Weapon of the Proletariat," a 1927 synecdoche of macho workers.[195] In 1929, Spartakiad, a Red Olympics, featured wrestling: Piddubny returned as a Communist hero. The workers from the Metallicheskii Factory (LMZ) together with Vyborzhets built the enormous Durnovo sports complex, featuring a football stadium, basketball courts, boxing, and judo rings.

After "initiating" socialist competition, Putin was soon entrusted with another sensitive mission, agitating for collectivization. In fall 1930, Putin's brigade of 20 workers left for a village, Nizhnee chuevo in Muchkapski district, Tambov region. Putin went to the houses (*izby*) of the poorest peasants to explain the benefits of collectivization. A local kulak, Goloshumov, threatened Putin. Undeterred, Putin's men held a boisterous meeting where ninety out of one hundred peasants voted for collectivization. In true Putin-style, this account was embellished: after the meeting Mikhail, fearing a kulak might try to stab him, walked alone to his lodgings avoiding all houses. Suddenly, he was attacked by three wolfhounds. Luckily, in the -33 degrees celsius frost, Mikhail was wearing a thick military jacket. He managed to shoot the dogs with his revolver. The perpetrators, Goloshumov and

---

[193] V. Ol'khov, *Za zhivoe rukovodstvo sotsialisticheskim sorevnovaniem* (VTsSPS, 1930), 21.

[194] Vasilii Akshinskii, *Kliment Efremovich Voroshilov* (Politizdat, 1974), 146: V. M. Ivanov and M. V. Rosliakov, *Nash Mironych: Vospominaniia o zhizni i deiatel'nosti S. M. Kirova* (Lenizdat, 1969), 443; and S. V. Krasnikov, *S. M. Kirov v Leningrade* (Lenizdat, 1966), 93.

[195] Aleksandr Putin, *Rod prezidenta V. V. Putina*, 249.

a local priest, were arrested. Thus was founded the kolkhoz "Kranyvyborzhets" which operates to this today.[196] Putin's name was attached to tirades supporting collectivization. In one, he asserted that the kulaks were conducting counterrevolutionary agitation, "spreading rumors that there would be flogging on the collective farms," ushering in a new kind of serfdom; the state would forcibly collect hair from peasant woman; men and women would be forced to sleep side-by-side under one thirty-meter-long blanket."[197]

Kirov, who voiced worries about the influx of unruly peasants to the factories, would have found Putin an invaluable enforcer.[198] From 1927 to 1929, Mikhail Putin resided at 18, Sixth-Sovetskaia Street, walking distance from Vyborzhets. There Putin, who took to dressing like Voroshilov, received visits from Kirov.[199] It was Kirov who was instrumental in formulating and propagating competition.[200] "We need to get rid of everything ostentatious, ceremonial, statistically exaggerated," Kirov recommended, by focusing propaganda on Vyborzhets.[201] Putin had enough authority to suggest ideas about how socialist competition be conducted. He criticized some unrealistic obligations. For example, one clause of Putin's contract demanded workers graduate from correspondence study at the Polytechnic Institute. Putin, doubting workers would be attracted to such goals, eliminated this condition.[202] Thus Putin must have played a considerable behind-the-scenes role in creating competition and would have been well compensated.

---

[196] M. E. Putin, "Nasha rabochaia brigada v derevne," in A. I. Vdovina (ed.), *Obnovlenie zemli* (Molgvardiia, 1984), 784–86.
[197] M. E. Putin article in *Partrabotnik* (1930), cited from Stepanov, *Rabochie Leningrada*, 219.
[198] S. M. Kirov, *Izbrannye stat'i i rechi* (Gosizdatpolit, 1957), 562–63.
[199] *Ves' Leningrad* (1929), 495, https://vivaldi.nlr.ru/bx000020019/view/?#page=11 96; *Ves' Leningrad*, (1927), 363, https://vivaldi.nlr.ru/bx000020161/view/?#page=981; and Zhdanok "Teorema."
[200] Lebedeva and Shkaratan, *Ocherki istorii sotsialisticheskogo sorevnovaniia*, 95; Eskin, *Osnovnye puti*, 103; and E. K. Bobrova and I. A. Lipilin, *S. M. Kirov i leningradskie kommunisty* (Lenizdat, 1986), 186–88.
[201] Pompeev, *Khochetsia zhit'*, 89–92.
[202] S. B. Poles'ev, *Po leninskim adresam* (Lenizdat, 1969), 240–41.

The Soviets eventually acknowledged that competition could not depend on enthusiasm alone.[203] Those, like Putin's brigade, that played the game earnestly did well for themselves. Boris Kruglov, after receiving an elementary school education, graduated from the Workers' Faculty, then the Institute of Civil Engineers. Pavel Mokin graduated from the prestigious Technological Institute. Mikhail Grigor'ev became a Party secretary at a factory. Aleksei Goriunov graduated from the Leningrad Shipbuilding Institute. Aleksei Ogloblin became a manager of a Donbass mine. A still-young Mikhail Putin in 1931 was awarded the Soviet's highest honor, the Order of Lenin.[204] Propaganda emphasized that Putin no longer had to get up early in the morning for work.[205] During the early 30s, Mikhail married Mariia Alekseevna Tsvetaeva (1910–70).[206] He graduated from the School of Trade Unions in 1933 and became an administrator over the council of trade unions *(Lenoblprofsovet)*. In 1937, the Party made him boss of the Soiuzspetsstroi Construction.[207] Putin, by 1935, lived in an elite, "fairy tale" apartment on Angliiskii Avenue next to the Kirov Theater, surrounded by famous ballerinas.[208]

His factory entered dark times. Shock workers broke up union opposition, thousands of workers were fired, and in 1937 many

---

[203] Lebedeva and Shkaratan, *Ocherki istorii sotsialisticheskogo sorevnovaniia*, 115; and I. M. Dakhiia and A. I. Velikanova, *Leningradskie rabochie v bor'be za sotsializm* (Lenizdat, 1965), 197.

[204] S. I. Tiul'panov, *Industrializatsiia Severo-Zapadnogo raiona v gody vtoroi i tretei piatiletok (1933–1941)* (LGU, 1969), 371–72; and V. G. Zakharov, *Ocherki istorii Leningradskoi organizatsii KPSS* (Lenizdat, 1980), 220–21.

[205] V. Druzhinin, *Udarniki goroda Lenina* (Lenpartizdat, 1934), 70–75; and Mikhail Putin, "Desiat' let nazad," *Pravda*, no. 118, 19 April 1939. In the latter article, Putin is pictured with his brigade relaxing in posh suits.

[206] Mariia hailed from a large family from Valdai. Her father Aleksei was a schoolteacher. A pre-wedding photo taken in Valdai shows a svelte, poised Mariia dressed in style, and heels, next to a plainer sister. Her people often stayed at Mikhail's apartment in the '30s; T. Zhdanok. Email with author, 10 July 2021.

[207] M. E. Putin, "Dogovor Ruda," 179; and "Pervoe bolee reshaiushchii," 17–19.

[208] *Ves' Leningrad* (1935), https://vivaldi.nlr.ru/bx000020160/view/?#page=1031, 334. According to Tat'iana Zhdanok, Putin was also in charge of Kirov's funeral commission, and later became a deputy in the Leningrad City Soviet; Tat'iana Zhdanok, email to author, 10 July 2021.

Polish workers were executed.²⁰⁹ Lying low, Mikhail Putin was clever enough to avoid Stalinist excess. Putin penned an anodyne article on Gorky's visit to the factory.²¹⁰

During the war, Mikhail Putin supervised construction projects in Leningrad. A co-worker E. I. Panteleeva recalled: "In 1942 at the 40-hectare farm of Special Unit No. 40 (OSMCh-40), we saved many from hunger. It was located in the village Sel'tsy" (now Voeikovo, about 20 km drive from Ladozhskaia metro station). The Nazis were 18 kilometers away. Panteleeva recounts: "We heard artillery, at night we saw the yellow-green light of enemy illumination rockets. I remember [Putin] because the Order of Lenin shone on his chest."²¹¹ Putin also managed repairs of the city water supply and (in Trust 38) supervised the construction of bunkers and ditches in Kupchino (which was close to the front).²¹² In a memo, Putin is charged with shifting workers from bomb shelters and bread factories to plumbing work in apartments, a matter of life and death in wartime Leningrad.²¹³ On 29 April 1944,

---

²⁰⁹ A. V. Kol'tsov, *Kul'turnoe stroitel'stvo v RSFSR v gody pervoi piatiletki* (Izdatel'stvo Akademii Nauk SSSR, 1962), 92; Lazareva, "Kommunisty Vyborgskoi storony," 90–92; and A. Ia. Razumov and D. I. Bogomolov, *Leningradskii martirolog: 1937-1938* (Rossiiskaia natsional'naia biblioteka, 1995), vol. 4.

²¹⁰ M. E. Putin, "K godovshchine smerti A. M. Gor'kogo," *Leninskii put'*, no. 40, 23 May 1937, 43.

²¹¹ K. A. Nikitin, V. S. Lekhnovich, and N. R. Ivanov, *V osazhdennom Leningrade: vospominaniia uchastnikov geroicheskoi oborony* (Lenizdat, 1974), 200–02.

²¹² S. P. Kniazev (ed.), *Na zashchite nevskoi tverdyni* (Lenizdat, 1965), 207–08; and A. A. Riadov, "Postroeno leningradtsami," in I. A. Leitman (ed.), *Inzhenernye voiska goroda-fronta* (Lenizdat, 1979), 88.

²¹³ "Reshenie Lengorispolkoma o remonte vodoprovoda i kanalizatsii v zhilykh domakh Vasileostrovskogo, Primorskogo i Oktiabr'skogo raionov" (6 August 1942), in A. N. Chistikov et al. (eds), *Stenogrammy zasedanii ispolkoma Leningradskogo gorodskogo Soveta. Zapisi obsuzhdenii, zamechanii k proektam, reshenii noiabr' 1941–dekabr' 1942 gg. Sbornik dokumentov* (TsGA SPb., Izdatel'stvo "Art-Ekspress," 2017), 260, https://spbarchives.ru/documents/10157/18919/%D1%81%D0%B1%D0%BE%D1%80%D0%BD%D0%B8%D0%BA.pdf/7d47718d-a1b1-4b74-b77d-40a5959aa1ae. Achieving the rank of senior lieutenant, on 3 June 1932 he received the medal "For the Defense of Leningrad"; "Lichnaia kartochka predstavliaemogo k vrucheniiu medali 'Za oboronu Leningrada'" (3 June 1943), available at "Putin Mikhail Eliseevich 1894 g. r.," Arkhivy Peterburga, https://medal.spbarchives.ru/person?docId=444026.

and in again in 1947, Putin returned to Vyborzhets to celebrate militarized anniversaries of the contract.[214] Tragically, Mariia and Mikhail's son, Dmitrii, died at a young age during the war. After the war, Mikhail left Mariia for another woman. They soon divorced.[215] In the 1950s Putin supervised restoration and housing construction in the Vyborg area of Leningrad.[216]

After World War II, Mikhail Putin became a trusted elder, one of Le Play's *starchi*. In *Pravda*, he was lionized, along with Stakhanov, as a hero.[217] While Stakhanov, a notorious rogue, was feted from afar, Putin, living "a humble life," continued agitating up to age 75.[218] Unlike other labor heroes, Putin was consulted by scholars.[219] A typical propaganda piece relates: "Time passed and the labor veterans aged, but they never forget their factories. A gray-haired man with the Order of Lenin on his chest often visited Vyborzhets: Putin. The shop was changing before his eyes: no cramped, dark cells anymore. Powerful, high-performance tube mills stand along the wide, bright aisles: Putin's profession has disappeared." Putin befriended his successors: "people of high technical culture."[220] Chatting with them, Putin was known for giving off-the-cuff speeches as if reliving his youth. Putin recounted: "The competition awakened the thought of the worker, made him look at the factory with different eyes, with the eyes of an owner."[221] In 1937, the city installed a marble memorial plaque with the names

---

[214] "Za dostoinuiu vstrechu 1 maia," *Izvestiia*, no. 86, 13 April 1949; V. A. Ezhov and I. N. Yablochkin, *O podvige Leningrada strokami khroniki* (Lenizdat, 1989), 543; and Amosov, *Pokoleniia*, 164.

[215] Scraping by as a janitor, Mariia's last years were lonely and bitter. Her family buried her in 1970; T. Zhdanok, email with author, 10 July 2021.

[216] L. S. Shaumian (ed.), *Leningrad-Spravochnik* (Bol'shaia Sovetskaia Entsiklopediia, 1957), 683; and I. E. Vorozheikin, *Letopis' trudovogo geroizma* (Politizdat, 1984), 61–66.

[217] "Prazdnik radostnogo truda," *Izvestiia*, no. 83, 7 April 1969, 1.

[218] "M. E. Putin," *Pravda*, no. 64, 5 March 1969, 1–2.

[219] Baevskii, *Politicheskii i trudovoi pod"em*, 199–200.

[220] Poles'ev, *Po leninskim adresam*, 240–41.

[221] Kabanov, *Ocherki istorii*, 151. For other remembrances of Putin visiting his factory: Elena Katerli, "Dorogoe tvorchestvo," *Izvestiia*, no. 102, 30 April 1954; and S. R. Gershberg, *Dvizhenie kollektivov i udarnikov kommunisticheskogo truda* (Politizdat, 1961), 64.

of Putin's brigade at the factory entrance.[222] A Vyborzhets stamp appeared in 1957.[223]

Putin became a valuable tool for indoctrination. "The participation of the veterans of the Revolution and labor [...] is extremely important in educating working youth on revolutionary and labor traditions."[224] University students would be bused to Vyborzhets and "introduced to the latest equipment" and sometimes Putin himself.[225] On 25 November 1958 on the eve of the 21st Party Congress, at the storied Tauride Palace 1,500 people gathered for a meeting [slet], broadcast by radio.[226] Komsomol youths sat together with labor veterans. "What a truly wonderful fusion of generations!" exclaimed Putin, now an elderly, slightly stooped man in glasses. The youth ardently applauded.

> And Putin himself applauds, then takes off his glasses for some reason, puts them on again [...] "[In 1929] everyone's heart was seething with joy [...] How many five-year plans have been fulfilled and over-fulfilled since that time! [..] Today, I feel young again, just like you. I'll tell you," he smiled slyly, "the secret of youth." This consisted in being consulted by the youth. "I gaze into your faces and see an amazing relay race of generations, inexhaustible loyalty to the party, loyalty to the homeland, and an indefatigable thirst to serve!"[227]

---

[222] "V chest' velikogo pochina," *Pravda*, no. 68, 10 March 1963; Iu. Ovchinnikova, "Pervyi dogovor na sotsialisticheskoe sorevnovanie," *Ogonok*, no. 26, 23 June 1957, 16; Zuev, "Vyzyvaem na sotsialisticheskoe sorevnovanie," 122–29; and "Krasnyi Vyborzhets," memorial'naia doska, *Sankt-Peterburg Entsiklopediia*, 1 January 2015, http://www.encspb.ru/object/2805587634?lc=ru.

[223] V. Iu. Solov'ev, *Pochtovye marki Rossii i SSSR* (IzdAT, 1998), 147.

[224] S. M. Lepekhin, "Vospitanie rabochei molodezhi na revoliutsionnykh i trudovykh traditsiiakh," in G. V. Vorontsov (ed.), *Nauchnye zapiski Instituta povysheniia kvalifikatsii prepodavatelei obshhestvennykh nauk pri LGU*, vol. 2 (LGU, 1969), 123.

[225] E. G. Alekseeva and L. I. Tolstova, "Iz opyta vospitatel'noi raboty prepodavatelei kafedry istorii KPSS so studentami vo vneuchebnoe vremia," in P. R. Sheverdalkin (ed.), *Voprosy metodiki prepodavaniia istorii KPSS v vuzakh* (LGU, 1974), 111; "Estafeta," *Agitator* (1979): 7–11; B. Novotorov, "Pervymi podniali znamia...," *Neva* 3 (1979): 216; and Senin, "Budem sorevnovat'sia!," 177.

[226] Lebedeva, *Partiinoe rukovodstvo*, 181.

[227] A. Itigin, "Reportazh iz budushchego," *Neva* 1 (1959): 181–83. See also: A. L. Mil'shtein and M. M. Ol'shanskii, "Leningradskaia partiinaia organizatsiia v bor'be za razvertyvanie dvizheniia brigad kommunisticheskogo truda,"

One stock propaganda piece was Putin mentoring younger workers, notably Nikolai Voronin. At a rally on 19 November 1958 at Vyborzhets, Voronin's brigade gathered in the "red corner" of the workshop to greet Putin. Voronin promised to "continue the work of our fathers, to multiply their traditions [...] In accepting new commitments, we take a sacred oath to live and work as Ilyich [Lenin] bequeathed. We challenge the Komsomol and youth brigades of the same enterprises that 30 years ago accepted the challenge issued by Vyborzhets." "The torch has passed," intoned Putin solemnly.[228] Voronin thanked Putin for his "valuable" advice.[229] "Taking this baton into our young hands, we pledge to carry it with honor, to be worthy heirs of the old guard of Vyborzhets."[230] A typical propaganda vignette featured youngsters seeking elder Putin's wisdom:

> On the "memorable evening" of November 19, 1958, two students strolled across Leningrad to the Vyborzhets factory to ask Nikolai Voronin to introduce them to Putin. The young Komsomol were "noticeably worried." "Maybe he won't attend." But after waiting, Mikhail Eliseevich entered the room. "All, as if in agreement, stood up." Voronin hugged Putin. "Look, Misha. Your heirs want to consult with you." Voronin brought in a chair for Putin. The youth pleaded: "We want to live in a communist way at work, in studies, in everyday life [...we want to compete]. But striving and doing are different matters. Do we have a moral right to compete? [...] we would like to consult with you, Mikhail Eliseevich. It is good to listen to elders." Tears sprung to in the eyes of workers. Voronin theatrically laid a sheet of paper in front of Putin. "Our obligations are written here [...] they now concern the young builders of communism."
>
> Everyone was waiting for what Mikhail Eliseevich would say. Propping up his heavy head with wide, weary palms, Putin was silent. A minute passed, then another. The labor veteran was lost in thought. "Why doesn't he speak?" the guys asked themselves. "Doesn't he believe us?" No, Mikhail Eliseevich believed and understood that if not today, then tomorrow, and if

---

Uchenye zapiski kafedr obshchestvennykh nauk 2 (1960): 65–66; and G. S. Merkur'ev, *Brigady i udarniki kommunisticheskogo truda* (Uchpedgiz, 1962), 30.

[228] Iu. A. Lavrikov and E. V. Mazalov, *Ocherk ekonomicheskogo razvitiia leningradskoi industrii za 1917–1967 gg.* (Lenizdat, 1968), 317–18.

[229] Nikolai Voronin, "Po zavetam Il'icha," *Komsomol turmushi*, 1 January 1959, 9–11; and V. E. Poletaev, *Rabochii klass SSSR, 1951–1965* (Nauka, 1969), 333.

[230] Amosov, *Pokoleniia*, 372.

not this brigade, then another will answer the call. It is as inevitable as tomorrow's sun rising [...] Putin understood perfectly, but he wanted to say something so weighty that it would sink into young fiery souls. Rising, he spoke slowly, but firmly: "Dear comrades! Nowadays working conditions are changing: Technology frees us from hard work, forces us to study, and creates unprecedented opportunities not only for increasing material goods, but also spiritual goods. Above all is the growth of communist consciousness. We laid the foundational stones of communism: we unfurled the banners. And now that communism has come to life, shouldn't these banners lead us forward? And shouldn't young people, talented and heroic, be heirs and continue the great initiative of the most revolutionary class in the world!"[231]

Figure 6. Mikhail Putin advises N.N. Voronin (Putin is second from the right, Voronin is on the far left). Source: *Leningradskaia panorama* 1 (1987): 5.

By the 1960s times had changed: the Aleksei Kosygin reforms were based on technological progress, not theatrical "competition." A typical socialist competition manual of the period stated: "Rationalization has become the law of the working class [...] the result of a deep study of the scientific foundations of production. Modern production with a predominance of machine time over auxiliary time, with a regulated rhythm, extremely limits the possibilities of increasing labor productivity through intensification."[232] Sidestepping his role in Stalinization, Mikhail

---

[231] A. A. Surov, *Odnogo kremnia iskry* (Molgvardiia, 1963), 58.
[232] F. G. Krotov and O. I. Shkaratan, *Rabochii klass—vedushchaia sila stroitel'stva kommunizma* (Mysl', 1965), 160; E. F. Pashkevich and O. I. Shkaratan, *Velikoe*

Putin was wise to play the sage who "barely recognizes his native factory."

Mikhail Putin was often called to give speeches at ceremonial events at Vyborzhets. After the "Song of Lenin," he delivered many memorable talks.[233] For example, in 1967, the 50th anniversary of the Revolution, Vyborzhets held "October Readings" featuring soldiers in formation. Putin greeted the soldiers, presenting each with a badge of Vyborzhets. Then the soldiers and young workers went to the factory museum.[234] Putin recounted the history of competition. Then he handed a pennant to some Komsomol youth who had just won a competition. Accepting the pennant, a young foreman uttered: "I assure you that we will justify the high trust of the old generation!"[235]

Mikhail Putin was celebrated as a figure of historical import.[236] In encyclopaedias, "Putin" appeared next to Alexander

---

dvizhenie sovremennosti: vozniknovenie i razvitie kollektivov i udarnikov kommunisticheskogo truda (Nauka, 1964), 223–47; and B. K. Alekseev and L. Abramova, *Partiinaia organizatsiia i rabochie Leningrada* (Lenizdat, 1974), 220.

[233] G. S. Merkur'ev and E. I. Savost'ianov, *Brigady i udarniki kommunisticheskogo truda* (Uchpedgiz, 1962), 101.

[234] E. M. Dvorianskii and A. A. Yaroshenko, *V ognennom kol'tse* (Ėėsti raamat, 1977), 231.

[235] N.a., "Rabochie Leningrada v bor'be za sotsializm i kommunizm," *Nauchnye zapiski Instituta povysheniia kvalifikatsii prepodavatelei obshchestvennykh nauk* 2 (1969): 123.

[236] L. S. Rogachevskaia, *Dvizhenie za kommunisticheskii trud: istoriia i problemy* (Mysl', 1968), 53; B. N. Ponomarev, *Istoriia SSSR: s drevneishikh vremen do nashikh dnei* (Nauka, 1966), t. 8, 492; G. P. Eliseev, *Molodezh' i sotsialisticheskoe sorevnovanie* (Ekonomia, 1969), 20; D. M. Zabrodin, *Ocherki istorii SSSR: 1917-1941* (Vysshaia shkola, 1978), 232; A. F. Khavin, *Kratkii ocherk istorii industrializatsii SSSR* (Politizdat, 1962), 154–55; S. R. Gershberg, *Rukovodstvo Kommunisticheskoi partii dvizheniem novatorov promyshlennosti, 1935-1941* (Politizdat, 1956), 22–23; Iu. A. Zakharov, "Zastrel'shchiki s vyborgskoi," *Sotsialisticheskoe sorevnovanie* 2: 28 (1979): 43–44; S. V. Raik, *Moskva-Leningrad: sorevnovanie trudovykh kollektivov dvukh gorodov* (Moskovskii rabochii, 1976), 53; L. S. Gaponenko, *Vedushchaia rol' rabochego klassa v rekonstruktsii promyshlennosti SSSR* (Mysl', 1973), 97; and V. N. Il'inskii, *Geral'dika trudovoi slavy* (Politizdat, 1987), 36–37.

Pushkin.[237] His achievements were taught in schools.[238] The Museum of Revolution in Moscow featured a large display on Putin.[239]

Soviet workers competed for the prestigious Putin prize while the Komsomol youth competed for the Kruglov prize.[240] During the Gorbachev period, the prizes continued to be awarded with the Putin motto "produce more, without harming quality."[241] At one team meeting, it was recounted: "Gusev gazed at his guys gloomily, but suddenly, smiling, announced, 'Why get hung up?' The Riazanovite factory won the Putin prize this time! But after all, Putin worked with us in this factory, which means we will achieve our goal next time. We are successors of Putin's mission."[242] Putin was interviewed on radio, for example, by the head of the Leningrad Radio bureau, Matvei Frolov.[243] In 1976, workers glowingly recalled him.[244] In 1978, a Soviet TV program "Our Biography," which broadcast hour-long episodes covering the main events of each year (1917–77) showed a "1929" installment that featured Putin and the importance of propagating his legacy.[245] The 1975 film *Spring of*

---

[237] L. S. Shaumian (ed.), *Leningrad. Entsiklopedicheskii spravochnik* (Bol'shaia Sovetskaia Entsiklopediia, 1957), 683.

[238] V. A. Ezhov, *Kak gotovit'sia k priemnym ekzamenam v VUZ: istoriia SSSR* (Leningradskii universitet, 1960), 107–08; P. N. Pospelov, *Istoriia Kommunisticheskoi partii Sovetskogo Soiuza* (Politizdat, 1965), v. 4. pt. 1, 595; A. V. Kornilov, "Istoricheskaia missiia sovetskogo rabochego klassa," *Prepodavanie istorii v shkole* 4 (July 1967): 29.

[239] M. P. Chernov, *Bor'ba partii za sotsialisticheskuiu industrializatsiiu strany i podgotovka sploshnoi kollektivizatsii sel'skogo khoziaistva* (Moskovskii rabochii, 1964), 169; and Nikitin, *Muzei*, 157.

[240] "Estafeta," *Agitator*, 7–11; Senin: "Budem sorevnovat'sia!," 177; and A. V. Koshurin, "Dostizhenie vysokikh konechnykh rezul'tatov—glavna'a tsel' v sorevnovanii," in A. I. Miliukov (ed.), *Sorevnovanie i khoziaistvennyi mekhanizm razvitogo sotsializma* (LGU, 1979), 125.

[241] N.a., "Premii sovetskikh profsoiuzov," *Magnitogorskii metall* 83 (July 1982) 15: 1.

[242] Gurinovich, "Kyl'ia pochina," 22–23.

[243] A. Zakhartsev, "Leningradtsy sami vyzvalis' spasti Rossiiu," *Voenno-promyshlennyi kur'er* (March 2019), https://www.vpk-news.ru/articles/48893.

[244] P. D. Kondiukova, *Gordost' Rossii: Rasskaz o geroiakh desiatoi piatiletki* (Sovetskaia Rossiia, 1978), 193.

[245] "Nasha biografiia. God 1929," *Nasha biografiia* (1976-77), available at *Sovetskoe televidenie. Gosteleradiofond* Youtube channel, https://www.youtube.com/watch?v=x-mU-pdZahg.

Labor featured a recording of Putin and footage of children at the Vyborzhets museum.²⁴⁶

Figure 7. Mikhail Putin. Source: *Krasnovyborzhets*, 10 January 1969, 2.

Putin's endeavor was considered crucial for the Humanities. A Soviet art critic claimed that the "Vyborzhets challenge" of 1929 provided a model for modern international artistic movements.²⁴⁷ Another Soviet academic wrote: "Competition gave rise to a new type of labor collective, gave rise to a new type of person, the working commander of production. And this determined the main direction of our literature, our art, determined their innovative essence."²⁴⁸

---

²⁴⁶ This segment is available online: *Vesna Truda* (1975) part 1 (at 7:00 min.), https://www.net-film.ru/film-7614/
²⁴⁷ M. M. Musin, Sovetskaiia kul'tura i dukhovnyii mir cheloveka truda (Sovetskii Pisatel', 1979), 249.
²⁴⁸ M. A Dudin, "V razvedke—pesnia i dusha/ Pisatel' i piatiletka," *Sovetskaia kul'tura i dukhovnyi mir cheloveka truda* (Sovetskii Pisatel', 1979), 29; I. I. Kolomiichenko, *Torzhestvo leninskikh ideii o sotsialisticheskom sorevnovanii* (Vishcha shkola, 1982), 47; and n.a., "Fundament ekonomiki," *Leningradskaia panorama* 1 (1987): 5.

Putin's achievement was also a philosophical breakthrough, creating "production democracy"[249] and a "new worker."[250] "Socialist competition and the Stakhanov movement were not only of purely practical importance [...] Competition develops creativity, influencing one's worldview and way of life. Indicative is Vyborzhets: the illiterate worker Pavel Moiken, who could barely sign the contract, became an engineer."[251] Competition continued to be a popular dissertation topic until 1990.[252]

Putin was commemorated at the highest levels. At the 21st Party Conference, after Comrade N.S. Khrushchev's report, speeches highlighted Vyborzhets victories.[253] Secretary Brezhnev seemed especially fond of competition. "We all rejoice," said Leonid Brezhnev at the 25th Party Congress, "Lenin's ideas of competition have taken deep roots."[254] Brezhnev noted how symbolic it was that Mikhail Putin before his death presided over the pledge of Voronin's brigade and that the heirs of socialist competition continue to bring fresh flowers to the bronze monument of Putin at the factory museum.[255]

When he died, in 1969, Mikhail Putin's obituary was printed on the first page of *Pravda*.[256] At his grave, in Leningrad's North

---

[249] See, for example: V. N. Kiselev, *Sotsial'naia funktsiia sotsialisticheskogo sorevnovaniia* (Profizdat, 1980); and V. G. Smol'kov, *Sorevnovanie i kommunizm. Metodologicheskie i sotsial'nye problemy* (Izdatel'stvo Moskovskogo universiteta, 1970).

[250] A. V. Kornilov, *Na reshaiushchem etape* (MGU, 1968), 167.

[251] A. R. Dzeniskevich, *Rabochie Leningrada nakanune Velikoi Otechestvennoi voiny* (Nauka, 1983), 157.

[252] V. G. Smol'kov, *Sotsialisticheskoe sorevnovanie v usloviiakh razvitogo sotsializma* (Mysl', 1974).

[253] E. V. Mazalov, *Na putiakh tekhnicheskogo progressa: iz opyta raboty Leningradskoi partiinoi organizatsii* (Lenizdat, 1962), 218.

[254] Kuzakova, *XVI Konferentsiia*, 79–81.

[255] N.a., "Na osnove vsemernogo vovlecheniia mass...," *Sotsialisticheskoe sorevnovanie* 2, no. 28 (1979): 45.

[256] A. Balatin, "Geroi s vyborgskoi vyzov krasnogo Vyborzhtsa," *Pravda*, no. 64, 5 March 1969, 1; and M. S. Krutyniv, "Putin M. E.," *Leningradskaia pravda*, 8 January 1969, 2–3. Putin outlived all the members of his brigade; B. I. Stukhalin, *Velikim imenem ozareno* (Pravda, 1970), 253.

Cemetery, there is a memorial bust by E. V. Tonkova (1976).²⁵⁷ In 1997, the Vyborzhets director, recalling Putin, claimed "socialist competition still continues as the spirit of market competitiveness [*konkurentnost'*]."²⁵⁸ This section has demonstrated that Mikhail Putin was well connected to the Party elite and became a revered socialist sage.

Figure 8. Mikhail Putin. Source: *Leningradskaia Pravda*, no. 6, 8 January 1969, 6.

From Putin to Putinism

According to Aleksandr Putin, by 1995, around one hundred Putins lived in St Petersburg, but from 1930 to 1970, there were only two or

---

²⁵⁷ L. S. Eremina, and I. M. Piriutko, *Istoricheskie kladbishcha Peterburga* (Chernysheva, 1993), 520.
²⁵⁸ "Krasnyi Vyborzhets," Evropa-TV (1997), https://www.youtube.com/watch?v=AokkRa9T-Xw.

three Putin households in the city.²⁵⁹ During the famine years, at the height of Mikhail Putin's fame, Vladimir Spiridonovich and his wife Maria received life-saving permission to move out of Pomimivo and register in Leningrad. While Vladimir served in the navy, Maria worked, perhaps at the Vyborzhets state farm growing carrots and cabbage.²⁶⁰ During the blockade, she lived with "some relative" near the Fontanka River.²⁶¹ This, assuredly would be with Mikhail Putin. In 1942, his apartment at the Skazka House was destroyed by bombing and Mikhail moved to a nearby apartment, at Fontanka Street 109, room 73.²⁶² Off-and-on they continued living with "relatives" until Vladimir landed a good job at the Egorov factory and they were given an apartment on Baskov Lane, a block from the Summer Gardens. (In "yet another coincidence, to which we have become accustomed," Russian state-controlled media reported in 2004 that Mikhail Putin's grandson, Viktor, was living on Baskov Lane.)²⁶³ Befitting a Putin, the future president, was born in the city's prestigious maternity ward, Snegireva. Mikhail's wife informed all her relatives about the birth.²⁶⁴ Vladimir talked little with his father, who was scarred by the war.²⁶⁵ But he used to visit a "relative"—perhaps Mikhail?—who recounted family history.²⁶⁶

The rise of Vladimir Vladimirovich Putin has always been a puzzle; but his biography makes more sense if he received Mikhail's helping hand. While nepotism was discouraged, the Soviets did promote "worker dynasties." Propaganda articles highlighted the "wonderful" Vyborzhets families of Denezhko, Voronin, and

---

259 Aleksandr Putin, *Rod prezidenta V. V. Putina*, 242.
260 Gevorkian et al., *Ot pervogo litsa*, 8.
261 Ibid.
262 "Lichnaia kartochka." This housing complex was the former residence of Prince Engalychev; "Dom kniazia Engalycheva," *City Walls. Arkhitekturnyi sait Sankt-Peterburga*, https://www.citywalls.ru/house1694.html?s=5rrd5up844l1m85c6l8kaiikv7.
263 N. a., "Priz imeni Putina vruchali esche 75 let nazad," *NTV*, 30 April 2004, https://www.ntv.ru/novosti/44113/.
264 Zhdanok, "Teorema."
265 Psychologist Kenneth Dekleva, who has published a number of psychological profiles of Putin and other political leaders, concludes that Putin's father never served as a role model; email to author, 18 December 2020.
266 Gevorkian et al., *Ot pervogo litsa*, 6–7.

Duninin. Mikhail Putin was regarded as a pater familias of the "school of communist labor."[267] At Vyborzhets, family dynasties enjoyed the "authority and deep respect of the collective. The display of such glorious labor traditions of hereditary working families in lecture and propaganda work is important in educating young people and instilling in them a love of work."[268] Mikhail's efforts to guide struggling Vladimir would thus have received official blessing.

Inter-generational sports was also a part of Soviet indoctrination.[269] Mikhail "kept in touch with his native factory," helping to build a good club and stadium.[270] From time to time, Mikhail met his old Sanitas wrestling mate Sergei Vasil'evich Dashkevich (1896–1953). Dashkevich went on to take Judo courses under the legendary Vasily Oshchepkov at the Moscow worker-peasant militia school.[271] In 1937, Oschepkov was repressed.[272] In order to set oneself up teaching Judo in Leningrad, it would certainly have been helpful to be connected with someone with Putin's sway.

It seems likely that Mikhail Putin may have been instrumental in helping Dashkevich's pupil, Anatolii Rakhlin establish the Judo Club currently located across the street from Vyborzhets factory.[273] In the 1960s in the USSR, the idea of a Judo (or Sambo) club, directed by a Jew and open to the public, would have been unheard of. Perhaps Mikhail Putin may have helped establish Rakhlin's club, which was located in the Yusupov Palace, close by his home. This unique club was named "Pipe-builder" (*Trubostroitel'*)—Mikhail's profession. The authorities would surely have demanded a vigilant

---

[267] Zuev, "Vyzyvaem na sotsialisticheskoe sorevnovanie," 122–29.
[268] B. A. Pokrovskii, "XXI S"ezd KPSS i zadachi Kommunisticheskogo vospitaniia," in A.F. Shishkin (ed.), *Voprosy marksistsko-leninskoi etiki* (Politizdat, 1960), 18–19.
[269] Amosov, *Pokoleniia*, 375.
[270] M. E. Putin, "Dogovor Ruda," 179.
[271] V. N. Grishenkov, *Dziudo. Stranitsy istorii. Chast' 2* (BGUFK, 2014), http://www.judo.lv/pdf_library/!dzju-do_2_rus_all_last.pdf, 44, 83.
[272] M. N. Lukashev, Sotvorenie sambo: rodit'sia v tsarskoi tiur'me i umeret' v stalinskoi (Budo-Sport, 2003).
[273] "Nasledie trenera," *Zolotoi Luch* (2016), https://www.youtube.com/watch?v=Wr1Lh7U53D0.

eye keep watch over this unprecedented undertaking.[274] Perhaps it might even be the case that Mikhail selected for this role the young Vladimir, who had been struggling in school, and who was among the club's first group of students in 1964.[275]

Times had changed: in place of peasant-brawlers, cultural heroes became scientists and scholars, as epitomized by the beloved nerd Shurik, from Gaidai's comedies of the 1960s. In the city, fighting was as unheard of as in today's South Korea. Vladimir was estranged from his father, adrift in a school system demanding deep mathematics, and sensitive about his height.[276] It is reasonable to assume that he would have thrown himself at the chance to follow in the footsteps of the iconic Misha the Wrestler. Certainly, martial arts shaped Putin's personality as much as any other activity.[277] He became a Hachidan in Judo (8th level). According to embellished accounts by Rakhlin's son, Mikhail—the current president of Russian Judo—the strict Rakhlin allowed no favors *(poblazhki)*. This

---

[274] Many lurid tales are told of Vladimir Putin's youth so that, at the least, it would seem that the Sambo club would have given him the reputation of a hooligan; Dmitrii Volchek, "Putin byl naglym dvorovym patsanom. Vospominaniia kaskadera," *Radio Svoboda*, 16 November 2019, https://www.svoboda.org/a/3 0271194.html.

[275] "VIII Traditsionnyi iunosheskii turnir po dziudo pamiati Zasluzhennogo trenera Rossii Anatoliia Rakhlina proidet v Sankt-Peterburge v zakrytom formate," *Regional'naia sportivnaia federatsiia dziudo Sankt-Peterburga*, 27 October 2020, https://www.spbjudo.com/news/viii-tradicionniy-yunosheskiy-turnir-po-dzyudo-pamyati-zasluzhennogo-trenera-rossii-anatoliya-rahlina-proydet-v-sanktpeterburge-v-zakritom-formate.

[276] Putin, for example, began his feud with the oligarch Vladimir Gusinkii after being called "Shorty"; Leonid Velekhov, "Vladimir Kara-Murza: 'Ia ne smog pobedit' nashikh zakhvatchikov," *Radio Svoboda*, 5 November 2016, https://www.svoboda.org/a/28095371.html.

[277] Kenneth Dekleva, "The Many Faces of Vladimir Putin," *Cypher Brief*, 22 January 2010, https://www.thecipherbrief.com/column_article/the-many-faces-of-vla dimir-putin-a-political-psychology-profile. Putin's judo partners went on to create their own dynasties and now form a key bloc in modern Russia's power elite; Aleksei Navalny, "Putin's Palace," 20 January 2021, https://www.youtube.com/watch?v=ipAnwilMncI. At least one member of the club married into the Putin family; Pavel Sedakov, "Bednyi rodstvennik: pochemu drug Putina Viktor Khmarin ne stal milliarderom," *Forbes*, 21 October 2013, https://www.forbes.ru/kompanii/infrastruktura/246369-bednyi-rodstvennik-pochemu-drug-putin a-viktor-khmarin-ne-stal-milliar.

straightened out the spoiled Vladimir, but training and the 40-minute trolleybus commute left little time for study.[278] Rakhlin, acknowledging Putin's limited academic potential, recommended that he enter community technical college (*Vtuz*): Putin had no chance of passing any entrance exam.[279]

Instead, Putin inexplicably entered the international section of the law faculty at Leningrad University, a notorious bastion of golden youth.[280] Here students interacted with foreign students, read "petty-bourgeois" scholars, and took subjects such as "International Organizations," "State Law in Bourgeois Countries," and "International Trade in Capitalist Countries."[281] All this was strictly limited to "verified" youth, and certainly not open to a nobody who was also a brawler and who fraternized with Jews,[282] at

---

[278] A newspaper reporter in 2000, when Russian journalism was still open, claimed to have seen Putin's school report cards which contained many Cs *(troiki)*. If true, this would have hindered his entrance into Leningrad University. No report cards have ever been divulged to the public; n.a., "Neizvestnye fakty iz zhizni Vladimira Putina," *Argumenty i fakty*, no. 3, 19 January 2000, https://aif.ru/archive/1636081. See also: Blotskii *Vladimir Putin*, 107. The school Putin attended specialized in chemistry, yet Putin has never demonstrated a mastery of the sciences.

[279] N. A. Zen'kovich, *Putinskaia entsiklopediia* (OLMA, 2006), 382.

[280] Anton Ivanov, "Iurfaki v SSSR," *Zakon.ru* blog, 20 April 2017, https://zakon.ru/blog/2017/4/20/yurfaki_v_sssr. Knowledgeable commentators have found it unimaginable that Putin would have been accepted to the law faculty with "no protectors and no influential parents *[keinen hochrangigen Patron und keine einflussreichen Eltern]*"; Victor Timtschenko, *Putin und das neue Russland* (Diederichs, 2003), 28. The entrance exam, which covered the official version of Communist Party history, was oral.

[281] In the mid-1960s, the international division of the Leningrad law faculty experienced an influx of foreign students. Many professors there specialized in pre-revolutionary Russian legal traditions: Anatolii Sobchak was an expert on the "bourgeois" diplomat Friedrich Martens; V. S. Ivanenko, *Kafedra Mezhdunarodnogo Prava*, St. Petersburg: Neva, 2011 http://law.spbu.ru/Libraries/c64a1507-2b1d-4adc-a64b-5875a5da40d7.sflb.ashx. This implies, at the least, that all students would have been thoroughly vetted by the 3rd department of the 5th Chief Directorate of the KGB, specializing in "ideological diversion" among university students and faculty.

[282] Foreigners in the Soviet world were under constant surveillance. For the East German case, see: Timothy Garton Ash, *The File: A Personal History* (Random House, 1997). The law school was attended by future members of the Soviet elite. Notably, Putin's classmate was Aleksandr Bastrykin who had graduated

a time when the 1967 Arab-Israeli War had caused a wave of anti-Semitism in the Soviet world. Clearly, Putin's entrance required connections *(blat)*, and we may speculate that it may have been Mikhail Putin who pulled the strings. Mikhail, old Leningraders whisper, must have written the required recommendation letter for Putin to enter the KGB.[283] Thanks to the miniseries, *17 Moments of Spring*, featuring the urbane spy Maksim Isaev, an erudite able to outwit Nazi nuclear physicists, the KGB became a dream career for the Soviet elite in the early 1970s. Nonetheless, Vladimir Putin continued to neglect his studies by focusing on martial arts.[284] According to Dmitrii Gantserov, a recruiter working in the 3rd department of the 5th Chief Directorate of the KGB, Putin from his freshman year, was considered a prime candidate out of an already elite group of law faculty students. The Leningrad KGB headquarters gave a green light to Putin's candidacy based on a review of family relations *(proverka dal'nikh rodstvennikov)*. For the final acceptance,

---

from the rarefied School 27 on Vasil'evskii Island and became the chief of the Russian Investigation Committee.

[283] During the years 2007-2014, the author heard this rumor several times from disinterested, yet well-informed people within Russia. The only alternative account of Putin's entrance into the KGB seems far less credible. According to this account, law professor Anatolii Sobchak was a KGB informant, who relied on the student Vladimir Putin for collecting information. Putin's skill came to the attention of KGB handlers; "Yurii Shutov. Na smert' svidetelia," *Open Russia*, 15 December 2014, http://openrussia.org/post/view/1514/; and Dmitrii Gordon, "Sokursnik Putina Shvets: Sobchak byl agentom KGB," *Dmitrii Gordon YouTube channel*, 14 February 2018, https://www.youtube.com/watch?v=YVY 8svheYHo. This version, which was put forth in the 1990s, by mobster Yurii Shutov, suffers several deficiencies. How did young Putin first gain enough clout to become a valuable informer? Why have none of the victims of his treachery ever come forward? As a "rat," how has he maintained the trust and loyalty of childhood friends and classmates? Ultimately, he would have only been one informer amongst countless others. See further on surveillance in the socialist bloc, Peter Keefe, *Chatter: Uncovering the Echelon Surveillance Network and the Secret World of Global Eavesdropping* (Random House, 2006), 120-40; and Evgeniia Al'bats, *Mina zamedlennogo deistviia* (Russlit, 1992).

[284] An evaluation of Vladimir Putin from the mid-1970s noted few achievements besides a dedication to sports. This would have been odd for an elite Soviet student; "V Peterburge pokazali kharakteristiku KGB na Putina," *RBC.ru*, 31 October 2019, https://www.rbc.ru/politics/31/10/2019/5dba1f7b9a7947148026 be82.

during Putin's last year of study in 1974, Gantserov was ordered to make a thorough review of Putin's family background by personally interviewing family members. Other than this, Gantserov mentions Putin was accepted to one of the most competitive jobs in the USSR because he was not found to be an alcoholic or womanizer. Befitting a princeling, the main job interview was conducted at a swank Caucasus-themed restaurant in the center of town.[285] The shadow of Mikhail would continue to give Putin a leg up.[286] Key members of the Putin elite such as Valentina Matvienko would have heard Grigorii Romanov, the first secretary in Leningrad, herald Mikhail Putin as a hero who "our whole country follows today."[287]

Putin's behavior, "the bored kid in class," is typical for the Russian princelings.[288] As is the case for the majority of post-socialist societies, the leader's princeling status is essential for acting as guardian and arbitrator over the ruling dynasties. This is what drove Putin's rise to power.[289] Amid a reactionary backlash, Putin protected the legacy of his former boss, the Mayor of St. Petersburg, Anatolii Sobchak, as well the business and political interests of his

---

[285] Gantserov was interviewed by Blotskii in 1999; Blotskii, *Vladimir Putin*, 265–66, 286–87.

[286] During the period from 1997 to 2004, the author studied at the State University of St. Petersburg, where he came into contact with many people from Putin's milieu, including several who enjoy close contact with Putin. It was an open secret that some of the university staff and faculty received their positions thanks to family ties and that often these people had connections to Russia's security organs. Starting in the 1970s, among Putin's entourage, nepotism became both widespread and accepted as the norm. On nepotism in the KGB, see: Vladimir Kuzichkin, *Inside the KGB: Myth and Reality* (London Deutsch, 1990), and Sergei Kostin, *Farewell: The Greatest Spy Story of the Twentieth Century Vladimir Ippolitovitch Vetrov* (Amazon, 2011).

[287] "Pervoe bolee reshaiushchii" (1980), 17–19; G. V. Romanov, "Moguchaia sozidatel'naia sila sotsialisticheskogo sorevnovaniia: Doklad na Vsesoiuznoi nauchno-prakticheskoi konferentsii 12 aprelia 1979," in G. V. Romanov, *Izbrannye rechi i stat'i* (Polit. Lit-ry, 1983), 415.

[288] Steve Holland, "Obama Describes Putin as 'Like a Bored Kid'," *Reuters*, 10 August 2013, https://www.reuters.com/article/us-usa-russia-obama-idUSBRE9780XS20130809.

[289] Chris Monday, "Ot partiinogo kommunizma k semeinomu podriadu," *Ideology and Politics Journal* 1, no. 9 (2018).

wife, Liudmila Narusova, and daughter Kseniia.[290] Based on this reputation, Valentin Yumashev, Tat'iana Yeltsin, and other members of Boris Yeltsin's family urged the president to select Putin as successor in 1999.[291] Symbolically, in Russia's exclusive Nikol'skoe Cemetery, directly opposite the grave of Anatolii Sobchak stands the tombstone of Viktor Mikhailovich Putin (6.11.1946–7.1.2010).[292]

Although "socialist competition" draws a blank from today's students, it would surely have created a model for governance in Vladimir's mind. If the young Vladimir did grow up in Mikhail's orbit, as I have suggested here, then he would also have witnessed how Mikhail cleverly used his sporting skills to thrive under Stalin, Khrushchev, and Brezhnev, winning prowess, respect, prestige, and power through his display of strength and masculinity. We may never manage to put in place a full and accurate genealogy and biography for Vladimir Putin, but it is intriguing to consider the possibility that his journey through life and to the presidency may owe its shape to an important but now-suppressed connection to his once famous namesake.

---

[290] Valeri Todorov, "Kseniia Sobchak o sud'be svoego ottsa, banditskom Peterburge i proshlom Putina," *Lenta.ru*, 14 May 2018, https://lenta.ru/articles/2018/05/14/sobchakosobchake/; Ekateriana Burlakova, "Sviazannaia s Sobchak krabovaia kompaniia voshla v spisok sistemoobrazuiushchikh," *Vedomosti*, 27 April 2020, https://www.vedomosti.ru/business/articles/2020/04/27/829113-sobchak-krabovaya-kompaniya; Dmitri Vachedin, "Naval'nyi: Sobchak za vydvizhenie obeshchali 'ogromnye den'gi'," 18 March 2018, https://www.dw.com/ru/навальный-собчак-за-выдвижение-обещали-огромные-деньги/a-43030782.

[291] Timothy Colton, *Yeltsin: A Life* (Basic Books, 2008), 340–76; "Ziat' Yel'tsina Valentin Yumashev naznachen sovetnikom Putina," *Current Time TV*, 2018, https://www.currenttime.tv/a/29313492.html; and Timtschenko, *Putin*, 65–74.

[292] Judging from the match of the grave photo produced by AI genealogy sites, this seems to be Mikhail Putin's son.

REVIEWS

Elizabeth Buchanan (Ed.), *Russian Energy Strategy in the Asia-Pacific: Implications for Australia*. ANU Press, 2021.

In this edited volume a variety of authors bring to the reader's attention the full extent of Russian foreign energy policy in the Asia-Pacific. The book will be of particular interest to those keen to understand the drivers, patterns, and evolution of Russian energy-related issues as well as the increasing uncertainty of energy security and competition in the region with a view to determining the implications for Australia.

The first part of the book provides a general overview of the energy landscape in the Asia-Pacific. Stoichi Itoh introduces the reader to the primary energy demand and consumption in the region. He gives useful background on the politicization and intensifying competition among energy producers for market share and among consumers for supply routes. Morena Skalamera develops further a perspective on energy interaction patterns and offers a detailed analysis of the growing Russian interest in capturing a larger market share in Asia. The author illustrates with insight Russia's attempt to establish cooperation with Japan, South Korea, and China as the fastest-absorbing gas buyers and reasonably underlines the emergence of intense competition for Australia in the region.

The second part of the book provides insight into the Russian foreign energy policy. Through the concept of a "grand strategy"—a term that the author uses to frame the overarching energy strategy and achievement of long-term goals—Jakub Godzimirski investigates the relationship between Russian strategy and the country's energy resources with a particular view to Asia. He offers a detailed analysis of Russian energy resources as a means, instrument, and goal of Grand Strategy. From these angles the author's investigation is extremely convincing in demonstrating that Asia's role as a generator of means is still relatively marginal. Numerous energy deals and partnerships with Asian actors as an instrument contribute to reducing Russia's dependence on

European energy markets, and to the transfer of funding and technology from Western partners (pp. 79, 81). Jakub Godzimirski concludes that extending the lifespan of the Russian energy sector will rely on securing mid- and long-term access to growing Asian energy markets. Peter Rutland has taken up the task of exploring interrelation of the domestic political regime of the "petrostate" and the long-pursued status of being an "energy superpower" in the post-Crimea 2014. He centers his discussion around the argument that the use of energy as a "weapon" became increasingly questionable and steadily diminished due to the fracking revolution, the rise of China, and the challenges of climate change. Keun-Wook Paik provides rich statistical and valuable data concerning the strategies, challenges, and performance of Russia's oil and gas entities: Rosneft, Gazprom, and Novatek. While largely descriptive, his informative chapter develops a deeper understanding of the achievements and prospects of Sino-Russian oil and gas cooperation. As the author implies, despite many ups and downs and mixed results, "Sino-Russian oil and gas cooperation will play the pivotal role in opening the era of Russia's Asia-Pacific policy" (p. 139).

The next two chapters making up the third part of this volume cover Australia's Asia-Pacific energy interests. John Blackburn builds up a picture of the patterns of Australia's energy security policy and examines the National Energy Security Assessment (NESA) as well as presenting a detailed view on fuel import dependency and strategic fuel reserves. The author underlines the lack of strategies, policies, and plans for energy security and points out the significant challenges for future investment in the Australian LNG market due to the larger proven Russian gas reserves and lower-priced Russian gas exports to the Asian markets. The author argues that the development of a hydrogen strategy could improve the national energy security and benefit the Australian economy. Stephen Fortescue gives us a view of Russia's development of coal export to the Asia-Pacific, its economic feasibility and projections. The availability of coal, coal producer companies and logistics to the Asian-Pacific markets are also under scrutiny here. The author suggests that Russia as a significant exporter of coal to the region faces nevertheless a high level of indebtedness, and low budgetary and infrastructure funding in the sector. On the contrary, Australian coal competitiveness is conditioned by capability to "cover for low margins when prices are low by ramping up volume" (p. 180).

The final two chapters of the book switch the focus to future developments in the Russian energy strategy in the Asia-Pacific. Maria Shagina takes care to highlight the impact of the Western sanctions imposed on the energy sector on Russia's foreign energy strategy. The author presents a vivid picture of the unfavorable effect of the financial restrictions and technology-related sanctions on Russia's long-term projects. By extending focus on import substitution as Russia's response to sanctions the author argues that limited success of this strategy is caused by insufficient financial support from the government, poor inter-sectoral coordination and cooperation, the lagging of research and development institutions, and rent-seeking. The Asian countries, in turn, provided some expertise, financial support, equipment, and services. However, there is still a wariness towards sanctioned Russian individuals and entities. Tatiana Romanova investigates Russia's new Energy Security Doctrine, approved in 2019. The discussion here moves on to such issues as geopolitical/market paradigms, energy mix, and geography and diversification. The author implies that the groups of examined issues represents much more continuity than change in the Russian energy discourses.

Overall, the edited volume joins debates about Russia's move into the Asian energy market and the extent to which this affects the growing energy requirements in Australia's emerging Asia-Pacific arena. The book is thought-provoking, written with competence, and extremely convincing in demonstrating that Russia's expanding diversification to the East, its cheaper energy resources and geographical proximity to Asia's growing market represent substantial implications for Australia in the light of lack of its own energy export strategy. The book is a solid empirical analysis for everyone interested in energy patterns of interaction and rivalry in the Asia-Pacific.

INNA CHUVYCHKINA
Institute of Scientific Information for Social Sciences (INION), Russian Academy of Sciences

Juliane Fürst, *Flowers Through Concrete: Explorations in Soviet Hippieland*. Oxford University Press, 2021.

Juliane Fürst has followed her study of "Stalin's last generation" with an ambitious attempt to capture a more elusive, if more colorful piece of late Soviet life: its own "flower children." Using personal and state archives alongside extensive oral history interviews—conducted not only in Moscow and Petersburg but places as far as Israel and the United States—*Flowers through Concrete* tells a fascinating story about communities that may well have been "marginal" in late Soviet society, but whose lives and fates were deeply entangled in the system against which they rebelled.

Not unlike the Soviet Union that provided their natural habitat, the Soviet hippies—like hippies the world over—are too often described with reference to their end, to communities drifting apart and degraded by drug addiction and early deaths. Fürst refreshingly refuses to reproduce this tired narrative and instead focuses on the vibrant, if complicated, lives of her subjects. Often speaking in their own words and shown in a variety of lively photographs, the Soviet hippies and the world they built are the center of this story. Unafraid to write openly of her own subjective position as author and interviewer, Fürst also intersperses frank discussions about limited, problematic archival sources and conflicting testimony from her respondents.

The book is divided into two sections. The first tells a more conventional history of the hippie movement in the Soviet Union, from its origins in the mid-1960s, through its maturation into a "system," complete with its own rituals, capable of social reproduction, and arguably outlasting its Western inspiration, in large part not despite but because of increasing (but inept) attempts at state repression. The second section is divided into chapters organized around several central themes of hippie life, from questions of ideology and material culture, to those of "madness" and the state of pure joy or "kaif" the hippies sought in drug use, rock music, or sincere being-in-community. It is in these chapters that Fürst's central claims about the inextricability of the Soviet hippies from their late socialist habitat are shown in clearest detail.

Examples of this "constant interplay with late Soviet reality" (32) range from the Komsomol organizing skills and ideological training apparent in early hippie community-building to the complex discussion of how "madness" was used by the authorities to punish and marginalize non-conformists and also by hippies themselves to avoid military service.

By far the most unique chapter is the final look at the female hippie or "gerla." The chapter confronts head-on the challenges of reconstructing this history, as hippie women themselves insisted that there were no significant differences between male and female hippie experiences. The appearance of children—a consequence of "free love" in a society without widespread access to contraceptives—often forced more hippie women to seek a rapprochement with mainstream society in search of medical care or to avoid custody battles. More than in any other part of the book Fürst herself enters the narrative here to acknowledge the fact that she brings to the project a range of experiences and views on feminism and women's history that differ from those of her subjects. Rather than subordinate the Soviet hippies' views to her own, she openly addresses the tension between her own and hegemonic Russian interpretations of second-wave feminism. The resultant discussion not only illuminates one of the key reasons that the experience of the female hippie was harder for the historian to trace, but also articulates the complexities of viewing Soviet gender relations through a Western lens. Historians of gender and sexuality will find much of value in how Fürst navigates this tension.

In the end, *Flowers Through Concrete* is a unique synthesis of the deeply personal and the highly political. Partly a collective biography of exceptional personalities, the book also draws compelling lessons about the role of countercultures in authoritarian regimes and the nature and complexity of "late socialism." The author describes a network of hippie communities who may have tried to "drop out" of Soviet society but were so entangled in it that they were both shaped by it and helped shape it in turn. But most of all, what may strike readers most is the empathy and care with which the work was carried out, suggesting the author is not exaggerating when she admits that she too has been influenced by these people who so venerated peace, love, and sincerity.

BRENDAN MCELMEEL
PhD candidate
University of Washington

Hubertus Jahn (ed.), *Identities and Representations in Georgia from the 19th Century to the Present*. De Gruyter Oldenbourg, 2020.

Attempting to cover issues around the identity and representation of Georgia since the 19th century is a hugely challenging task, for a number of reasons. Firstly, these issues have not been covered systematically and comprehensively in the previous scholarship, either in-country or international. Secondly, this is a topic that requires engagement with the debates over nationalism studies not only in relation to the Georgian independence struggle but also in relation to the dominant actors in the region (Russia and Turkey, in particular). Thirdly, Georgian studies (Kartvelian studies, Kartvelology) lacks anthropological analysis and methods for researching the cultural practices of various social groups and communities present in Georgia.

Being a compilation of materials prepared by a number of Georgian and international scholars, this collection of analytical chapters appears to be an important collective work aimed at providing an overview of identities and representation issues in Georgia through the wide range of issues raised by the authors in relation to singular events and figures as well as an attempt to analyze them in wider perspective in the light of national, gender, colonial and religious identities. The added value of this publication is the fact that it has been developed by a number of scholars who approach the topic from Georgian, local and country-wide, as well as global perspectives.

The book presents a compilation of works oriented towards scholars with expertise in a range of disciplines within Kartvelian studies. The editor of the volume, Hubertus Jahn, has contributed a wide-ranging introduction to the Georgian context, presenting the different stages of Georgian nationhood creation and development since the 19th century, situated between dominant political bodies – the Russian and Ottoman Empires. The book has a particular focus on Russian influence, later represented by the USSR and the Russian Federation.

The first chapters examine representations and perceptions of Joseph Stalin both in public discourse, via analysis of the political and cultural context at local and national levels in Georgia, as well as through a case study of the Stalin museum in Gori in present-day Georgia. Lasha Bakradze in his chapter explains why Stalin's figure is still popular in the Georgian narrative and explores how it has been employed in Russian and present-day Georgian propaganda. In her contribution, Katrine Bendtsen Gotfredsen, along with reviewing Georgian governmental attempts to reframe the narratives on Stalin, outlines the process of de-politicization and ambivalence that is present in informal practices of various Georgian social groups.

Most of the book's chapters contemplate the debates on nationhood creation and colonialism past and present in light of the Georgian experience. Malkhaz Toria's chapter examines the Likhni declaration as a decisive event in the Georgian-Abkhaz conflict in the late 1980s before the Soviet collapse. Using Brubaker's theoretical approach to conflicts between ethnic and national groups, Toria analyzes which factors contributed to the escalation of the situation in the late 1980s and considers its relationship to the USSR's collapse and the subsequent evolution of Georgian-Abkhaz relations, as well as looking at the Russian Federation's role in these events.

The chapter authored by Nutsa Batiashvili concentrates on Georgia's collective experience of colonial identity on the margins of an "empire." Here, "empire" has been chosen as a key word to analyze cultural contexts and social formations in relation to liminality, the in-betweenness experienced by Georgia over the last two centuries.

As mentioned above, a focal point of the current work is the nation-building path that Georgia is still going through. Several chapters search for the roots of this process from a historical perspective, analyzing key events in Georgian history since the 19th century, the rise of Russian dominance, and the history of language policy in the Georgian territories. For instance, the chapter on Iakob Gogebashvili's natural method and its contribution to pedagogy development in Georgia under the Russian domination, discusses how native language learning goals became, according to the chapter's authors Timothy K. Blauvelt and Anton Vacharadze, later "paradoxically subsumed to assimilation," more often appearing in tandem with "great Russian chauvinism."

Special attention is paid in the volume to social groups that are excluded from the central discussion on Georgian issues both in nationhood and culture studies. Martin Demant Frederiksen, in a chapter entitled "Meaningless people. Atheism, subjectivity and unrepresented identities in Georgia" based on a case study of the Atheist's Club, analyzes the debate on atheism as a social phenomenon in Georgia and places this practice in opposition to the religious practice of the majority. Khatuna Gvaradze's chapter examines the connections between the women's question in the late 19th and early 20th centuries and Georgia's national movement, showing how the women's movement was part of the wider fight for Georgian independence, and describing roots and trends that were relevant to the Georgian women's movement and how it has functioned up to now.

This is a thought-provoking and very relevant collected volume that offers the reader insights into the contexts of present-day Georgian nation building, and into the factors that influence the acquisition and employment of political and cultural practices in Georgia, both by state bodies and informal groups and individuals. The book as a collective work of renowned international and Georgian researchers fills an important gap in current studies on Georgia. It would be great to have more such works concentrated on contemporary minorities (national and ethnic minorities, LGBTQ communities, migrants and refugees, elderly and young people) and their identities and representations in Georgia. The authors aimed to analyze national, gender, colonial and religious identity through the historical perspective of nation-building and relations of different ethnic groups as well as through external policy-building, particularly towards Russia. The work is worth reading and will surely help to raise further research questions relevant for understanding not only the past but the present.

OLGA KHABIBULINA
PhD candidate
Institute of Slavic Studies
Polish Academy of Sciences

Natalia Knoblock (ed.), *Language of Conflict: Discourses of the Ukrainian Crisis*. Bloomsbury, 2020.

Since the 2014 Maidan Revolution and Russia's annexation of Crimea, the Ukrainian crisis "has provoked a flurry of propaganda, as well as emotional and sensational material, from both professional media and amateur content creators," according to Natalia Knoblock. Her edited volume, entitled *Language of Conflict: Discourses of the Ukrainian Crisis*, consists of thirteen chapters by linguists, journalists, literary scholars, and language teachers. These contributions analyze social, political, and military conflicts in public discourse on the Ukrainian crisis, using a discourse-analytical approach to examine aspects of language that people encounter in their everyday lives, through political speeches, television, social media, "state" traditions, and other sites of discursive practices.

The scope of *Language of Conflict* is broad, encompassing the role of discourse in reflecting and constructing multiple, often contradictory, discourses around the Ukrainian crisis as it has unfolded since 2014. The authors take the position that participants categorize and frame various aspects of the crisis through their existing worldviews, and that this shapes their interpretations of events relating to the crisis. The book analyzes how various social groups in Ukraine have responded to these events, and how this response is reflected in their narratives. With a focus on the linguistic and extralinguistic features of categorization, stance, positioning and framing, (de)legitimation, manipulation, and strategies for coping with antagonism and war, the chapters draw attention to the discourse participants' deliberate, or responsive, communicative activities. The overarching hope underpinning the text is that, by shedding some light on the linguistic aspects of the Ukrainian crisis, and by highlighting destructive or problematic discursive practices, the research could promote a more responsible use of language by drawing attention to different points of view and, ultimately, building a bridge between them.

Language of Conflict is multidisciplinary, utilizing a broad range of approaches and methods. Natalia Knoblock's previous publications showcase her research on the intersection of language and politics, and this research focus is reflected in the methods applied to contributions in the volume. The majority of its studies are situated within critical discourse analysis and critical metaphor analysis. Daniel Weiss' chapter, for example, on competing discourses around Ukrainian nationhood in Russian politics, examines the discursive embedding of different types of metaphors into government statements, parliamentary and television debates, and newspapers, across four different languages: Ukrainian, Russian, Polish and Czech. Another example is Olga Baysha's chapter on antagonistic discourses of the Euromaidan, in particular, the use of the signs "jumper," "kolorad," "maidown," "panhead," "sovok," "vatnik," and others, in both pro-Maidan and anti-Maidan memes on Facebook. Liudmila Arcimavičienė's chapter on metaphor is another example, as it investigates identity and conflict in former Ukrainian President Petro Poroshenko and Russian President Vladimir Putin's speeches. Some contributions employ corpus linguistic approaches, such as Tatyana Karpenko-Seccombe's chapter, which employs a cross-linguistic corpus-assisted comparative discourse approach to analyzing Russian and Ukrainian parliamentary debates from 2014. Others use multimodal approaches, such as Alla Tovares' chapter on the recreation of Zaporizhian Cossacks' letter-writing on YouTube, which she considers a form of "collective creative insurgency." Each chapter reflects distinct communicative features that, when taken together, begin to approach the overwhelmingly complex task of representing what Knoblock refers to as the "manifold, fragmentary and often contradictory reality of the Ukrainian discourse and the conflict upon which it centres."

The variety of studies in the book highlights the complexity of the situation and the diversity of perspectives and voices that have been influencing one another since the protests that preceded the Ukrainian crisis began in 2013. These voices often perpetuate existing concepts and further polarize already divided mindsets, making the underlying goal of the book, to bridge the gap and to facilitate compromise between perspectives, especially important. While the Ukrainian crisis has, in the past, been analyzed from political science and communication studies perspectives, *Language of Conflict* brings attention to the linguistic aspects of this conflict, including its political rhetoric and in-group and out-group relations, and cultural phenomena that is influencing the discourse. The studies could inform important work on early detection and prevention in conflict studies by demonstrating the ways in which discourse antagonizes and polarizes particular groups. In this way, the studies are not only useful for those interested in language as it relates to the Ukrainian crisis, but for anyone interested in the broader relationship between language and conflict from a political, social, or military perspective.

Language of Conflict is a diverse, yet nuanced, volume that reflects the broad spectrum of agent-mediated perspectives that make up the vast fabric of discourse on the Ukrainian crisis. The studies in the volume will likely be of interest, not only for linguists, but also for political scientists, communication scholars, genocide and human rights scholars, social anthropologists, and historians whose research focus is on Eastern Europe.

ELISE WESTIN
PhD candidate
University of Adelaide

Andrei Kozyrev, *The Firebird: The Elusive Fate of Russian Democracy* with a foreword by Michael McFaul, former US Ambassador to Moscow. University of Pittsburgh Press, 2020.

In his colorful and highly readable autobiography *The Firebird: The Elusive Fate of Russian Democracy*, Andrei Kozyrev, who was the first post-Soviet Foreign Minister of Russia in 1991–96, gives an incisive and personal eyewitness account of the epochal transformation when the mighty Soviet Union was irreversibly dissolved and succeeded by fifteen formally independent and sovereign republics. Among them first and foremost is Russia, incomparably more influential, ambitious and powerful than any of the others.

Andrei Kozyrev had the privilege of belonging to President Yeltsin's innermost circle, a self-confident and tight-knit cabal of nine Kremlin top officials enjoying the personal trust of and practically daily interaction with the President, who himself gave it the name "the President's Club." Kozyrev tells us that the Club members had exceptionally intense and frequent access to the President. They "met each other in an informal atmosphere almost daily at dinner, occasionally at lunch, and in the early morning on the tennis court"—simply a uniquely advantageous vantage point for chronicling the relentless Kremlin rivalries, the rumors, the intrigues, the perpetual power struggle at the top that Kozyrev scrupulously observed at close distance, mercilessly analyzed and took an active part in.

Andrei Kozyrev's account mirrors the dramatic but—miraculously!—largely peaceful transition from the moribund Soviet superpower, led by the visionary but progressively ever more powerless Mikhail Gorbachev, to a resurrected yet anarchic and chaotic Russia. Kozyrev was present during the August 1991 coup attempt against Gorbachev, when Soviet armed forces overwhelmed the urban scene of Moscow in their attempt to seize the emblematic Russian White House. This is when the charismatic, towering Yeltsin rose to the circumstance and seized the moment, resolutely stepping onto a tank to address the crowd assembled all around, a watershed moment in post-World War II history, instantly eternalized in countless press photographs distributed around the world.

This courageous and highly symbolic act was Yeltsin's national-scale as well as global political break-through. Metaphorically speaking, Yeltsin never stepped down from that tank, until he decided to abdicate from the Russian Presidency by the turn of the millennium 1999–2000.

Kozyrev also participated in the truly epoch-making negotiations at Brezhnev's legendary former hunting lodge in Belavezha near Minsk, when the political leaders of Russia, Ukraine, and Belarus agreed to dissolve—or, to use a more graphic term, bury—the Soviet Union. Kozyrev tells us that it was he himself who made the historic phone call from a simple, ordinary landline telephone —the only available means of communication—and was put through to the President of the United States George H. W. Bush to inform him of the demise of the Soviet Union.

For half a decade, Andrei Kozyrev had the immeasurable advantage of working in close proximity to President Yeltsin, both in the Kremlin and on official visits abroad, which definitely makes his autobiography a rare source of firsthand inside information about this unprecedented phase of contemporary history, jam-packed with developments of lasting impact.

Kozyrev's book is full of stories, anecdotes, reflections, both domestic and international, some of lasting interest, some more ephemeral. One such anecdote, not widely known, refers to the "KGB initiative," named after the Russian, German, and US foreign ministers Kozyrev, Genscher, and Baker, launched in order to keep former Soviet nuclear scientists busy in Russia and the other CIS countries, so as to have fewer incentives to work on contracts for proliferation-prone countries such as Iraq or Iran. A theme of more lasting impact that Kozyrev highlights is the nationalistic resonance of issues concerning ethnic Russians living in ex-Soviet countries but outside Russia, most poignantly Ukraine. Khrushchev's off-the-cuff decision in the 1950s to transfer Crimea to Ukraine was never well received among Russians and revanchist sentiments surfaced immediately after the break-up of the Soviet Union. Kozyrev's account is a sober, if discouraging, reminder of this intractable problem that was fueled by the dissolution of the Soviet Union and has since only become ever more acute.

After serving as Foreign Minister for five years, Andrei Kozyrev resigned and walked out from the Stalin-era Foreign Ministry skyscraper—by chance built the same year that Kozyrev was born— on Smolenskaia Ploshchad' by the Moscow river in the center of the Russian capital, one of the so-called Seven Sisters making an indistinguishable imprint on the Moscow skyline. Kozyrev then successfully ran for a seat in the Duma, the Russian Parliament, for the Northern naval port city of Murmansk. After serving one Duma term, Kozyrev retired from political life to pursue a career in private business after which he emigrated to the United States where he still lives, working as Professor of International Studies at Stanford University.

More than anything else, internationally Andrei Kozyrev will be remembered for his unprecedented two-part plenary speech at the December 1992 Ministerial Summit of the Conference on Security and Co-operation in Europe (CSCE) held in Stockholm, Sweden. When Kozyrev took the floor he shocked the assembled Foreign Ministers and their aides by "announcing serious changes to the foreign policy of the Russian Federation." Adding to the dramatic effect, Kozyrev went on to elaborate: "The space of the former Soviet Union cannot be regarded as a zone of full application of CSCE norms. In essence, this is a postimperial space, in which Russia has to defend its interests using all available means, including military and economic ones."

The audience was dumbfounded. You could hear the proverbial pin drop on to the floor. Yet, by informal agreement with the CSCE chair, Sweden's then Foreign Minister Margaretha af Ugglas, Kozyrev was, against all protocol, given the floor a second time when he explained that his first intervention had only served to illustrate "the sort of changes that are typically demanded by the centrists [Kozyrev's term for the moderate, middle-of-the-road elite] in Russia. Of course this is just a pale simulacrum of the U-turn in strategy that the real opposition would make if it seized power. I wanted you to be aware of these demands." Kozyrev then went on to present to the bewildered, yet relieved, CSCE foreign minister collective "the actual policy of the Russian Federation as defined by our President."

Andrei Kozyrev's chronologically conceived memoir has ten chapters, divided between three main sections entitled "Russia versus the Soviet Union, 1991," "Climbing a Steep Slope, 1992–1994," and "The Downward Slope, 1994–1996," reflecting the rapid rise and fall of Russian democracy.

The book is capped by an Epilogue called "Can Russian Democracy Rise Again?," where Kozyrev concludes that "the failure of the reforms was not inevitable," but that "Burdened with Soviet concepts and habits, Yeltsin, after an initial effort to enact profound change, in many ways retreated to the old habits of governing. His flaws were matched by the inability of the democrats to act without him; to overcome their personal rivalries... This was our major error, and the key reason why Russia's democracy failed. My reformist friends and I share responsibility for that failure." Still, Kozyrev wants to end his analysis on a more optimistic note: "The Firebird of Russian democracy has arisen many times—in 1905, 1917, and 1991. Sooner or later the Russian people will rise up again and reclaim the Russia they deserve." Sadly, there is currently not much sign of this. Kozyrev is aware that some consider him naive. By choosing to label his memoir "Firebird," Kozyrev bravely exclaims that he does not wish to hide his optimism under the rug,

Both as Foreign Minister and as a Duma deputy, Andrei Kozyrev consistently followed an ardent pro-Western policy line that earned him many vicious, shrewd, and resourceful political opponents. The book details the domestic tug-of-war between the committed pro-Westerners such as Kozyrev and the more traditional-minded Soviet power-brokers who gradually gained the upper hand. The main message of Kozyrev's book is that Russia missed a historic opportunity when it discontinued its initial democratization and Westernization effort, sliding backwards to a Soviet-style social order.

Andrei Kozyrev makes good use of his inside information. Throughout, he makes every effort to be evenhanded with Yeltsin and his shortcomings. Kozyrev is very discreet about Yeltsin's well known alcoholism, but occasionally lets it be alluded to between the lines. Kozyrev starts out as a devoted Yeltsin fan, but gradually becomes progressively more alienated and ciritical. With Gorbachev the evolution is the reverse: from harsh criticism to ever greater sympathy, even admiration for the politician who, by spearheading glasnost and perestroika, pioneered the reform effort required for the historical transition from the straitjacket of Soviet communism and planned economy to market conditions and gradual political pluralism needed for Russia's social progress and economic well-being.

If this sounds very much like current mainstream political analysis, it is, in fact, the case that the overarching lines of thinking in Kozyrev's book are not prone to shock anybody familiar with this phase in contemporary Russian history. The added value of Kozyrev's particular take is his immediate firsthand experience and his profound personal commitment to and dedicated involvement in the political change for Russia that he is seeking.

MANNE WÄNGBORG
Minister-Counsellor at the Embassy of Sweden,
Moscow (1998-2003, 2009-2010)
Sweden's Consul-General in Kaliningrad (2006-2009)
and Ambassador to Kazakhstan (2010-2014)

Anna Matveeva, *Through Times of Trouble: Conflict in Southeastern Ukraine Explained from Within.* Lexington Books, 2017.

The events that have taken place in Ukraine since 24 February 2022 have brought Eastern Ukraine to the front pages of the world's newspapers. The Donbas, where the Russian offensive is concentrated since the beginning of April, has acquired global name recognition. However, as many Ukrainians and some external observers repeatedly point out, war has been ongoing in Ukraine since 2014. *Through Times of Trouble* accounts for the genesis and the early stages of this little mediatized and scantily studied war.

It explores this particular conflict through the perspective of the secessionist actors, endowing them with the agency that is rightfully theirs and that successfully allowed them to establish alternative structures of power to the Ukrainian state. It also shows what the mechanisms of escalation of a particular crisis are: while war is not inevitable, Matveeva's book traces the different events, triggers, personalities, and enabling environments that led to the violent creation of the DNR and LNR. The wider framework, understood as the Russian annexation of Crimea and Russian policy towards (Southeastern) Ukraine, matters but, while dutifully included in the book, it does not take central stage. Much has been written on how external forces have shaped the Donbas and, in light of the 2022 Russian invasion, much more is set to come. This book reminds us that history is not solely crafted in the capitals.

The book successfully contributes to different fields, including political science, war studies, and area studies. How do new political entities come to be? The book shows how closely the establishment of new entities (such as the DNR and LNR) can be enmeshed with the development of a new political project, which rests on ideologies, communication, popular and external support. In the early days, both project and entities are dynamically morphing creatures, shaped by an array of people, interests, and events. They are characterized by complexity, contradictions, and chaos, and do not follow linear trajectories. The two appear to feed on each other, emerging almost simultaneously from the potentiality of territorial disruption and re-shaping of boundaries, exemplified by Crimea's secession from Ukraine.

In this context, the factor of violence, and its organization, plays a dominant role. As such, the book strongly inscribes itself into a wider War Studies literature and does so by painstakingly developing a little known and under researched case, with a strong focus on its local dynamics. It tackles an array of issues that are at the center of the field's attempts to better understand the determinants of war, such as looking at processes of mobilization and at the role of motivation and ideology. It accounts for the diverse trajectories of combatants, underlining the variety of their backgrounds, whether geographical, motivational, or professional. The book does not simplify their stories, not does it lump combatants into a few easy-to-grasp categories, but it accounts for the complexity of the experience and, at times, for the randomness of it all.

Matveeva has interviewed ex-combatants and Donbas residents, politicians on all sides of the divide(s), experts, journalists, and analysts. The array of respondents who "speak" through the book and who are otherwise non-existent to an English-speaking public is remarkable. This method of exploring a particular case through the people who live in it and shape it, more or less violently, is what characterizes much of the author's previous work, whether in Central Asia or in the Caucasus. She has repeatedly brought the voices of the local actors to the academic literature and to a more policy-oriented readership, and here she does so once more. However, the book is far from being a straightforward anthropological account of the conflict in Southeastern Ukraine: Matveeva's additional contribution is in making sense of her respondents' narratives through the mobilization of political science and IR theories.

At the same time, the book is precious to scholars who work on the region through an Area Studies perspective. A key merit of the book rests in the fact that it accounts for the identity and communal changes that have occurred in Southeastern Ukraine at least since the early 2010s, stressing the dynamism of local identities and logics of belonging. This is in line with an attempt to move away from a more static understanding of identity in Ukraine and the post-Soviet region more widely, that refers to the pre-1991 asset as an almost immutable and final determinant of contemporary dynamics. So, if a collective identity in Donbas strengthens in the context of an independent Ukrainian state, a renewed *Novorossiia* project could emerge in the aftermath of the 2014 Maidan events and Russia's takeover of Crimea. How this happens is thoroughly traced in the book.

Anna Matveeva's book was published in 2017. While the situation that we are confronted with in (Southeastern) Ukraine has dramatically changed in 2022, *Through Times of Trouble* is a precious documentation of what happened beforehand and makes a solid argument as to why it matters.

GIULIA PRELZ OLTRAMONTI
ESPOL, Université Catholique de Lille

David Rainbow (Ed.), *Ideologies of Race: Imperial Russia and the Soviet Union in Global Context*. McGill-Queen's University Press, 2019.

Ideologies of Race: Imperial Russia and the Soviet Union in Global Context is an edited collection that provides a much-needed intervention in the literature on race in Russia. The authors outline two major analytical issues with contemporary approaches to studying race in the field. First, the literature relies too heavily on Western European examples of race, racism, and racial hierarchy. Thus, because of this reliance, Russia is often characterized as not engaging in racial categorization or racism. Furthermore, Russia is often analyzed in a vacuum due to Russia's "lack" of a Western European racial ideology. This unique case makes comparison with other European racial regimes a pointless exercise.

Analyzing race is a matter of how not whether it functioned in the region. As David Rainbow and his contributors show, researchers on the Russian empire and the Soviet Union benefit from examining race in the region within a transnational frame. As Rainbow argues in his stellar introduction, the volume "offers a way to account for particularities without falling into exceptionalism" (20). By approaching race as an ideology—"those configurations that both constitute a view of the world (or some aspect of it) and also matter to, and in, society"—the volume opens a space to investigate race and racialization in Russia. It demonstrates that Russia did have ideas of race, racial categorization, and hierarchy despite the absence of a legal form of racial identification in the Russian Empire and the Soviet Union.

Moreover, the volume engages with a broad spectrum of literature on race both within and outside the field. The 2002 *Slavic Review* forum on race that featured articles from the late Eric D. Weitz, Francine Hirsch, and Amir Weiner, looms large in the historiographical engagements of the pieces. Multiple essays directly address the 2002 forum and argue that characterizing elements of Soviet nationality policy as racial policy flattens important distinctions between the Nazi and Soviet regimes. Instead, these essays show that Soviet engagement with racial policies and categorization does not conflate the Soviet approach with that of the Nazis. Rather, these essays exemplify why Western European-centered approaches to understanding racialization and racial violence preclude appropriate comparisons between the Soviet Union and other Western and non-Western racial regimes. In other words, studying race and racialization in Russia and the Soviet Union contributes to a more comprehensive understanding of race and realization in a global context.

The volume is well-organized and relatively cohesive, considering its engagement with imperial Russian, Soviet, East Asian, American, Brazilian, and Caribbean historiographies. The book is divided into four sections, and each section includes a chapter on the Russian empire, one on the Soviet Union, and then closes with a chapter that places the preceding two chapters into a global context that ties them into conversations about race in more "traditional" locations of racial thinking: Germany, the Atlantic, Brazil, and the United States, respectively. Rainbow's powerful introduction provides a comprehensive discussion of the primary historiographical debates the volume engages in Russian and Soviet history and connects these debates to significant debates in race and sociology of race, including George M. Frederickson's definitive *Racism: A Short History* and sociologist Howard Winant's theory of the "globality of race."

The volume includes essays from titans studying race and racial politics, including Alaina Lemon, Vera Tolz, Marina Mogilner, and Eric D. Weitz. Two standout essays include those on Romani and Korean subjects. Brigid O'Keeffe's article on Roma during the Stalinist period illustrates how Soviet nationality policy required human malleability while operating on the assumption of ethnic and national essentialism. She draws on the Moscow Gypsy Theater and the short-lived All-Russian Gypsy Union to show how Roma activists were faced with the dilemma that to gain the benefits of Soviet "affirmative action," they had to lean into the worst Russian imperial and Soviet stereotypes about Roma as dirty, untrustworthy, and nomadic people. O'Keeffe persuasively argues that "race was not the operative category for Soviet citizens engaged in nationality politics does not disqualify race as a productive category for analyzing Soviet nationality politics" (155). Another fascinating contribution is Susanna Soojung Lim's chapter on Korean intellectual Yun Ch'iho and the role of Russia in creating the "White Pacific" through its engagement with Korea, China, and Japan. Lim's essay demonstrates an important gap in the contemporary literature on race in the Russian empire and the Soviet Union—the racialization and treatment of Asians in the Russian Far East. She shows that imperial Russian intellectuals perceived Koreans, Chinese, and Japanese people as a singular East Asian race and that Russian fears of "Pan-Mongolism" had continuity into the Soviet period exemplified by Stalin's deportations of Koreans from the Far East because they were perceived as a minority willing to collaborate with the Japanese. Still, these are only two examples of the new historical, sociological, and anthropological methodological approaches to studying race featured in this work.

Overall, I highly recommend this volume to advanced researchers and students alike. The essays introduce readers to the growing body of literature on race in the field and provide a global context for understanding the particularities in the Russian and Soviet cases. One of the few weaknesses is the lack of a conclusion. Rainbow's introduction is strong but ending the volume with the fourth section's last analytical essay leaves the reader to wonder how to think through the analytical connections presented in the previous essays, particularly the importance of approaching race as an ideology. Still, this is a minor shortcoming. This well-written and well-organized collection of essays should become a standard text for studies on race and racialization in the Russian empire and the Soviet Union.

KIMBERLY ST. JULIAN-VARNON
PhD candidate
University of Pennsylvania

Josephine von Zitzewitz, *The Culture of Samizdat: Literature and Underground Networks in the Late Soviet Union*. Bloomsbury Academic, 2021.

As the author states in her introduction, her work is "a book about people," with a focus on the "informal networks that gave birth to the samizdat phenomenon." There is a growing literature on this phenomenon (the book's bibliography provides a good introduction to this literature). There is room, however, for analyses that throw light on various neglected aspects of this phenomenon, and the author largely succeeds in producing an interesting volume that does not focus on samizdat texts and their often well-known authors, but on those who prepared and circulated samizdat, making it accessible to its avid readers. A good example of this focus is Chapter 3 of the book, which focuses on the typically obscure samizdat typists whose painstaking labor was crucial in view of the "underground" nature of samizdat production. Another interesting feature of the book is the author's effort to survey a sample of those involved in samizdat networks in the past, a highly time-sensitive task given the age of those connected to these networks in the now long-defunct USSR. Those interested in the networks which ensured the circulation of samizdat in the Soviet Union (Soviet Russia in particular), can benefit a great deal by reading this well-written and insightful book.

Nonetheless, a few critical comments. As the book's sub-title indicates, the author's supposed intent was to discuss samizdat in the Soviet Union as a whole. The book, however, focuses almost exclusively on Russian-language samizdat, and on its production and circulation in Moscow and Leningrad (the main centers of samizdat production), although a few other centers (e.g., Odesa) are occasionally mentioned. Those reading this book thus will have no idea that there was a "national question" in the USSR, and that samizdat documents and publications circulated in Ukraine, the Baltic states (Estonia, Latvia, and Lithuania), Armenia, and Georgia in the native languages of these republics. It would be unreasonable to expect even the most skilled and multilingual author to discuss samizdat networks in the above-mentioned republics and other non-Russian areas of the Soviet Union. Still, the author of this book should have done more to clarify the book's limitations, and to specify that its focus is on Russian-language samizdat.

Likewise, the book devotes some attention to samizdat materials, of a religious nature, produced in non-official Russian Orthodox circles. No mention is made, however, of the widely circulated *Chronicle of the Catholic Church in Lithuania*, the longest-running and best-known samizdat periodical in Lithuania (81 issues appeared between 1972 and 1989). Similarly, the extensive underground publishing activity conducted by unofficial Baptist groups, Jehovah's Witnesses, and other "non-conformist" religious groups, is completely neglected.

The above comments do not detract from the value of this book. When introducing books they have written, however, authors should not only specify what is covered in these books, but are well advised to also clearly state what is **not** discussed in the books because of a lack of time and space, language skills, and other limitations.

IVAN (JOHN) JAWORSKY
Professor Emeritus (Political Science)
University of Waterloo

Jessica Zychowicz, *Superfluous Women: Art, Feminism, and Revolution in Twenty-First-Century Ukraine*. University of Toronto Press, 2020.

Art and activism are intrinsically interconnected. Good art can convey a powerful message about injustices and shortcomings of the world by appealing to our feelings and emotions. By doing so it can inspire us into action that can in turn result in political and social change. Artistic activism blends the creative power of arts with the dynamic energy of public campaigns. Found across countries and periods it has a variety of applications and forms ranging from anti-war posters to songs against racism and xenophobia. *Superfluous Women* by Jessica Zychowicz provides an insight into the multidimensional and complex character of artistic activism by taking artistic expressions of women's rights activists in modern Ukraine as a distinctive unit of analysis. Chronologically the book concentrates on the turbulent decade that lays between the two pivotal events of Ukrainian history—the Orange Revolution in 2004 and the Euromaidan in 2013/14. Both events were marked by large-scale protests and subsequent shifts in the national political system and national self-identity.

Many historical events and revolutions are associated with the leading role of men. Those are often portrayed as charismatic figures with great intellect, militancy, and resolution, empowering them to change the world. Zychowicz shifted the focus on the role of women in the turbulent events of modern Ukraine—Femen protests, confrontational art that challenges the moral principles of a society that has already lost morality. Historical "masculine" methods of changing the world through violence and battles have a lesser impact on a society used to atrocities and cruelties during revolutions. The patriarchal society based on religion and post-Soviet ideology assigns women a secondary role after men in revolutionary transformations.

In exploring the development and impact of female artistic activism, Zychowicz commenced her analysis with the Femen group, well known outside the country for its provocative public protests against religious institutions, sexism, homophobia, and many other national and international issues. Femen challenges the moral foundation of society by combining together body art and social rebellion. The author locates the origins of Femen's politically motivated display of the female body in Ukrainian art of the Soviet period. She observes that some conceptual artists employed the female form in the 1970s–'80s to capture the making of power.

Femen's activism has also been shaped by the modern influences of pop art and mass-media technologies. The following chapter shifts focus on the development and action of Ofenzywa, the largest women's rights group that has emerged in independent Ukraine. As a major source of evidence the author relied on artistic work by Yevgenia Belorusets, a writer and photographer who played a leading role in the group. Belorusets's photos provided Zychowicz with multiple meanings of the collective identity and purpose of Ofenzywa. She shows that the group focused its street and other protests on the commemorations of International Women's Day that in public view embedded the legacies and values of the communist time. The book continues by exploring the themes of public exhibitions organized by HudRada and Revolutionary Experimental Space—two groups of Ukrainian artists who condemned government-supported restrictions in creative expression, free speech, and public freedom. The book ends the main discussion by exploring how public spaces, historical monuments, and movies can be used as a medium of exchange for new ideas and information that could provoke civic action.

While the book does provide a competent analysis of contemporary Ukrainian female artistic activism, it is not an easy read, especially for the reader who has limited knowledge of the post-1991 history of Ukraine. In this respect, to better conceptualize the topic and set up its background, the author could have included a separate chapter to provide a brief account of major political events and major political players over the past thirty years. Alternatively, a few smaller accounts of relevant historical events could have been included in the existing chapters. While the study provided a comprehensive examination of the meanings of multiple pieces of artwork, it did not make a systematic effort to assess the capacity of the artwork in question to enact social or political changes in Ukraine. The general impression is that the women's artistic activism had a rather small impact on broad society. There is a limitation in the book's coverage as well. While the book title suggests a focus on the whole territory of Ukraine, the story, in fact, is overwhelmingly centered around activist groups based in Kyiv, the country's capital. Surely there may have been similar developments in other parts of Ukraine—large cities, especially in the western part of Ukraine, traditionally had stronger cultural ties with Europe due to geographical proximity. The book is well referenced with endnotes, yet it would have also benefited from the inclusion of a separate list of primary sources used in the text. Despite these comments, Zychowicz has created an informative account of art activism in Ukraine, making a valuable addition to the literature in the field.

YANA OSTAPENKO
La Trobe University

Vladislav M. Zubok, *Collapse: The Fall of the Soviet Union*. New Yale University Press, 2021.

Throughout the early 1980s, virtually no Western scholars or policymakers foresaw the fall of the USSR. Today, more than three decades after the disintegration of the one-party rule, the breakdown of the command economy, and the loss of the Kremlin's control over the republics, these events remain shrouded in mystery. The extensive literature on the end of the USSR identifies several contributing causes, including the crisis of the Soviet economy, the movements for national independence in the Soviet republics, and the external pressures resulting from the Cold War. The debates regarding the relative weight of these factors—involving professional historians and policymakers alike—are ongoing. Zubok's meticulously researched book is an important addition to these debates and another attempt to unravel the puzzle of the collapse.

The USSR *circa* 1985 faced numerous challenges such as the stagnating economy, ethnic tensions, and bureaucratic inefficiency. These challenges worried the Soviet leadership, but most did not feel them to be life-threatening. Gorbachev, however, believed that these challenges were severe enough to justify a series of far-reaching reforms. According to Zubok, the ideas underpinning these reforms were outdated and inadequate, and their design was flawed. As a result, these reforms—such as the partial economic liberalization and transfer of powers from the CPSU to the competitively elected legislative bodies—resulted in the destruction of the extant political and economic structures from within. The 1988 Law on Cooperatives created a major loophole in the Soviet financial system, leading to uncontrollable inflation. The new political institutions created by Gorbachev, such as the Congress of People's Deputies, were incapable of governing the USSR. Similarly, Gorbachev's decision to renegotiate a new Union treaty to unite the republics in a voluntary decentralized federation paved the way for the USSR's dissolution.

Zubok views the collapse not as inevitable, but rather as resulting from a sequence of contingencies. Gorbachev and other reform architects were unable to recognize their errors and modify their course. The book outlines several critical junctures where different actions by the key actors could perhaps have saved the Union in some form. Gorbachev repeatedly asked the Congress of People's Deputies to grant him additional powers to negotiate with the republics and implement economic reforms. While these requests were approved, the Soviet leader failed to use his massive constitutional powers to change the situation. This hesitance proved to be fatal for the USSR.

Perestroika and *glasnost'* opened the Soviet politics to numerous new actors and organizations. The book introduces many of these voices, but without de-centering Gorbachev. For Zubok, the personality of the last USSR president was one of the major factors in the USSR's demise. Similar to his role model Vladimir Lenin, Gorbachev attempted to create a polity and society which had never existed. However, the last Soviet leader constantly rejected the violent and dictatorial methods that were largely responsible for Lenin's success as a revolutionary and a state builder. During most of his years in power, Gorbachev succeeded in his difficult balancing game, enacting substantial changes but avoiding backlash from the hardliners. Ultimately, however, Gorbachev's reforms alienated the Communist *nomenklatura*, while the counter-elites rallied behind the more radical leadership of Yeltsin. According to Zubok, it was the weakness of the USSR leadership, not the strength of the opposition in Russia and the other republics, that was ultimately responsible for the terminal crisis of Soviet statehood.

A major strength of the book is the careful examination of the Western impact on the Soviet collapse. Zubok does not exaggerate the role of the West, arguing persuasively that the external factors were secondary to the internal causes of the collapse. However, as the USSR entered the final year of its existence, international factors were crucial in shaping the behavior of major Soviet elites. Many in Putin's Russia continue to believe in an American conspiracy to destroy the USSR. This belief is baseless, as the documents show that the US leadership was surprised and dismayed by the USSR's disintegration. It is also true that the US leadership was narrow-minded and unimaginative in using their substantial soft power to assist the peaceful transformation of the Soviet society. Zubok's command of the non-Russian sources, such as diaries of the American and British policymakers, and his ability to weave them into his narrative, sets his book apart from many other accounts of the collapse.

Zubok's analysis is largely devoid of inaccuracies and omissions. One flaw of the narrative is the excessive focus on the dynamics at the Union's Russian core (and the Gorbachev–Yeltsin rivalry) at the expense of the republican arenas. The role of the nationalist movements—especially in the Baltics and Ukraine—in the process of the Soviet collapse is downplayed at times. For example, Zubok's insistence that the Ukrainian independence referendum of 1991 was a reflection of the Soviet collapse, rather than a contributing cause, is at least questionable. Overall, *Collapse* is an important contribution to the debates regarding the causes of the Soviet dissolution, a major historical event that continues to impact global politics.

DIMA KORTUKOV
PhD Candidate
Indiana University, Bloomington

ABOUT THE GUEST EDITORS

GERGANA DIMOVA is a lecturer in politics at the Florida State University London Program and a senior researcher at the Graduate Institute of Geneva. She received her PhD from Harvard University and has subsequently assumed research and teaching positions at the University of Cambridge and at the University of Winchester in the UK. Her book monographs are *Democracy beyond Elections* (Palgrave, 2019) and *Political Uncertainty (ibidem*-Verlag, 2022). Her academic articles have been published in *Demokratizatsiya, Observatorio, Global Media Journal,* and others. Her expertise has been featured in the Atlantic Council, Huffington Post, the LSE Policy Institute, Global Risk Insights, and Bulgarian TV and radio. She serves on the editorial board of *Democratic Theory* and is the convenor of the Anti-Politics Specialist Group of the UK Political Science Association.

ANDREAS UMLAND is an Analyst with the Stockholm Centre for Eastern European Studies at the Swedish Institute of International Affairs in Stockholm, Associate Professor of Political Science at the Kyiv-Mohyla Academy, as well as editor of the book series *Soviet and Post-Soviet Politics and Society (ibidem*-Verlag, 2004–). His articles have appeared in, among others, *e-Foreign Affairs, e-Foreign Policy, e-The National Interest, Harvard International Review, World Affairs, Survival, Political Studies Review, Perspectives on Politics, European Political Science, Journal of Democracy, Terrorism and Political Violence, European History Quarterly, Europe-Asia Studies, Problems of Post-Communism, Communist and Post-Communist Studies, The Russian Review, Nationalities Papers, Journal of Slavic Military Studies, Demokratizatsiya, Internationale Politik, Österreichische Zeitschrift für Politikwissenschaft, Zeitschrift für Politik, Osteuropa, Sirius, Politicheskie issledovaniia, Sravnitel'naia politika* and *Voprosy filosofii*.

About the Contributors

TOR BUKKVOLL is a Senior Research Fellow at the Norwegian Defence Research Establishment. He specializes in contemporary Russian and Ukrainian security and defence policies. Among his latest publications are "Why Putin Went to War: Ideology, Interests and Decision-making in the Russian Use of Force in Crimea and Donbas," *Contemporary Politics* 22:3 (2016); "Fighting on Behalf of the State—The Issue of Pro-government Militia Autonomy in the Donbas War," *Post-Soviet Affairs* 35:4 (2019); "The Threat of War and Domestic Restraints to Defence Reform—How Fear of Major Military Conflict Changed and Did Not Change the Ukrainian Military 2014–2019," *Defence Studies* 20:1 (2019) (with Volodymyr Solovian), "The Emergence of Russian Private Military Companies: A New Tool of Clandestine Warfare," *Special Operations Journal* 6:1 (2020) (with Åse Gilje Østensen); and "Private Military Companies – Russian Great Power Politics on the Cheap?," *Small Wars & Insurgencies* 33:1–2 (2022) (with Åse Gilje Østensen).

RUMENA FILIPOVA is Chairperson and Co-Founder of the Institute for Global Analytics in Bulgaria. She received a DPhil and MPhil in International Relations from the University of Oxford and a BA in Politics, Psychology and Sociology from the University of Cambridge. Her main research interests focus on the politics and international relations of Central and Eastern Europe, with a particular reference to questions of identity, Constructivist IR theory, media and disinformation, and the authoritarian influence exercised by Russia and China in the region. Her new book is entitled *Constructing the Limits of Europe: Identity and Foreign Policy in Poland, Bulgaria, and Russia since 1989* (ibidem-Verlag, 2022). It examines the reasons for the differential integration of Central and East European countries into the Euro-Atlantic community after the collapse of communism, focusing on the importance of national-state identities and historically conditioned conceptions of "Europe" as shapers of external behavior.

ABOUT THE CONTRIBUTORS

KERSTIN S. JOBST is Professor of Eastern European History at the University of Vienna. Her main focus is on the history of Ukraine, Poland, Russia, and Crimea. Her most recent book is *A History of the Crimea: From Iphigenia to Putin* (De Gruyter Oldenbourg, 2020) (in German). English and Ukrainian translations are in preparation.

MYKOLA KAPITONENKO, PhD, is an Associate Professor at the Institute of International Relations of Kyiv National Taras Shevchenko University, where he is also Director of the Center of International Studies. He has been invited as a visiting professor to the University of Iowa, and has taught at the Diplomatic Academy of the Ministry of Foreign Affairs of Ukraine. Since 2015 he has been co-editor of *UA: Ukraine Analytica*. He is a consultant to the Committee on Foreign Policy and Inter-Parliamentary Cooperation of the Parliament of Ukraine. His main research focus is conflict and security studies; and Ukrainian foreign policy. He is the author of *International Relations Theory* (2022), *International Conflicts* (2009), and *Power in International Politics* (2013) (in Ukrainian). In 2012 he was awarded a National Prize of Ukraine in Science.

MARTIN MALEK holds a PhD in Political Science from Vienna State University. Since 1997 he has been a (civilian) researcher at the Institute for Peace Support and Conflict Management, then at the Institute for Strategy and Security Policy, both of the National Defence Academy (Vienna). He has held several internships in research institutes and think tanks in Germany, Russia, Ukraine, and the US. His areas of expertise include state failing theories, theories of separatism, theories of ethnic conflicts, security and military policy in the Commonwealth of Independent States (especially Russia, Ukraine, South Caucasus), post-Soviet language policy, military-industrial complex and arms trade in the post-Soviet republics, NATO–CIS and EU–CIS relations, and Eurasian energy policy. He is the author/editor of several books and some 300 articles, published in a dozen countries.

ABOUT THE CONTRIBUTORS

ION MARANDICI, PhD (Rutgers University 2017), studies the political economy of reforms, comparative foreign policy, voting, unrecognized states, and perceptions of China in the US. His publications include articles in *Nationalities Papers, Problems of Post-Communism, Eurasian Geography and Economics, Demokratizatsiya* and chapters in collaborative volumes.

CHRIS MONDAY is an associate professor at Dongseo University (South Korea) where he has worked for sixteen years. After completing an undergraduate double-major in Math/History from UC Santa Cruz, Chris Monday taught math in the Peace Corps in Turkana, Kenya. He studied Russian history at UCSC under Peter Kenez. From 1996 to 2004, he lived continuously in Russia where Chris received a PhD in economics from the University of St. Petersburg. (His academic adviser was Leonid Dmitrievich Shirokorad.) Since then, has traveled to Russia almost every year: a 2014 sabbatical was spent there. He is a native of LA.

PETER RUTLAND is a professor of government at Wesleyan University in Middletown, Connecticut. He is vice president of the Association for Study of Nationalities. He writes on post-Soviet political economy and nationalism. In 2021 he co-edited a special issue of *Nations and Nationalism* on "Digital Nationalism" and of the *Journal of Baltic Studies* on "Nation-Building in the Baltic States," and wrote an article on "Racism and Nationalism" for *Nationalities Papers*.

GRETA LYNN UEHLING teaches in the Program in International and Comparative Studies at the University of Michigan in Ann Arbor. Her scholarship is broadly concerned with international migration and forced displacement. Major projects have examined the experiences of refugees, asylum seekers, and the internally displaced. Her current project explores the subjective experience of military conflict and forced displacement in Ukraine. Uehling holds a PhD in cultural anthropology from the University of Michigan and completed a post-doctoral fellowship with the Solomon Asch Center for the Study of Ethnopolitical Conflict at the University of

Pennsylvania. Her first book is *Beyond Memory: The Deportation and Repatriation of the Crimean Tatars*. Her forthcoming book is *Everyday War: The Conflict over Donbas, Ukraine* with Cornell University Press. She is the author of numerous scholarly articles and book chapters.

JAN ZOFKA is a historian of Eastern Europe and Researcher at the Leibniz-Institute for the History and Culture of Eastern Europe (GWZO) in Leipzig who completed a PhD on the social background of post-Soviet separatisms in Transnistria and Crimea in 2015. His recent research focuses on transnational dimensions of socialist industrialization processes during the 1950s. He is currently working on a project on technology transfer between China and Eastern Europe during the Cold War. He is the author of the monography *Postsowjetischer Separatismus: Die pro-russländischen Bewegungen im Dnjestr-Tal und auf der Krim (1989–1995)* (Wallstein Verlag, 2015) and "The Transformation of Soviet Industrial Relations and the Foundation of the Moldovan Dniester Republic," *Europe-Asia Studies* 5 (2016); as well as more recently "Technokratischer Internationalismus. Kohle-Experten der DDR der 1950er-Jahre in globalgeschichtlicher Perspektive," *Geschichte und Gesellschaft* 2 (2021); "Chairman Cotton: Socialist Bulgaria's Cotton Trade with African Countries during the Early Cold War (1946–70)," *Journal of Global History*, published online September 2021, and "China as a Role Model? The 'Economic Leap' Campaign in Bulgaria (1958–1960)," *Cold War History* 3 (2018).

***ibidem*.eu**